Passion for Provence

22 Keys to La Belle Vie

Gayle Smith Padgett

EAGLE
OWL
PRESS

PASSION FOR PROVENCE: 22 KEYS TO LA BELLE VIE

Published by Eagle Owl Press
1225 E. Sunset Drive, Suite 145
Bellingham, WA 98226

This book is a memoir. It reflects the author's present recollections of experiences over a period of time. Some names and characteristics have been changed, some events have been compressed, and some dialogue has been re-created.

Cover design by David Regan
Author photograph by Julien Daguet

Visit the author's website at www.gaylesmithpadgett.com

First edition

ISBN: 978-0-9994295-0-1

To

Ralph Henry

Author's Note

This book is based on my recollections—however imperfect—of real-life experiences. For privacy purposes, some names and identifying details have been changed. However, Ralph really *is* Ralph.

Contents

Introduction

Falling for France is as easy as sipping a glass of pale rosé on a sun-dappled *terrasse* overlooking a shimmering Mediterranean cove. Moving to France is more complicated.

Peter Mayle did it, famously recounting his French adventures in *A Year in Provence*, published in 1989. I read the memoir over twenty-five years ago while sitting on a Mediterranean beach at Saintes-Maries-de-la-Mer. It was magical to be in luscious Provence on my honeymoon, but enjoying *A Year in Provence* while *in* Provence made the special event even more memorable.

In the years that followed, I eagerly awaited each of Mr. Mayle's delightful publications. In fact, he signed one of them for me at my local bookstore in Virginia. I was charmed by his warmth and wit, as well as his scarlet socks. While I was writing this book, a recollection of those spirited *chaussettes* prompted me to send him a long-overdue fan letter. As his birthday was imminent, I tucked my note inside a fanciful birthday card. To my delight, he wrote back. Not only was his response a gracious thank-you for a thank-you, but it included sage publishing advice. I framed the letter—it inspires me every day.

For my husband and me, a permanent transition to France was gradual. From our home in Heidelberg, Germany, where we lived and worked for many years, we'd head to Provence as often as possible. After retiring in 2010, we finally moved here—first to Aix-en-Provence and then in 2012 to Saint-Rémy-de-Provence.

This memoir, *Passion for Provence: 22 Keys to La Belle Vie*, tells the tale of our French adventures—so far.

Chapter 1

Bonjour, Provence

The United States to Europe — Fall 1992

"*Petite question* … can I drink wine with these medications?" I asked Dr. Durand, who was kneeling at my side on a hotel room floor in Saint-Rémy-de-Provence. Even in my dazed state, the physician's youthful, bronzed face and sandy blond locks registered. *Oh là là!* I was feeling better already.

"*Ah, madame,*" he said, his gaze drifting to the sunny window and the dramatic Alpilles peaks beyond.

I held my breath. Don't you dare say *non*, I silently begged, locking my eyes on his baby blues. It was the first day of a week-long vacation in Provence, and my hubby and I were looking forward to indulging in all its luscious bounty, particularly some Côtes de Provence wines.

He continued, "*Mais seulement … le vin français.*"

"Oh, only French wine? Not a problem! *Merci beaucoup, docteur,*" I grinned, allowing my body to de-clench. What a relief! The doc had given me a terrific gift, a green light to fully savor

1

our Provençal escape. Technically, for us newlyweds, this trip was much more than an ordinary getaway. It was our *lune de miel*—our honeymoon—and the very beginning of our love affair with France.

❧

The sun was shining that autumn day in 1989 in Arlington, Virginia, the day Cute Guy showed up. My future husband entered the picture at the mammoth brick condominium complex, called Fairlington Villages. With over two thousand units in the north sector alone, the slate-roofed, gabled historic landmark, dating from the 1940s, spread across acres of rolling hills. The vast housing development, graced with majestic oaks, doubled as a huge, leafy park that included multiple swimming pools, as well as basketball and tennis courts.

I was at the main tennis center watching a match, sitting at the base of a shade tree next to the sidewalk that ran along the courts. My position was slightly elevated, so I had a greater field of vision than from the benches below. Good thing I'd moved to higher ground, because some significant action was happening and it was not on the courts.

From my perch, I noticed a guy with a mop of curly brown hair saunter down the sidewalk in a soggy T-shirt and baggy shorts revealing long, muscular legs. Then he did what sweaty guys do—he grabbed the front of his shirt and lifted it to wipe the perspiration off his forehead. If a guy with a "kegger" does this, the exposure of his overextended belly can be downright scary. When this guy did it, however, he exposed a taut, tanned "six-pack" and toned pecs partially covered with a dark shadow of chest hair. I gasped, not out of fright, but with what-a-hunk delight. Cute Guy, whom I judged to be almost six feet tall, made himself comfortable on a bench nearby. A red-alert alarm sounded in my brain, compelling me to mosey on over, drape my arms around his shoulders, and plant a smooch on the delectable curve where neck meets shoulder. Such were my impulses, anyway.

Instead, I regulated my breathing to avoid hyperventilating my way to blackout mode, which would have jeopardized my hastily formulated plan of getting to know him. With all the poise I could muster, I positioned myself at the opposite end of the mystery man's bench. When a tennis player smashed a powerful overhead, I emitted a loud "Wow!" Cute Guy's head swiveled my way, and that's all it took.

As we chatted about the match, my mind and eyes drifted away from the court. My senses were occupied registering every detail about Cute Guy, now known as Ralph. Unfortunately, our tête-à-tête was brief, as he had to drive to a conference in Norfolk, several hours south. We walked together to his bike, where we said goodbye. Then my intriguing new friend rode down the hill toward home—with only my first name and without my number. I had managed to ascertain he was unattached, but I didn't have any other information. Would I ever see this intelligent, articulate, attractive, easygoing, funny, sporty guy again?

Two weeks later Ralph was back at the courts, and so was I. Not such a coincidence, really. I had scarcely abandoned my post since that first meeting. (Begrudgingly, I had taken breaks for work and some ZZZs.) When I caught a glimpse of him, he was about fifty feet away, standing by the drinking fountain next to the clubhouse. Much to my dismay, there was a young woman next to him, and they were chatting. She looked to be in her early thirties, several years my junior. Long golden legs and hair to match. Voluptuous. As more of a shrimp at five foot four inches—if I rounded up—with shoulder-length brown hair and less robust dimensions, I might have felt intimidated. Strangely, I wasn't.

A jolt of confidence exploded in my head and energized my feet. I didn't know this gal, but I *did* know she was history. As I started walking toward Ralph, my pace quickened, along with my heartbeat. Closing in on thirty feet, I shouted his name, startling myself, because I hardly ever remembered names. I waved, clamping my eyes on his. We exchanged smiles. When I reached him, the girl had disappeared. Well, I didn't see her. I may have squeezed in between the two of them and pivoted around to face Ralph. That way she could easily read the message on the back of my shirt that read, "He's mine. Byeee!"

During our eighteen-month courtship, Ralph learned I was a Washington state native and a Spanish and Latin American Studies major who had studied in Mexico and Colombia. Though originally my sights had been set south of the Rio Grande, I'd headed to Germany to work before settling in Virginia. For my part, I discovered that in addition to shooting hoops and playing tennis and the piano, my North Carolinian beau was a mathematician who harvested backyard vegetables and baked delicious sourdough bread from a family recipe. He also could waltz and rumba me 'round the dance floor, as well as entertain me with his quirky, wry wit.

A case in point was his theory of guys' names, comprised of four categories. Category One names belonged to the leading man and were crisp and commanding like Rick, Rhett, or Dirk. Category Two names were for the leading man's best friend—solid and reliable names like Jimmy, Roger, or Bob. Category Three names were assigned to the jerk neighbor—Harvey, Dwayne, and Chester. Category Four names were cartoon characters like Rollo, Bubba, and Spike. Ralph was convinced his was a Category Three name. There was more bad news, he lamented. He was doubly burdened with a *pair* of Category Three names, his middle name being Henry.

Another unique dimension of Ralph's personality was his passion for birdwatching. I'd known people who watched birds at a feeder through their kitchen window, but I'd never met anyone who ventured into the wild *looking* for birds. Ralph even had a bird list. All serious birders have one, as I came to know. Whenever he spotted a new bird, he made a note in his trusty bird book bible, *Peterson's Guide to Birds of North America*. He regularly visited his favorite local haunt, Huntley Meadows, and frequently headed to notable birding areas farther afield like Chincoteague, Virginia, and Cape May, New Jersey. Though I hadn't been bitten by the birding bug, it was exciting for me to see my guy so excited when he spotted a new winged creature or got a good look at a rare one. But the more new birds he identified, the fewer there were to find. What to do?

Though I'd often raved about the few years I'd worked in Europe—all the exceptional cultural and travel opportunities to be had—I was taken by surprise when Ralph announced one night he had received a US government offer for a position as a cost analyst in Heidelberg, Germany, and felt inclined to accept. Now my convincing tales about the glories of a European lifestyle were proving damaging to my case. Crestfallen, I realized my beau was bound for distant shores—alone. Softly I asked, "What about—uh—me?"

He gave me a quizzical look and said matter-of-factly, "We're getting married, of course."

"What did you say?" I asked, not believing I'd correctly heard him pronounce *the* M-word.

Shortly thereafter, Ralph delivered a more romantic proposal—on the bench at the tennis courts where we'd met. I didn't say yes immediately. First, I took a deep breath. I wanted to revel in the dreamy moment and ensure a composed response. Before my exhale was complete, I gushed, "Oh-yes-oh-yes-oh—YES!"

After getting legal in Old Town Alexandria at the historic Old Presbyterian Meeting House, we started our own history, one to be filled with plenty of foreign adventures. Soon after taking a leave of absence from my job teaching English to international students and renting out the condo, we were winging it over the Atlantic to Heidelberg. The beguiling city of the famous operetta *The Student Prince* was conveniently located an hour from the French border and just eight hours' drive from Provence.

More than a year passed in Heidelberg before our delayed honeymoon in the south of France. Ralph was keen to press his binoculars into action in the Camargue where the Rhône River fans into a wide delta before spilling into the Mediterranean Sea. I, on the other hand, was eager to experience the landscapes that inspired some of my favorite painters, especially Cezanne, Van Gogh, Matisse, and Picasso. My anticipation of our trip was further enhanced by the publication of Peter Mayle's *A Year in Provence*; the tale of a British couple trading hectic jobs in London for retirement in Provence had captured my imagination. To be free to roam around sunny, southern France with all the outdoor markets, quaint villages, and charming bistros—that was more than a good life. That qualified as a life par excellence, one we'd try to emulate on our week's vacation. The book, however, wasn't a practical travel guide with lists of places to stay and eat. For that we relied on a friend's trip report, which included loads of insider tips on hotels and restaurants. Because it was off-season, we didn't feel the need to book anything. Armed with some Michelin maps, we headed south.

The first night we spent in striking Annecy, the Pearl of the French Alps, set on the northern tip of breathtaking Lake Annecy. Ralph, however, barely caught a glimpse of its stunning beauty, as he was fully occupied with food poisoning, probably caused by a chunk of way-past-due cheese I'd dug out of the fridge and tossed in our picnic lunch. What was I thinking? I don't know who felt worse. Since he was still feeling a tad poorly the next morning, I did all the driving. We hit a few *bouchons* or traffic jams, so it was five hours later by the time we made it to Arles, the gateway to the Camargue. By then, my clutch leg and back were screaming for a break from my standard transmission Honda CRX. But the squeals from those body parts went unheeded, as I needed to respond to an urgent nature call. I creatively squeezed the little car into half a normal parking space in front of a café, where I made a mad dash for *les toilettes*. A few minutes later I was feeling significantly better, when the proprietress began railing at me for using her facilities without first buying something. "This isn't a rest stop on the *autoroute!*" she scolded.

The owner was easily appeased with an order of two espressos, after which we went in search of our digs. The recommended accommodation wasn't the charming enclave we had imagined. Unless *charmant* meant peeling paint, a creaky bed, a concave mattress, threadbare towels, rusted faucets, and no doubt, a starving family of fleas. We moved on as quickly as possible—before anything could bite us. In a small village east of Arles, we found a stylish *chambre d'hôte* holiday complex run by one Monsieur Oiseaux, recently transplanted from Paris. Perhaps he'd had a tough move, because he was in a grumpy funk despite the gorgeous weather. If Mr. Birds had been a bird, I'd have pegged him as a vulture who'd arrived late at the carcass feast. Since he was having a cranky day, I did not attempt to describe the droll irony of his name and a major motivation for our trip. No matter, though, because he had what we'd come for—an attractive room—not to mention inviting lounge chairs positioned around an expansive pool surrounded by olive trees, shimmering under French blue skies.

Unfortunately, Mr. Oiseaux's property was full that night, but he did have availability the next night and for the rest of the week. We reserved the room and continued east, ending up in Saint-Rémy-de-Provence. There, we stumbled upon the most conveniently located hotel, a stone's throw from *centre ville*, as well as a *docteur* and a *pharmacie*, which we would soon need. Exhausted after a three-flight trudge up the stairs, I'd heaved my overly laden suitcase onto the bed with one grandiose effort and promptly passed out, falling over backward. Ralph later told me I wasn't frothing at the mouth, but my eyes had rolled back and my jaw locked. Frantic, he'd raced downstairs and screamed in English at the desk clerk until she realized he meant *doctor, now!* and soon Dr. Durand was hovering over me. He determined the episode had resulted from hyperventilation triggered by the pain that had shot through my leg.

The episode was entirely my fault. In a last-ditch effort to get in shape for our honeymoon, I had gone into overdrive at the gym. During a rushed session, I'd neglected to properly adjust the weights on a machine, causing an overstretched, if not torn, back muscle. After the long clutch workout on the

Autoroute de Soleil, my tormented muscle, agitated further by the suitcase-heaving, was compelled to vehemently object. Dr. Durand prescribed some muscle relaxants and painkillers, assuring me I'd be fine for the week.

Our agenda now needed to be reworked since pampering my back was a priority. Slow-mo became our motto. For hours we meandered by car through the expansive Camargue. We made frequent stops to marvel at the masses of fuchsia flamingos feeding peacefully, oblivious to the clippity-clop of horses trekking back to the noontime feedbag and the herds of bulls milling around in yonder pasture. In the whitewashed seaside village of Saintes-Maries-de-Mer, we stopped at a brasserie for a simple lunch of *salade de chèvre chaud*, goat cheese melted on toasted baguette rounds placed on salad greens, and a carafe of pale rosé. Afterward, Ralph roamed the marshes behind the sandy shoreline, spotting legions of herons, egrets, gulls, and oystercatchers. I relaxed on my beach towel, content with my *A Year in Provence*, watching demure waves tiptoe up and slip back out to sea.

Another day, we passed through the quaint village of Maussane. On the outskirts, eagle-eyed Ralph spotted a sign for Mas de Mistral, an olive oil producer. Olive oil being a local specialty, we both agreed it merited investigation, so we followed the red arrows. Our detour wound us through the countryside, past vast olive groves and grazing sheep. At the end of a rutted-out dirt track, we pulled up in front of an old farmhouse. Inside, we found the young owner filling bottles with golden liquid from a dispenser like a beer tap and sticking on the labels—all by hand. We sampled the pure, fresh concoction—no comparison to the supermarket versions—and bought a couple of tall liter bottles.

After leaving the olive oil *domaine*, this time I was the one who spotted a tempting sign, one that spoke not to my taste buds but to my heart—*poterie*. The outside area by the store's parking lot was loaded with gigantic garden pots, each the size of a pied-à-terre. Inside the shop, we found an extensive variety of glazed forms in blaring primary colors but also some subdued, rustic models with discreet medallion bas-reliefs. The style I fell for was urn-shaped with a blotchy glaze, produced by an artisan named Monsieur Briand from Anduze, a town a couple of hours northwest. Unbeknownst to Mr. B., that was the day I began contributing to his retirement fund.

During the week, we strolled the plane-tree-lined *périphérique* that circled Saint-Rémy's historic center, crammed with dozens of cafés buzzing with patrons leisurely sipping espressos from tiny cups, wine from squat urns, or cloudy, licorice-flavored *pastis* from tall glasses. Inside the medieval *centre historique*, we discovered a maze of winding alleyways filled with chic clothing shops, home design boutiques, and contemporary art galleries. But the most impressive revelation was the Wednesday weekly market. It enveloped the entire town from the main square, Place de la République, to the Place Pelissier, dominated by the beautiful sixteenth-century Hôtel de Ville, the town hall. On Place Favier, by the graceful fountain with a curved bench base, a young entrepreneur wove slender satin ribbons into a bouquet of lavender, forming a wand. She picked up an elongated work of art that resembled a skinny maraca and gently squeezed the bulb, explaining to her customer that the lavender scent would last years. I *had* to have at least one of those delicate beauties, but I rationalized three before moving on to the other artisans.

I found an astounding variety of stalls displaying exquisitely crafted leather goods, fringed *foutahs* in a thousand vibrant hues

10

for use as beach or pool towels, iconic straw shopping baskets, inventive jewelry, olive wood platters, *chapeaux*, soaps in dozens of scents and hues, original watercolors of Les Alpilles mountains, two-meter-long rolls of fine linen fabric, plus piles of quilted covers called *boutis*—a shopping paradise.

Not being much of a market man, my hubby had been people watching from the church steps while I completed my reconnaissance of the artisan section, but he joined me to admire the edibles on Place Pelissier. The stunning array of *fruits et légumes* was just the beginning. There were chubby *poulets rôtis*, thigh to thigh, on a trio of spits. Fresh slabs of glowing pink salmon. Massive bowls mounded with glistening black and green olives stuffed with anchovies, almonds, or red peppers, or spiced up with herbs de Provence. Stacks of crusty rounds of bread studded with figs, walnuts, or olives. *Saucissons*—made from not only *cochon* but also boar, deer, and *taureau* (bull)—laced with hazelnuts, pistachios, or mushrooms. With all the stalls cramming the square, a weathered stone fountain with four graceful, water-spewing dolphins was barely visible.

Leaving the chaos of the market, we drove five minutes up the hill to Van Gogh's peaceful clinic, Saint-Paul-de-Mausole. It was during the artist's time here that he painted *The Starry Night*, one of his most famous works. From the painter's bedroom window, we could see, just as the master himself had, the rows of lavender in the garden and the twisted cypress landscapes in the distance.

Another day, we admired the elaborate Roman arch at Les Antiques, flipped through international magazines at the *presse*, selected goat cheese cloaked in peppercorns at a quaint cheese shop, and chatted with the tourist office staff. They raved about time-honored village events, such as the annual *transhumance*.

Thousands of sheep and goats, guided by their masters in traditional dress, lap the town before heading to higher pastures for the summer. Not to be missed, they said. We marked our calendar for the following spring. How effortless it was to ease into the languid Provençal pace, stopping to smell the roses and sip the rosé.

Saint-Rémy offered so much in such a compact space, just steps away from Les Alpilles. Clearly, we realized, this Provençal enclave of only ten thousand citizens punched far above its weight in terms of natural setting, amenities, and ambience. And only an hour's drive away was the Camargue with all its amazing wildlife—the icing on the *gâteau*. With a Roman antiquity here, a Van Gogh scene there, outdoor markets, walks in Les Alpilles, vibrant Mediterranean cuisine, and vineyards to eternity and beyond, we were smitten.

Despite my brush with the medical community, our trip assessment was unanimous—long live the joie de vivre of Provence. Though retirement was a long way off, the Provençal spell had been cast.

Untether your inner joie de vivre.
Oh, the adventures you'll have, the memories you'll make. Giddyup.

Chapter 2

Flirting with France

Heidelberg and Provence — 1992 to 2010

Once we'd seen Provence, we eagerly gave in to its charms. A two decade-long dance of seduction with the south of France ensued.

When vacation time rolled around during our working years in Germany, Ralph and I couldn't resist heading south. We reveled in those week-long excursions to Provence. South of Lyon where the Provençal landscape begins to unfold, revealing its majestic cedars and golden-stone hilltop villages, a giddiness would come over us.

On one occasion, we based ourselves in the Venice of Provence, the delightful antiques town of L'Isle-sur-la-Sorgue, built around a network of canals. Its Sunday market has a special dimension. In addition to all the stalls overflowing with the typical *marché* wares—soaps, fabrics, baskets, and scarves—stretched out along the main canal, a vibrant flea market sells

13

everything from tiny teacups of Moustiers-Sainte-Marie fame to massive cherrywood armoires.

From L'Isle-sur-la-Sorgue, it was easy to explore the hilltop villages of the northern Luberon—Gordes, Roussillon, and Ménèrbes, of Peter Mayle fame. Once after a plat du jour of *moules frites* (mussels and fries) in the author's village, we lingered at the hard-packed dirt *boules* court to watch a few rounds of the game, played with heavy metal balls nearly the size of grapefruit. Of the six mature fellows playing, all wore faded nondesigner jeans and either work boots or faded jogging shoes. Five sported black berets, positioned at a jaunty angle. They stood at the sides of the court focused on the one beret-free man with his knees slightly bent and feet together inside the half-circle drawn in the dirt. The man expertly tossed a ball that came to rest next to the small red target affectionally called *le cochonnet,* meaning piglet. The talented player bore a striking resemblance to Monsieur Mayle. Maybe it *was* him. Or perhaps my rose-tinted glasses had seen too many glasses of rosé. Hmm.

In between week-long vacations, we loved popping over the border into France for a delicious *déjeuner* with friends. In just an hour from our home in Heidelberg, we could be in the tiny town of Lauterbourg. We always ordered the same delicious dish—*tarte flambée*—TF for short. It's a thin-crusted rectangular pizza, topped with crème fraîche, shredded onions, and crispy bacon chunks. It was de rigueur to wash the TF down with a dry, spicy, local Alsatian Riesling. Afterward, we'd push our carts up and down every aisle in the enormous supermarket, Cora, picking up lots of Frenchie goodies—crusty baguettes, blocks of butter blended with salt crystals from Guérande, and, of course, bottles of local bubbly, Crémant d'Alsace.

Occasionally we'd spend weekends in Paris. From Heidelberg, reaching the City of Light by train was a snap. Within a few hours we could be strolling through Luxembourg Gardens, trying on berets at Galleries Lafayette, eating seafood *choucroute* at Bofinger, or visiting Monets at the Musée d'Orsay. One particular hotel made these excursions especially delightful. A perk of our professional association with the US government was permission to stay at the French Officers' Club with its upscale amenities. Not only did our room come with an Eiffel Tower view, but at the time we designated, breakfast was delivered to the room—crispy, buttery croissants, a big pot of rich coffee, a jug of hot, foamy milk, plump soft-boiled eggs, silky *beurre*, and an assortment of yummy *confitures*—all of our favorites. And how did they know? The night before, we'd noted our *petit déjeuner* preferences on a dainty card with a cord attached, handy for dangling on the doorknob. Getting spoiled, French style, involved no learning curve whatsoever. Apparently, we were naturals.

Aside from quick train trips to Paris, we trekked west to magnificent Mont Saint-Michel in Normandy, and south to Beaune in Burgundy. Champagne being my adult beverage of choice, Épernay, the Capital of Bubbly, was a must-see too. After an informative and delicious tour of the Moët & Chandon Champagne estate—it concluded with a generous tasting—I paid tribute with a bow to the ingenious monk who started it all, Dom Pérignon, standing tall and bronzed in the main courtyard.

Farther afield, we traveled to the teensy island of Île de Groix off the Brittany coast. There, for the first time, I experienced a meal served *en papillote*, a paper bundle, served in a plain restaurant connected to a hostel filled with young oceanographers on a research junket. As I opened the little pouch, a billow of steam escaped, revealing a mound of curried *moules* topped with thyme twigs—a striking and heavenly combination.

That dish wasn't the only surprising juxtaposition. We discovered that our youthful, mustached bike rental guy doubled as a philosopher. There were numerous bicycle rental shops on the island, but not one advertised *bicyclettes*, ordinary bicycles. They all rented *vélos*, which looked exactly like ordinary bikes to us. After tooling around the island and turning in our rented two-wheelers, I asked the shop owner to explain the difference between the two bicycle terms. I expected a one- or two-word answer like "fatter tires." Instead, his smile vanished and his eyes narrowed. As he leaned forward on the counter, he stroked his mustache and said, *"La différence entre la bicyclette et le vélo … ah, c'est très, très subtil."* He had obviously given the topic substantial thought and appeared primed to launch into the deeper recesses of a complex issue, which was probably tied to French national identity or the meaning of life. Or maybe they were one and the same, a concept he would also try to explain. Since we had a ferry to catch, we convinced the philosophizing proprietor we were satisfied with his *subtil* insight and hightailed it to the dock. Since then, whenever something culturally perplexing surfaces, instead of digging for the definitive answer, which would most likely prove futile, we relegate the issue to our *très-très-subtil* list. Voilà, harmony is restored.

On a subsequent visit to Provence, we stayed near Carpentras, but drove an hour over to Saint-Rémy for its Wednesday market—*that* I couldn't miss. Unsurprisingly, I found it as vibrant as I had the first time. While I happily lost myself wandering among the stalls, Ralph hiked up into Les

Alpilles looking for bird rarities like the Egyptian vulture and Bonelli's eagle. His search was to no avail, but any day birding is a good day for Ralph. We were both happy campers. By the end of the week, we'd clocked some *vélo* saddle time riding to the glider field near Eygalières to watch the sleek planes lift off and float above the craggy Alpilles, played *boules*, ate our weight in goat cheese, and drank double that in rosé. What a life! We began to get just a hint of an inkling that we might like to retire here.

As the years rolled along, the French retirement idea stubbornly refused to go away. We'd been seriously dating France for a long time and the relationship had deepened. Every additional trip to Saint-Rémy reinforced our fantasy. We marched around Les Alpilles and the outdoor markets, visited our favorite olive oil producer in Maussane, and enjoyed a *dégustation* at Domaine de Valdition near Eygalières. We observed flamingos sifting mud through their beaks—that's what they're busy doing out there in the Camargue marshes, Ralph told me.

And of course, we enjoyed our favorite bistros. Excessive as it may have been, on one visit, we squeezed in two lunches in five days at Bistrot de Paradou, in the town by the same name. After the first meal early in the week, we couldn't resist reserving for Friday to experience the renowned aioli, a simple Provençal dish of steamed white fish, potatoes, and veggies. The star of the show, garlic mayonnaise, also called aioli, wasn't on the plate but was presented in a separate little tub—for safety reasons, we realized later. Since the aioli was contained in its own vessel, there was no pretending it could slide onto your fork by mistake. You had to knowingly go after it, and we did with abandon, recklessly. The seemingly innocuous mayo concoction was so lusciously decadent, it was easy for newbies like us to gobble it all up, rendering the small bowls shiny clean. Though a huge boon to our immune systems, the downside was that the powerful, garlicky punch the aioli packed didn't much lend itself to romance. Even blowing kisses was ill-advised. If we had both blown simultaneously and at close range, we would have risked singed eyebrows. Lesson learned; when it comes to reckless abandon, save it for the boudoir.

During our Provençal getaways, we soaked up the dreamy ambience like industrial-strength solar panels to keep us powered up while we were elsewhere. Retirement was on the horizon now, so the choice of where to homestead was soon to be ours. Why not choose France, so we could enjoy its joie de vivre every day? If we were so attached to the country, why not stop dating France and move in together? Granted, there would be some significant legal hurdles to jump—France's reputation for bureacracy was legendary. Still, we absolutely *loved* the idea. But did France? Did France want to cohabitate with *us*? To find out, there was wooing to do—in La La Land.

Brace for bureaucracy.
Much won't make sense to you,
but it does to somebody, and that
somebody is stamping your visa.

Chapter 3

Shackin' Up

Aix-en-Provence — Fall 2010

Live in sin with La Belle France—that was our plan. But to set it in motion, we had to make a case to France that we were worthy. And that meant heading for the French consulate in Los Angeles, because California was our official home of record. France doesn't allow expats to request permission to reside long term while said expats are physically *in* France. You have to ask politely from your own native land. And that solicitation must be delivered in the form of a fat dossier, packed with convincing data that you aren't just teasing, that your intentions are serious. Most importantly, it has to contain proof you have an abode to call home.

You'd think we would have figured out *where* in France we wanted to live during our two decades of ramblings, but we hadn't. Now that our French dream was taking shape, we took a cold, hard look at the starting point. Would it be our go-to town of Saint-Rémy? We'd always thought Saint-Rémy would

19

be *the* one, but were we riding high on emotion? Perhaps we needed to consider alternatives. Could it be picture-postcard pretty Obernai in Alsace, our favorite weekend escape while living in Heidelberg? We'd found a wonderful *chambre d'hôte* just a five-minute walk through vineyards to *centre ville* and often spent weekends there. In summer, we'd bicycle through the vineyards connecting the impossibly charming villages that make up the Alsatian *Route des Vins*. One of my favorite routes was the ride from Dambach-la-Ville to Ribeauvillé. Just outside of the fairy-tale half-timbered town—especially ravishing when crimson and coral geraniums gushed from every window box— is the renowned, historic Beauvillé factory, which produces incredible tablecloths and tea towels in magnificent colors and patterns. Ralph knew my attraction to the fabrics approximated obsession but took solace in the knowledge that my acquisitions would be held in check by the size of my bicycle basket.

And then there was beautiful Beaune, in Burgundy. Like the Alsace, Burgundy's bike routes through the vineyards were tremendous, even if they didn't include a textiles factory along the way. The scenery rivaled Alsace's vineyards, and during the *vendange*, the region would burst with energy. We once witnessed the end of the grape harvest in Volnay, where twenty-year-old grape pickers dressed in togas with grapevine wreaths on their heads took their party to the *rues*, sharing their luscious product with whomever passed by.

Before we left Europe as newbie retirees, we thought it prudent to give objectivity a nod and spend a week in both Obernai and Beaune en route to Provence. The fall of 2010, both *villes* forgot to put out their welcome weather mats. The chill factor and high gray-day count helped us come to a decision. As much as we'd enjoyed both towns over the years, for year-round living, there was no contest with France's sunny southern region. Onward we drove south.

Timing was not on our side, however, even in Saint-Rémy. When we arrived, not only was the sun in hiding, but the fierce mistral was howling like a terrible two-year-old having a major meltdown. Standing upright wasn't even possible. Most plans for outdoor activities like walking, birding, biking, and apartment-hunting were scuttled. We huddled inside. When we did venture out, we discovered that our favorite bistro had changed hands and my most coveted home décor boutique was shuttered for renovation. Even the remarkable weekly market failed me. Only a few brave marketers had set up shop. Reality had intervened in our sparkling fantasyland. We recognized that perhaps Saint-Rémy wasn't *the* place for real-life retirement for us. Downhearted, we returned to California without a French address.

✦

It wasn't long before a renewed, now-or-never mind-set blossomed. We had fantasized for a long time about living in France, and we knew that if we didn't embark on the adventure then, there was a real possibility it would never happen. Countless hours were filled with devising a plan to realize our dream, but we still didn't know where it would happen. Then, one morning, I awoke with an epiphany.

"Honey, how about Aix?"

"Aix-en-Provence?" Ralph said.

"Yes, Aix. Think about it. We had a super visit there several years ago."

21

"Oh, yeah—remember those terrific sandwiches from the pizza truck just off the Cours Mirabeau?"

"You bet I do—man, they were *dee*-licious!" I said. My thoughts drifted back to those grilled eggplant-zucchini-red-pepper focaccias. They were so packed with *chèvre* that when I took a bite, the melted goat cheese had oozed out and dribbled down my arm. Luscious bits of heaven they were. From our bench on the Cours Mirabeau, we had gazed down the main drag of Aix-en-Provence (pronounced *X-on-provonce*) through the green tunnel of plane trees to the magnificent Rotonde fountain. Water shooting out from graceful swans and dolphins formed perfect, gentle arches. Glistening spray as fine as silvery fairy dust cooled the grateful bystanders. A soft, jazzy melody wafted out of the renowned Deux Garçons restaurant, once frequented by Cezanne, Zola, and Picasso. The historic brasserie was crowded with a mix of chic Parisian-type patrons, serious business folks, and fresh-faced university students. The energy put a spring in our step. What a dreamy corner of Provence Aix was.

"It's maybe bigger than what I'd prefer, but it's walkable," Ralph noted.

"And it's not all hustle-bustle … it has its quiet, quaint corners," I added.

"And it's only thirty minutes to the sea, which is really good. There should be some good birding there. Yeah, it really does work. I think we should do it."

My "aha" moment set the wheels in motion to take another crack at launching the quest for our French retirement nest. The trip to Marseille was challenge-free and unbelievably, so was finding a furnished apartment in Aix. We discovered the "by-owner" ad on the tourist office website, which meant no realtor's fee. That was a relief, because typically the fee equates to a month's rent. It was only the second apartment we visited, and though a compact 67 square meters (just 720 square feet) and decorated with the owner's personal mementos, we didn't quibble. It had all the basics, including a bathtub, washing machine, and easy parking. There was no doubt it was *the* one. We knew it the moment we walked into the living room and saw the captivating view directly over the elegant city, the focal point being the imposing Cathédrale de Saint Sauveur. And the owner was lovely. When the slight woman with long brown hair and angelic eyes opened the door and smiled warmly, I felt an instant connection, as if we were soul mates meeting up after an extended separation. But it was even more than that. It was as if with one gentle glance this stranger absorbed all my anxieties about moving to a foreign city where we knew not a soul. Discovering Nathalie and her apartment with the *belle vue* fell squarely in the meant-to-be category. Our sad breakup with Saint-Rémy was behind us. We were now looking forward to a new relationship—with Aix.

Back in California, armed with our rental agreement, we got busy compiling our dossier for the French consulate in Los Angeles. That included documents confirming sufficient income, health insurance, and proof that our photos weren't stapled to the local post office bulletin board. Our appointment at the consulate was at 10:00 a.m. We left the house at 6:00 a.m., allowing four hours for a two-and-a-half-hour trip. The freeway was bumper to bumper, and we were going nowhere fast. We were nervous wrecks. If it hadn't been for the high-occupancy vehicle lane, we never would have made it. As it turned out, we had some time to spare. Once in the consulate waiting room, we passed the time waiting to be called to the counter by rechecking our dossiers for the umpteenth time. Ralph gasped.

"What's wrong, honey?" I said.

"I don't believe this. My photos are missing." His face was ashen.

"Oh my God! Now what?" I said in a hushed voice, trying not to attract attention.

We recalled we'd seen a big all-service pharmacy just down the block. If he ran fast, there might be just enough time to get another set of passport photos made and make it back for the appointment—just. If he didn't make it, we'd have to book another appointment, probably weeks away, and make another grueling trip to LA. And the French official reviewing our packet would probably give us a demerit or two for failure to organize ourselves. If we couldn't manage to put a complete dossier together, how on earth would we manage living in a foreign country whose language we had barely begun to grasp? As Ralph rose to put his coat on, he handed his folder to me. I opened it, flipped through the pages, then stuck my hand deep into the folder's pocket. And pulled out the packet of photos. Apparently, it had slipped out from the paper clip at the top of the page and slid down.

"Sweetie, look!" I held up the photos.

"Whew—what a relief!" Ralph murmured, letting out a big breath.

Just as our pulses were returning to normal, the official called us up to the glass-enclosed counter. We slid the dossier through an opening, and the no-nonsense French woman checked it for the appropriate components. "*C'est bon*," she said, and plopped it on a stack of similar-looking dossiers. "You will receive notice shortly."

Hoping for a more defined timeframe, I ventured, "*Quand, exactement?*"

"Shortly," she repeated in a don't-call-us-we'll-call-you tone.

Accepting that no more information would be forthcoming and realizing our cue to exit had been given, we responded with our much-practiced phrase, "*Merci beaucoup, bonne journée, et au revoir.*"

France held its cards close. There was no news for several weeks. Then a pair of special delivery packets arrived. They contained our temporary visas. We were good to go. Next stop, La Belle France.

3

Establish a French base camp.
From there, you can launch a quest
for your long-term nest.

Chapter 4

Raining Chats et Chiens

Handy with a chainsaw? Trained on a tractor? Good with goats?

If you are a house-sitter wannabe and these nifty skill sets highlight your curriculum vitae, an abundance of free house-sitting opportunities awaits. Simply sign up for a membership on a house-sitting website, specify where you want to go, and what you will do—feed dogs/cats/chickens/llamas/grandpa, etc.—and presto, you'll soon receive countless notifications of inviting offers from sophisticated citizens of the world with well-equipped, finely functioning designer homes in inviting areas where the weather is always primo, plants thrive, and pets cooperate. And hiccups are prohibited.

The house-sitting concept held particular appeal during our first summer in Aix in 2011. Our apartment lacked *climatisation* (air-conditioning) to combat the fierce heat, and the only

26

outdoor space consisted of a tiny balcony that barely fit two folding chairs and an undersized bistro table, much less an infinity pool. We were still coping with the US economic downturn, and we weren't yet certain whether Aix was *the* place for us or whether there was a more suitable home for our hammock—the one I'd bought as an anniversary gift years before at Saint-Rémy's market. Though it had crossed the ocean a few times, it remained a virgin hammock and was not getting any younger. So while needing to be prudent with our assets, yet anxious to explore, we welcomed excuses to vacate our overheated homestead. House-sitting clearly seemed a win-win.

Even though we didn't operate heavy equipment, babysit, or have a flair for farming, the odds were good we'd get some reasonable offers, as many homeowners simply wanted their home occupied, plants watered, or a small pet fed. I felt confident we could manage if we put our minds to it. I mean, how hard could it be? Ralph had grown up with a cat and I a dog. Plus, I boasted an impressive pet-sitting résumé.

While living in Heidelberg, Germany, during our working years, I had successfully cat-sat (technically, cat-fed) multiple times for my spunky Canadian neighbor, Lucille, who fiercely indulged her demanding kitty. Her outdoor cat, appropriately named Cleopatra, assumed she was the Queen of Cats and rightfully deserved the multicourse meals Lucille provided. Common cats would be a cinch, I reasoned, after having been put through my paces by Cleopatra.

During the Cleo-care period, a neighbor took the morning cat-feeding shift, and the night gig was assigned to me. On the first evening, I opened Lucille's back door around six and called out into the yard for Cleo. Taking her own sweet time, the kitty pranced into the premises. I presented the first of three courses—the dry food. Bowl filled, I stood back. The cat sauntered to the dish and simply stood there; her head didn't lower. I double-checked the detailed cat-feeding notes Lucille had prepared. Yep, first the dry food.

"Go ahead and eat," I told Cleo. She didn't. I stood there, leaning against the kitchen counter, waiting. Nothing. The cat stared at the food. "Please eat," I begged. "I can't wait here all night. I have my own dinner to prepare." The cat slowly swiveled her head and glared at me. "What?" I said. "What do you want?" She remained motionless. "Ah, now I get it. My presence is an invasion of your privacy, is it?"

Kitty, clearly annoyed, shot me a "Like, duh?" look.

"Okay, okay, prima donna, I'll leave you in peace," I said, retreating to the dining room. I couldn't see her, but I could hear her chomping the hard kibble. When the crackling stopped, I withdrew the dry food bowl and replaced it with the wet food and obediently left the room. Then the big treat—the cream. In an attempt to bribe Her Highness into being more punctual, I gave her a generous portion. When she'd licked the saucer clean, she moseyed around her domain—undoubtedly checking to see if the *help* had fingered anything. When she was satisfied all was in order, she stopped in front of the door, head held high as if supporting the crown she so richly deserved. That was my cue. I opened the door and stepped respectfully back. Kitty glided by. I was dismissed. Purrrfect.

Figuring I had earned my cat management stripes, I didn't hesitate when another friend in Heidelberg asked if I'd be part of her feline feeding team while she was on vacation. I was to do week one and a neighbor's son would take care of week two. The cat had freedom of movement through the pet-flap installed in the back door. All I had to do was to refresh the food and water bowls once a day. My amazingly trusting girlfriend always left her kitchen door unlocked, so I wouldn't even need to fuss with a key.

What a snap. I'd drive up to the kitchen door, fill up the water bowl, pour some dry food in the other bowl, and buzz back out. No waiting for the cat to grace me with its presence. No waiting for the cat to eat three courses. No waiting for the cat to lap the living room. The first few days went fine. Then, on the last day, I was about to blast out of the house, home free, when something out in the dining room caught my eye. I spotted a dark blob in the walkway alongside the large area rug—most likely an expensive one. Good grief, what could it be? I edged a bit closer to the threshold of the dining room to investigate. Whatever the clump was, it most certainly looked repulsive; it made me gag just to see it, even at a distance. No way could squeamish me do anything with it—yuck! I did manage to get close enough—while averting my eyes—to drop a sheet of paper towel over it so the follow-on feline feeding team wouldn't step in it accidentally. I left a note explaining my acute aversion to animal deposits. Surely it wouldn't be any big deal for the strapping young teenager to take care of it.

When my friend returned from vacation, she told me the kid hadn't wanted to mess with the mystery goo either and had passed it off to his mom. Raised on a farm, the lady was used to dealing with such muck, but apparently it had taken some doing. As did the partial resurfacing of the hardwood floor. Big oops. Many apologies flowed and my friend was infinitely gracious. She'd been considering spiffing up the dining room anyway—or so she said. The blob was later identified as regurgitated rodent.

Although that experience certainly didn't up my standing in the cat-sitting community, I did learn a valuable lesson that would serve me well down the road: all animal gigs henceforth would require a guck removal subcontractor on board, i.e., hubby Ralph, to deal with messy stuff when the need arose. Of course, the enticement would have to be compelling.

While sweltering away in Aix-en-Provence, I recalled that golden nugget cat-sitting lesson as I considered a new request for house-sitter services—a nearby friend needed a house-sitter for a week. The email stated that kitty care was required. Drat, no free *déjeuner*. And that meant a potential requirement for guck removal services, which meant persuading Ralph. I read on. The cat was of the outdoor variety, eating a bowl of dry food twice a day. It meowed to be let in and stood by the door when it wanted out. With no freedom of movement—closed-door policy was enforced and no kitty flap installed—there was a greatly reduced risk of "presents," I reasoned. But would a spacious home close to downtown be enough to convince my guck removal contractor? I wondered. Hold on, what's this? There was an expansive grassy area and—wait for it—a pool! I was already doing laps. Ralph agreed, and in short order, I made the deal. Ralph and I played our roles to the letter and so did kitty. Unfortunately, it rained most of the week, so there was little pool time, but sitting in the lush garden under an umbrella was utterly delightful.

Our next gig was again for friends, but this time in a Luberon house with a sweeping view of the countryside just on the outskirts of a picturesque hilltop village, two skips and a hop from enticing Moustiers-Sainte-Marie. Two independent cats reigned supreme. They enjoyed *carte blanche* mobility—through a kitty flap. Red flag alert—Gunk Patrol switched to

Ready-for-Duty mode. But gunk was the least of our problems. Our friends warned us that one of the two cats—from time to time, extremely rarely, highly unlikely, hardly ever happens—would deposit inside the house a small "gift" in the form of a mouse, which had been "toyed with" and undoubtedly would be in critter heaven at the time of discovery.

I bucked up and Ralph geared up, but I silently prayed that no "gifts" appeared. To be on the safe side, I held a kitty pow-wow on the first day to clarify the game plan of the Temporary House Management Company. On a regular basis, Supervisory Team Padgett would provide all kitties with sustenance and beverages (plus the occasional special treat!), and all kitties would provide us caretakers with absolutely *nada, rien, zilch*. No objections were noted, the meeting was adjourned, and off we scampered in our respective directions.

Not to be out-felined, we had a backup plan to be activated immediately on the off chance a kitty went rogue. Each morning, my husband would recon the hallway to ensure it was clear, and in the unlikely event that a "gift" was lurking there, he would sweep it onto a dustpan and take it outside to the field across the street; meanwhile, I would stay safely off to one side, out of the flight path. First morning, A-okay. Second morning, fine and dandy. Morning number three—*oh là là*, bad kitty. As planned, Ralph got the dustpan and swept the little carcass onto it. As he made his way into the living room, the little guy in the pan got a second wind and started squirming. Alarmed that he'd jump overboard, and wanting to avoid chasing a mangled mouse through the house with me squealing in the background, Ralph held the pan at arm's length, tilting it this way and that to counter the mouse's movements. Like a flare, Ralph shot through the dining room and kitchen to the outdoors. Whew, that was a close one.

But the day was not over. Later that afternoon, Ralph was changing clothes in the bedroom. From the corner of his eye, he saw a blurry, dark something swoosh by. Then he saw the real deal. Not an inanimate gift but a swift gift. He called out to me at the other end of the house, and I came running. As I got to one end of the hall, I saw Ralph rush out of the bedroom and slam the door to the toilet room, typically called the WC (water closet). "There's one in there," he said matter-of-factly, not wanting to distress me.

"One what?" I asked.

"Think mini Ratatouille—very, very mini, in fact."

"Ratatouille, as in the movie *Ratatouille*, where a long-tailed creature is a gourmet chef and wears a tall white toque on his furry head?" I asked, shaking my head in disbelief.

"Sorry to say … but yep. On the bright side, it's only the tiny field version, so no worries." Omigod. Action plan. I turned to one of the cats and pleaded for assistance. He purred. I took that as a yes. I held him with one hand and, in one swift movement, opened the door to the WC with the other and launched the kitty in. Silence. Instantly I felt a sharp pang of guilt followed by an icy slap of self-loathing. What was I thinking? It was one thing to be theoretically aware of the food chain but quite another to set the stage, and so blatantly. I cracked open the door to take a peek. The cat scampered out without any tell-tale tail dangling from its chops. Still, I wondered if possibly this mouse mission was a fait accompli? Quickly scanning the WC, my eyes fell upon the wee mouse, shivering in a shadowed corner.

Much relieved, I allowed my guilt to subside. But something had to be done. For house-sitters, this was one of those "other duties as assigned" scenarios. We moved on to Plan B. The lady of the house, an ardent animal lover, wasn't a fan of typical mousetraps but did allow the humane variety. We put some peanut butter in one of the mini-cage "mouse motels" and set it in the WC on the rug in front of the toilet. Hours later we cracked open the door. The peanut butter was gone, but the mouse was still on the mat, hoping for seconds. When our patience had run out, a lightbulb flashed on. Quick like bunnies, we removed the mouse cage, turned the small trash can over the mouse, and then, holding the rug tightly to the can, flipped over the rug-can combination. Ralph ran through the living room, keeping the bathroom rug clamped down tightly on the can, through the kitchen and out to the terrace, down the stairs, past the pool, and across the street to the field, where he freed the little guy to the wild. By the time he climbed back up to the terrace, a cold beer greeted him.

After those disagreeable critter skirmishes, I feared my usually accommodating hubby would be reluctant to make another foray into the world of cat-sitting. Surprisingly, he agreed to my next "opportunity"—the first from a stranger—discovered on a house-sitting website. It was located in Lagarde, a village north of Toulouse, not far from the Les Landes region where Ralph was likely to catch a glimpse of some unusual migrating birds. And there was just one independent yet obedient cat that was never allowed "play dates" inside the house—the owner promised we could bank on it. And the photos of the house on the internet looked lovely. We signed up.

En route to the house, we made some rewarding discoveries, including lively Pezenas crammed with antique stores and vibrant Narbonne with the Canal du Midi running right through it. Upon arrival at the house, we met the British owner, who had kindly prepared us dinner. Beforehand, she gave us the requisite house tour. All standard spaces, we thought, as we marched from one room to the next, except for a multistory worm complex tucked into a corner of the terrace, clearly a source of great pride for the owner. We were invited (but not required) to feed the grubs. When my stifled gag was misinterpreted as interest, she offered a lecture on its use and attributes. Produces fantastic fertilizer, apparently.

The owner departed early the next morning, at which point we took a closer look at our surroundings. There was no TV, microwave, or coffeemaker. Oops—a bit of an oversight on my part. Thank goodness, the internet worked well and the pretty garden had several sitting areas, though one was off-limits—the harsh serenade of some buzzing hornets signaled that message loud and clear.

We managed without the gadgets for four whole days. Except for a little hubbub when a bird went berserk after flying into the potbellied stove (Ralph set it free sans drama), all went without a hitch. The kitty followed her own agenda and, as promised, didn't make any "deposits" in the house. We biked all over the lush countryside and enjoyed some peaceful walks. I bought a beautiful aubergine-hued mohair throw at the expansive weekly market in Fleurance, had fun exploring Condom (best known for Armagnac and selfies in front of the city sign), savored simple meals at a cute café under the arcade in La Romieu, and spent tranquil evenings on the terrace at the little house, rosé in hand, following the sun as it melted into the verdant hillside.

It was early October, but the days were sunny with temperatures near 25°C (77°F). A balmy breeze drifted through the open windows. We were leaving the next day, so we organized the place and prepared our stuff to pack into the car. Early on the day of departure, I popped out of bed, eager to wrap up our current responsibilities and move on. Bleary-eyed, I shuffled down the hall to the attractive bathroom, in which an oval *baignoire* was set on the diagonal. I made a note to have one of those in our own home someday. As I was drying my hands on a towel hanging by the sink, a painful sensation ripped down the top my left hand as though it had been slit with a shard of glass. "Geez, that hurts," I said, wincing. I could see no broken glass on the counter. There was no blood, but the pain was increasing, so I ran some cool water over my hand, rubbing it gently and feeling for something sharp. Nothing. The pain deepened. Just then, a hornet flew out the window. Shrieking ensued.

Ralph was now at my side, trying to calm me as my hand turned red and swelled rapidly. I was breathing fast. Slow down, Gayle—you do *not* want to black out, I told myself. Ralph placed ice in a washcloth and pressed it to my hand. He then opened the laptop and typed, "How to treat hornet stings."

I wasn't showing signs of anaphylactic shock, so I could do nothing but ice it and down some aspirin. But what if I had a delayed allergic reaction? How long would I have if I needed emergency care? Ralph had a friend who'd discovered he was allergic to shrimp after consuming more than a few of the crustaceans at a fundraiser in Washington, DC. On the way home, he'd felt increasingly ill and made the prudent decision of going directly to the emergency room. Good thing. He got there in time, but just.

I wondered if they even had a doctor in that wee village tucked away in the French countryside? And what was the French equivalent of 911, anyway?

I paced and shook my hand and paced some more. Thankfully, the throbbing began to subside. Since it seemed as if I was going to survive without a hospital visit, we started packing the car. Good thing I'd done most of the cleaning the day before; it might have been a bit tricky with one hand. We left a fresh baguette for the owner next to a little note. I reported that the kitty and house were in fine form, but I'd had an unfortunate encounter with a hornet. The next day she emailed that she felt my pain—she also had been a hornet victim. I thanked her for her concern but resisted suggesting that along with a few other modern creature comforts, she might also want to consider acquiring a defibrillator. At least we hadn't been expected to cultivate the grub farm.

After that exciting adventure, I became much more selective about my house-sitting choices. When one popped up in gorgeous Annecy—with a sumptuous view of the lake—I couldn't resist. The owner had not one but two pooches, and their photos were utterly adorable. It was a terrific opportunity to experience authentic life on a lake. Plus, some friends in Puligny-Montrachet, near Beaune, would be visiting their daughter in nearby Geneva and would come down for an afternoon. After I repeatedly waved the lake-view photo in front of Ralph, he finally gave in, and we were on.

The little doggies were, in fact, the cuddliest little fluffballs imaginable. So cuddly that they cuddled with the owner all night, which we did not discover until we arrived. The owner asked if we minded if the doggies slept with us. I was horrified. Yikes, canines in our bed—no way! I didn't even want to think about where those paws had been. "At least, can they sleep in the same room with you?" the owner pleaded.

"Okay," we eventually conceded. We weren't thrilled but agreed to put the doggie beds in our room. The "kids" needed to be let out a lot, but they would always tell us, the owner said. They could run on their own in the garden, but outside the gate they needed the leash. And they didn't like to be left alone for more than a couple of hours. Oh, uh, okay.

We said goodbye to the owner the next morning. Then we played with our new charges. We let them out into the garden. We gave them treats. We let them frolic on the deck. We let them out into the garden again. We went on a long walk by the lake. Then the garden again. We watched a magnificent sunset together. They sat on our laps while we watched TV. We scratched behind their ears. Everybody was content.

Or so we thought. On day two of our four-day stay, I rose before seven to let the doggies out. There on the living room floor was not a regurgitated rodent, not a mouse, not a bird. Just one expansive puddle of pee—on the hardwood floor. And just inches from a large and possibly valuable woven basket, which I scooped up immediately as I made a mad dash to the kitchen for paper towels to mop up the mess. The two cute fluffballs were waiting expectantly by the door, tails wagging.

"Which one of you is responsible, and more importantly, why on earth did you do this? We're supposed to be buds!" I was exasperated, not to mention dismayed at having to kick off my day, not on the lakeside deck quietly sipping my cappuccino, but on all fours, enveloped in fierce cleaning-product fumes. Very much *not* buds, as it turned out. The next morning our charges expanded their repertoire—awaiting me in the wee hours of the morn was a puddle of pee *plus* a pile of poop—on a carpet, no less. That cleanup job took more than a little elbow grease. Thank goodness, the owner was returning the following afternoon—I was wearing a hole in her rubber gloves and running low on disinfectant. When I told her about the poop, she was ademant it was only barf—they always did their business outside, she insisted. Well, that was something, I thought. At least I was somewhat less disgusted, retroactively.

The Annecy trip made us seriously consider sitting out house-sitting altogether. As much as we loved exploring new regions, the attractive cost factor, the spacious interiors and gardens, our low tolerance for unexpected pet deposits had been tested and proven, again and again.

It was time we accepted the fact that many pets follow the same behavioral guidelines with sitters that schoolkids do with substitute teachers—raise hell while you can! So unless we wanted to invest heavily in hazmat gear, we should part ways with pet-sitting. At least that was one point of view.

On the other hand, perhaps we'd simply had a bit of bad luck. Would the next sit be the cat's meow? The odds of that happening would be, admittedly, slim to none. Regardless, I kept checking the house-sitting site, wishfully thinking that maybe, since we'd paid our dues (a couple of times over, in fact), our house-sitting ship might come in. And it did.

Surprisingly, our lucky number turned up not through the house-sitting site but from the international group we belonged to in Aix. Some members were seeking a dog-sitter while they were away in the Cotswolds. They lived in Lourmarin, a town we knew well, just forty minutes north. It was a precious town with an imposing château and renowned Friday market. I sensed a stellar house-sitting experience coming on.

Long ago, in Lourmarin, Ralph had seen a bee-eater, a gorgeous multicolored bird splashed with royal blue, sunflower yellow, and burnt chestnut. In fact, he'd seen an entire group of them, so I hoped he would consider repeating that rewarding experience. And he agreed, albeit reluctantly. I rang the British couple, and we were invited for lunch. As we drove up the driveway, my heart flipped. The place was magnificent—right out of *Côté Sud* home décor magazine—the stereotypical renovated-to-perfection Provençal farmhouse with a creamy stone façade, terra-cotta tile roof, and blue-gray shutters.

Our blind date, Marco, an ebony spaniel, bounded down the stone steps to the parking area, running around and hopping up and down and yapping away. Immediate bonding. The couple was gracious, the designer décor inspired, and the view over the château stunning. All indicators pointed to a joyful experience.

Marco slept in his own bed, thank you very much, just off the living room in view of the TV, thanks to the glass-door enclosure. When we left the house, Marco remained ensconced in his assigned space, contentedly watching his favorite reality shows. When we were there, we'd read on the comfy sofa by the picture window with Marco nearby on the windowsill soaking up the rays. During long walks, we'd let him off his leash and he'd run freely, chasing rabbits over hill and dale. And he always returned after a short while, just as the owners said he would. It was such a positive experience that a few months later we leapt at the chance to again watch over sweet, playful, obedient, and—best of all—considerate Marco, who returned his sitters' affection with no gifts at all.

After the Lourmarin sit, we went on hiatus from sitting—both house and pet. Ralph needed a break, and I took the time to reflect. Although during the house-sits, some traumas and mishaps rested squarely in the character-building column, regrets were few, and there were some stellar bonuses. It was gratifying to help out friends, and the sits expanded our travel horizons. One bonus gift in particular has kept on giving.

During a Luberon house-sit, over a country inn *déjeuner*, quite by chance we met a British couple. Finding our intended bistro closed, we'd followed signs to another. At the adjacent table, we'd overheard English. And roars of laughter. Before the cheese course, arrived, we'd discovered the pair had spent years abroad as educators in Bahrain, Peru, South Korea, and Mustique. Masters of reinvention, they now were managers of a huge estate, harvesting lavender and welcoming guests. Since then we've become fast friends, and not surprisingly. In addition to professional lives spent abroad, we shared some striking weaknesses—the south of France, pale rosé, and strolling in the hills, not to mention delectable *déjeuners* in the Provençal countryside. Even though our friends have since moved back to England, we keep in regular touch and get together as often as possible, visits that nourish the soul and, not regrettably, deepen the laugh lines. *Mille mercis*, serendipity.

Count on kismet to surprise.
When Lady Luck appears, be ready to greet her.

Chapter 5

Cock-a-Doodle-Don't

Aix-en-Provence — Summer 2011

Fans of the Five Basic Food Groups—salt, fat, sugar, alcohol, and caffeine—are thrilled with an Irish coffee sprinkled with a salt-encrusted peanut garnish for their evening meal. Everybody else, however, tends to gravitate to a more substantive repast, especially for *dîner*, which is what we were planning.

Taking a break from the search for our perfect place and from all the pet antics, we decided to get festive with our local chums and have a dinner party. The first question was how to navigate around everybody's specific dietary requirements and preferences, which included but were not confined to fat-free, gluten-free, meat-free, fish-free, shellfish-free, carb-free, egg-free, nut-free, lactose-free, sugar-free, not to mention low sodium and low fat. Don't. Just invite Sebastian—he ate everything. And not only that, he also waxed poetic about everything, including all manner of innards. He had never met a *pied paquet* or *tête de veau* he didn't like. I'm not sure where he put

41

it all—he appeared to have zero body fat on his wiry frame—but you could count on him to go for seconds.

So Sebastian, along with his equally accommodating wife, Jill, were coming to dinner. Sebastian was an Aussie and Jill, a Brit. They'd met in Singapore, became engaged while cruising the high seas, and married in Tahiti or some similarly exotic tropical isle. They'd been living in Aix-en-Provence for a few years after a foray to Paris, where Jill perfected her French, and a stint in The Hague, where Sebastian added Dutch to his repertoire of languages. One Sunday, we'd met them on a family ramble—a casual hike—organized by the international group we'd joined in Aix soon after our arrival. As new kids in the *quartier* and keen to expand our social network, we were thrilled to cross paths with Sebastian and Jill—such a spirited, globe-trotting couple.

What menu, though? What we needed was a lively lineup—dishes with flair to match Sebastian and Jill's keen sense of humor and adventuresome palettes. I hit on a Cinco de Mayo theme. After all, any month was a good month for Mexican food, and it would also give us an opportunity to capitalize on our California connection. During visits to Palm Springs, California, Ralph and I had been spoiled with terrific Mexican dishes, and we really missed them here in France. *Olé!* Mexican it was to be. The menu we crafted started with some zingy margaritas, spicy guacamole, accompanied by corn chips and salsa, followed by zesty chicken enchiladas, with a black bean/rice/hot pepper combo on the side, all garnished with plenty of fresh cilantro and a bloop of sour cream. The grand finale would star Kahlua over vanilla ice cream, adorned with a dark chocolate wafer. Voilà, a pretty decent attempt at a Viva Mexico menu, I thought, considering I was flying by the seat of my *pantalones*. I called Jill to double-check the meal particulars, including their tolerance level for spicy. Jalapeños? Not a problem! Of course not—it was Sebastian we were talking about.

One minor detail, however. Could I find all the necessary ingredients locally? Hmm. I remembered seeing corn tortillas around somewhere. In one of the big *supermarchés*, I figured. Crème fraîche could stand in for sour cream. Avocados were ubiquitous, as was cilantro, thank goodness. I realized I'd have to concoct my own salsa and enchilada sauce, not to mention scout out black beans, so some research was needed. And what about cheddar cheese? Yep, I recalled seeing that, or at least some cheese that emanated a bright orange, cheddar-like hue. Black olives, check. What about those packets of enchilada spices? Nope. Not around Aix, as far as I knew. I'd have to blend my own. Okay, so over to the laptop to locate recipes. After a few minutes of scrolling through some options, I settled on an appealing enchilada spice recipe, but it required a huge variety of ingredients. That was a surprise—I'd had no idea those little packets of spices we used to take for granted in the United States and that cost just a few pennies contained so many different types of spices, including turmeric. Geez, what was turmeric in French? Pondering, I looked it up. Good thing, too, as I couldn't have guessed that one—it's *curcuma*. I was going to be doing a lot of grinding. Oh yes, I needed a mortar and pestle too, so I added that to the list.

Sure enough, I had to run around to a bunch of different stores to get everything. In anticipation of the time-consuming prep, I started a day early with the spice grinding, sauce production, and chicken shredding. At least I saved a little time by buying a roasted chicken. So on the big day, I was well prepared—all I had to do was assemble, which was the fun part. I lined up all the enchiladas rolls side by side in the baking dish, smothered them in the enchilada sauce, topped them with the grated cheddar-like cheese, and stepped back to admire my handiwork. Awfully cute, I thought. I just hoped they were tasty as I popped them into the oven and set the timer.

While the main course was working up to a sizzle, I surveyed the scene. Table set. Candles lit. Roses fragrant. Julio Iglesias queued to croon. We were ready to shake those maracas and click those castanets. Okey-dokey, it was time to shed the apron. Always the responsible margarita maker, Ralph was sampling his concoction to ensure quality control. He handed a glass to me.

"I think you're going to like this," he said proudly.

Just as I was saying, "Yum, honey, it's really good—" the shrill *BZZZ* of the doorbell startled me, practically sending my margarita airborne. Setting my glass safely down on the counter, I turned to Ralph. "Let the festivities begin!" I flung open the door and walked to the top of the stairs to greet Sebastian and Jill. Bending over the railing, I saw bobbing heads climbing higher and higher, making their way up to our third-floor apartment. Huffing and puffing, they stopped at the landing below to catch their breath. "Just one more—you're nearly there," I reassured them. There they were—our freshly made friends in our very own French abode for our very first dinner party in France.

"Hello, daaahling," cooed Jill, looking as stunning as ever, her curves shown off to full advantage by a figure-hugging blue dress that matched her eyes and set off her lustrous blonde hair. *Bonsoirs* and *bises* (cheek kisses) were issued all around.

"*Bienvenue Chez Padgett.* Did you find a parking place okay?" Ralph asked.

"No, didn't need one. Thought we'd walk over so we could cruise home on autopilot—forgot about that strikingly steep hill, though. Is it new?" asked Sebastian in his typical deadpan manner.

"Ha! Only about a few million years ago," came my retort.

"Then you must be thirsty—a margarita?"

"*Absolument,*" they said in unison.

We'd barely settled in on the couch with our frosty drinks when I remembered dinner in the oven. "Oops, had better check my chicken enchiladas. Don't want them to burn. Back in a jiff." I rose to head to the kitchen.

"Hang on," Sebastian said. "Did you say *chicken?*"

"Yes, silly. Chicken enchiladas usually mean there's a portion of *poulet* in there somewhere," I replied sarcastically. I was on to Sebastian's kidding nature. But Sebastian wasn't laughing. His cheery demeanor had disappeared.

He put his margarita down, licking his lips, and said, "Seriously, I don't eat chicken."

"You kidder! What carnivore doesn't eat chicken?" I shook my head with a he-almost-got-me look.

"Me."

"No!" I insisted in disbelief.

"Yes, I mean no, I really don't eat chicken." The famous twinkle in Sebastian's eyes had vanished.

"But you eat everything. You even like that disgusting stuffed pig intestine—what's it called, oh yeah, *andou-ey-something*—for heaven's sakes!"

"*Andouillette*, you mean," Sebastian corrected me.

"That's it, *andouillette*." I repeated it so I could remember what *not* to order—ever. The name was so close to a rather tasty—usually grilled—Cajun-spiced sausage called *andouille* that I really had to concentrate on that one. Mixing them up would induce the gag reflex instantaneously.

"Well, yes, that's true, I do consume *andouillette*. Just not chicken," Sebastian said.

"Oh my God, Gayle, I'm so sorry," wailed Jill, mortified. She explained that while I was reviewing the menu with her, her brain had clicked off at the margaritas, so my reference to the chicken ingredient hadn't registered.

I had to think fast. Now what? I didn't have a Plan B. What the heck was I going to do? But what I said was, "*Pas de problème*—really! I have an idea. Come with me." I motioned to Jill to follow. We scurried off to the kitchen where, much to my great relief, I found ingredients for a spinach-cheese-bacon enchilada. Upon sampling the mixture, I proclaimed it quite tasty. Iron Chef, eat your heart out.

A few margaritas later, we all sat down to Mexican enchiladas, albeit Sebastian's were greener and *pollo*-free. He tucked into them with vigor and soon asked for seconds. I heaved a sigh of relief. I did wonder, though, whether Sebastian's "chicken thing" involved a beloved pet *poulet* that had made an ill-timed decision to cross a busy road. But fearing the story might feature flying feathers, I relegated the mystery to the back burner, keeping my inquisitive impulses quiet.

I pondered the close culinary call that had been our festive dinner party. Lacking a clairvoyant kitchen to guide me, I had very nearly been a main course short. Nothing like sending your dinner guests home hungry to endear you to them. That approach would certainly not help expand our social network in our adopted country. I made a note to self—require that future dinner guests sign off on the menu via a notarized affidavit. And bake back-up.

Feed new friendships.
Serving a buffet of tastes satisfies appetites and wins hearts.

Chapter 6

Puppy Love

Aix-en-Provence and Palm Springs, California — Fall 2011

Life in Aix-en-Provence was humming along. We were making
friends and getting to know the city. But it proved a challenge
to settle into our compact furnished apartment because it
turned out to be more of a treasure trove than a conventional
rental unit.

Our scholarly landlady was a Middle Eastern expert, and we
had become de facto custodians of her impressive resource
library and artifact collection. The built-in bookcases, which
covered two and a half walls of the large alcove adjacent to the
living room, were packed with thousands of neatly arranged
leather-bound tomes, most of which were in Arabic or Italian.
High on a wall in the living room was an imposing, three-feet-
tall warrior puppet-doll dressed in a red brocaded robe with
gold embellishments, its right hand wielding a wide sword. He
sported a thick ebony mustache, matching shoulder-length hair
and piercing eyes that said, "Don't make me use this sword or it

won't end well for you." We named him Oskar, and we had total confidence that he would maintain order.

In the dining room area, across from Oskar, stood a sturdy plastic table. When covered with a pretty linen tablecloth that fell to the floor, it masqueraded as a regular, indoor table and was completely functional. In front of a pair of throw-covered futons, positioned at a right angle, was an intricately etched oversized brass tray, supported by a folding wood base, that served as a coffee table. Since the area doubled as our TV-watching spot where comfort reigned supreme, we needed something to prop up our feet. I swapped out the brass tray for a makeshift ottoman that I fashioned from a cardboard box, stuffed with excess towels, covered with a folded blanket, and topped with another linen cover. I was especially proud of that repurposing job, because not only did I create a footrest, but I also freed space in the hall closet. Well done, *moi*.

The kitchen was thoroughly outfitted, including a late-model fridge adorned with magnets holding up masterful crayon drawings that had been created twenty-five years earlier by our landlord's daughter. They just weren't any kid's artwork; this particular child had grown up to become a competition-winning art curator, so I wanted to ensure her creations remained spatter-free. I found the treasures a safe home on a bookshelf, sandwiched between thick dictionaries. Maybe one day the artist and her mom would thank us for protecting the works—when they garnered a tidy sum on eBay.

Granted, the apartment wasn't going to win any *Architectural Digest* awards, but style hadn't been a priority for us, at least at the beginning. What *had* interested us was a single, crucial attribute—its French address—the requirement for our *cartes de séjour*. Now that we had those basics, our focus turned to refining our abode. Our already tiny place quickly began to shrink after we moved in. Not surprisingly, we were getting restless for more space and a real garden. After all, from the get-go, it was to be our starter apartment, not our forever abode. We weren't going to marry this apartment or Aix. We were still playing the field.

The search for a bigger place was ongoing, but nothing adequate came up. Months slipped away, and we were still there. But that time allowed us to get to know Nathalie, our landlady. She lived and worked in Paris but would come down on some weekends to visit her veterinarian boyfriend, Daniel. Both turned out to be absolute dolls. Early on, they invited us to go on a walk and picnic with them in the shadows of Mont Sainte-Victoire. Despite our lack of French skills, we bonded. In stressful times of family illness or intense overwork, which for them was the norm, we exchanged offerings of support. I felt instinctively that we could count on each other.

As a matter of course, when mail for Nathalie was delivered to the apartment, we'd drop it off at Daniel's clinic, which was located in a little village north of Aix near where we played tennis. After a match, despite being decked out in tennis togs, we'd stop off at the vet's office. I'd pop inside with Nathalie's letters and march to the desk, past all the impatiently waiting clients with their pets. It didn't take long for the nurses to recognize the lady in the rumpled tennis attire, and they always welcomed me warmly. If the doctor was in, they'd ask if I'd like to see him. Normally I'd decline because I knew how busy he was, but one day everything was different. My mother, now ninety-three, had become quite ill, so we were planning to fly to California and would be staying for six weeks. I wanted to explain the situation to the doctor, so I said, *"Oui, s'il vous plaît.*

50

C'est important.'' The nurse nodded solemnly and turned to fetch him.

Before I could take a seat, Daniel appeared. With a big smile, he offered both cheeks for the requisite *bises*. I started to tell him about our US plans, but I became choked up. Daniel glanced at all his clients and their masters and mistresses seated along the wall, then turned to me and said, "Come with me." Halfway down the hall, he stopped and opened a door. Standing back, he allowed me to go in first; he followed and closed the door. A small shaft of light was filtering through the blinds at the far end of the room, but otherwise it was dark and hard to make out where we were.

In the semidarkness, Daniel turned to me with a serious look, arms crossed in front of his chest, and asked in French, "How is your mother?" I began again to tell him as much as I knew. A protein in her blood was the cause of her severe illness. He nodded knowingly. I continued on about the transfusions and how they had helped for a while but couldn't go on forever. He nodded some more, encouraging me to continue. I explained that my mom was small and didn't eat much and seemed to be losing stamina. My emotions bubbled up, and I had to stop to restore my composure. It was then that I glanced from one side and to the other. Where were we, anyway? There was no desk and no examining table. What I did see was floor-to-ceiling metal shelving. Then I noticed lots of large, full sacks. Pet food? Could we be in a supply closet? A cold, wet sensation zinged my left leg. Then another. Startled, I jerked away and nudged Daniel as I emitted a slight whimper. He caught me and helped me steady myself. I looked down at the floor. Geez—it was a small dog licking my leg.

Daniel smiled and explained. *"C'est le chien de Nathalie. Il s'appelle Pinot. Il va rester avec moi pour quelques semaines. Charmant, n'est-ce pas?"*

So Daniel was taking care of Nathalie's poodle for a while. How considerate, I thought. *"Mais oui, Pinot est adorable,"* I said. And stealthy—I hadn't detected any movement before contact. But apparently little Pinot was also caring like his masters. Maybe he'd sensed my angst and figured I needed a hug, or a lick, in this case. Or he had a sodium deficiency and mistook my leg for a salt lick. Beyond Pinot was another, much larger version of Pinot, but he was content simply observing and not licking anything connected to me, for which I was most grateful.

I struggled to get a grip and finish my sad story. Daniel's demeanor was grave as he asked for some numbers relating to my mother's protein count. As I told him what I knew, searching for the words in French to describe a medical condition I didn't understand very well in English, all the tennis sweat on my legs was being removed courtesy of my landlady's puppy. A few licks later, Pinot was satisfied and retreated. Daniel thanked me for coming in and assured me he'd pass on all the details of our situation to Nathalie. He opened the door, allowing Pinot to tag along, and out we all went to the waiting room. In front of the menagerie and their owners, Daniel assured me that he and Nathalie would check our mail and watch the apartment while we were gone and that we should not worry. Thanking him profusely, I promised to email from California. After exchanging au revoir cheek kisses, as I was about to head for the door, Pinot tilted its head upward, gave a concerned look, and let out a small woof that I took as poodle-speak for "Hang in there." I nodded my *merci* and hustled to Ralph waiting for me in the car before I started boo-hooing.

⌇

We arrived in California the day after my mom had been given one of her now regular transfusions. She said it would be her last. She lied. But it was a fib we were grateful for because it bought precious goodbye time. Family and friends took leave from work and school to travel to Palm Springs and give my spunky mom one last hug and have a few last laughs. Often she would give them a little memento, usually something silly from her extensive Snoopy collection, the crowning glory of which was a functioning, rotary telephone in a box topped with a smiling foot-tall Snoopy, his left hand on his hip and the other holding a bright yellow receiver. (Not only was that our main telephone during my high school days, but it was also installed in a peculiar place—the hall closet, which my mom had turned into a telephone booth.)

While the Snoopy collection dwindled over the course of the next five weeks, I remembered something pooch-related I'd always admired but my mom would never let me have. It was a stylish, tasseled umbrella that my dad had given her for their first wedding anniversary. The cloth was deep amber and the faux tortoiseshell handle was molded into the sleek shape of a greyhound wearing a top hat. Since my teenage years or earlier, I was struck by what an elegant, unconventional gift it was. For me, it was emblematic of my dad's spirited personality and my parents as a happy couple—a dim memory but exactly how I wanted to remember them. Year after year, decades after my father had passed away, I'd periodically rummage around in my mom's closet until I uncovered the umbrella and I'd ask my mom if I could "borrow" it. She always answered firmly, "No, you can't have that—your dad gave it to me for our first wedding anniversary. Now put it back in the closet."

One afternoon while I was sitting with my mom on the edge of her bed, chatting quietly about random topics—from misguided city developers threatening to destroy historic Palm Springs buildings to the late delivery of the local paper, *The Desert Sun*—it occurred to me that I wanted her permission to finally gain official guardianship of that sentimental item. I suppose I wanted her to know that I'd take good care of something that was dear to her, a way of honoring our special relationship. "Hey, Mom," I said, "remember the umbrella Dad gave you on your first wedding anniversary?" I waited for her to guess why I'd raised the subject and prepared for her to object, as she always did.

"No, not really," she said, shaking her head.

Stunned, I finally let it sink in that she was, in fact, fading. I continued, "You know, the gold one with the handle in the shape of a dog? Does that ring a bell?"

She paused for a long moment. "You said an umbrella?"

"Yes. I asked you for it over the years, but you always said no. Maybe I could adopt it now?"

With a small burst of energy, she said, "If you can find it, go for it!"

Though I understood that her memory was bouncing furiously through her more than nine decades of life, I was disappointed she didn't seem to recall our feisty doggie umbrella repartees. But that didn't diminish how much I knew she and my dad had meant to each other, and that was what counted. As I thanked her with a gentle hug, her head came to rest on my shoulder and she cupped my hand. Time was running out.

꧁

On the sunny day she passed away a week later, the sky was clear and brilliant blue, a typically perfect Palm Springs winter day. It was the type of day that people from Canada and Washington and Michigan and other chilly parts gravitate to when the weather goes south up north. A few years before, we'd decided to have a sun-drenched winter getaway ourselves and had acquired a condo in Palm Springs. While in France, we'd rented it out to some of those snowbirds, and now a couple of those sun-seekers were expected in less than a week, the day we were scheduled to return to France.

In my grief-stricken zombie state, I did my best to prepare our condo, with Ralph carrying the heavy load. My mind kept wandering to my mom's memorial service, which was to take place at the end of the following month. While family and friends took charge of orchestrating that endeavor, Ralph and I returned to France to finalize some official business.

꧁

At home in Aix, I had a limited window of opportunity to finish the paperwork for my French driver's license. I needed to swap my US license for a French one—only a handful of states have a reciprocal agreement—to avoid having to attend an expensive French driving school and pass a complicated test, both of which terrified me more than crisscrossing the ocean a few times in a metal tube.

Even before I'd recovered from jet lag, I filed my driver's license dossier in Aix and made reservations to return to California. For the second time in just over two months, we launched into an extended absence. Our gracious downstairs neighbor took in our pair of plants, and we snagged a corner parking spot where we backed in our second-hand Renault, just in case it needed a battery charge when we returned.

On the day of departure, we rose early to have plenty of time for the Fort Knox-style lockup, a promise to our wonderful and security-conscious landlady. Even though the third-floor apartment had only two small bedrooms, there were seven doors, two or three locks each, including one that triggered a vertical iron rod that shot up and down when activated by an intricate key with multiple stubby spikes. Peace of mind was not an issue. Plus, Oskar was on duty.

The trip back to California was thankfully uneventful. All our energy went into helping with the final preparations for my mom's memorial and celebration of life services. Both were lovely. We returned to Aix, more energized than ever to live the life that brought us joy—a life in France.

Soak up support—whatever the source.
Even puppies and puppets can play for
Team Comfort.

Chapter 7

Nut Case

Aix-en-Provence — Spring 2012

"Wait, wait, *s'il vous plaît*," I called out to the tall surgeon
striding briskly down the corridor, having just left my husband's
hospital room in a Marseille clinic. One corner of his white coat
fluttered as he pivoted to see my face, tight with distress, a sight
he no doubt recognized only too well.

"*Docteur, excusez-moi*, I am so … worried. Will he be all
right?" I barely squeaked the words out, clutching his arm.

As he peeled my fingers one by one from his forearm, the
doctor, emanating a compelling gravitas, stared down at me, his
eyes boring into mine. Deliberately and slowly, he said in
English, "Madame Pah-*ZHETT*. This is the simplest thing I do.
The operation is twenty minutes. Your husband will be fine.
The nurse will find you when the operation is complete. You
must not worry." Much relieved, I thanked the confident chief
of neurosurgery and watched him continue down the hall to

finish his evening rounds. The *docteur* looked around fifty years old, which surely meant he had experience on his side. I knew he performed brain surgery, so yes, replacing a single herniated disk was probably a *promenade* in the *parc* for him. No doubt he could do it while playing a game of *boules* in said *parc*. I knew I had to relax. With a deep breath, I returned to Ralph, who would get a new nut in his neck the next morning.

※

The pain had begun a couple of months before when Ralph awoke with what he thought was an unhappy muscle in his upper back. He thought he'd probably slept on it wrong. Over the next few days, I applied my expert massage technique on the smarting muscle, and for a while, Ralph seemed fine. And then he wasn't. In the middle of a set at our tennis club, Ralph stopped in mid-serve. He couldn't go on, he said. The doggone pain in his upper back was growling loudly and ferociously. Professional help was needed.

Back at our apartment, we developed a course of action that began with asking around for physician recommendations. The first doctor we saw stuck some needles in Ralph's upper back à la acupuncture, but that procedure didn't prove effective, causing us more consternation. After that, we saw an internist who prescribed X-rays and the services of an osteopath. After a few treatments, Ralph's condition seemed to improve—and then became dramatically worse. Time for a CT scan and then an MRI.

The radiologist spoke English well, and so did his assistant—a congenial young Irish lass. But no verbal language was necessary to convey Ralph's situation. The radiography clearly revealed a disk that had not only sprung a leak, but had pretty much exploded, producing a sizable balloon of disk goo.

Ralph and I stared at each other in utter disbelief and then squinted at the photograph again. Yikes, how had *that* happened? We had no clue, but apparently Ralph's spine had quite literally harbored a weak link that had given out in spectacular fashion. So it was no mystery why the proficient young radiologist said what he said next: "You need a new disk, Monsieur Padgett. Dr. Galliano will give you one."

Without further explanation, the matter-of-fact Docteur Lanvin opened his notebook and began drawing a map. He looked up and said, "This is the best way to go to Marseille."

"Marseille?" Ralph said, staring at the emerging sketch.

"Yes. You'll take these photos to Dr. Galliano in Marseille. He's a great spine surgeon." Pointing to a little square box he'd penned, he said, "This is his clinic. It's a fine one—you'll see."

"Can't we just email the photos?" I asked, trying to quickly process both Ralph's serious condition and how I'd navigate Marseille's famously treacherous road network.

"Unfortunately, no—they're too big," he answered. "And besides, you must see Dr. Galliano. I'm calling his office now to let them know you're coming."

Carrie, the Irish assistant, said, "Downtown Marseille is a real mess because they're digging up the roads for the new trams. Marseille is a European Capital of Culture next year, and they're doing a lot of building, so you really can't drive through it." She continued, "You should go down by Aubagne and then to Cassis and backtrack to Marseille. The clinic is on that side of town, so it'll be so much easier than trying to cross Marseille, which is basically impossible."

Well, that was confidence boosting. Not.

So, as though spinal surgery for my husband wasn't terrifying enough, I now had to drive about an hour from Aix into the madness that was big-city Marseille traffic and along a coastal road to boot. Prior to this point, we'd never driven to Marseille. Why would we? There was no need, as the bus was simple and efficient. It took just a half hour from the conveniently located bus terminal, not far from the Aix train station. The bus would deliver us to the Marseille train station, from where we could hop the metro or take an easy stroll to the Old Port. And even if we were using the bus, we would time it to avoid the nightmarish backups that come with Friday afternoon. But now, on top of the everyday Marseille congestion, there would be tons of worker bees more frantic than ever to leave the city behind to start their weekend.

But before we could begin the dreaded trip to the surgeon in Marseille, I had to first take the radiography back to the osteopath, who was located directly in the middle of the historic center of Aix, a complex network of one-way and resident-only streets. Luckily, I found a parking space about a block from the ring road that circles the city. I told Ralph to sit tight—as if he was going to scamper off somewhere—and took off jogging through the cobbled streets, the precious CD of the radiography in my bag. After the osteopath viewed the photos, he proceeded to handwrite a lengthy missive for the surgeon. It seemed to take forever, and I was becoming increasingly agitated thinking about the impending surgery, not to mention the coastal drive to Marseille. At last, the specialist was satisfied with his detailed evaluation—fully aware that our famous Marseille surgeon would be scrutinizing it—and off I went, running, zig-zagging around and through masses of summer shoppers.

Aix is a superb shopping town, by the way. But no, I did not stop, or even pause to window-shop, as tempting as it was. I had a sick sweetie in the auto. Okay, truth be told, out of my peripheral vision I did catch a glimpse of advertisements for the upcoming summer sales, or *soldes* as they are called here. And yes, I did hope that I'd be able to take advantage of them in the not-so-distant future when life got back to normal. By the time I returned to the car, my veins were surging with adrenaline, which I badly needed in order to face the trek to Marseille.

Sometimes things work out in your favor, and this was one of those times. The drive wasn't nearly as bad as I'd anticipated, not even the cliff road between Cassis and Marseille. Thank goodness, there weren't sheer drop-offs without guardrails. It did get a little tricky negotiating the hairpin turns looping down into Marseille, but it was do-able—we were on the mountain side.

Once on the hospital grounds, I parked the car across from the main hospital entrance where we thought the surgeon's office was located. Ralph had to extract himself cautiously from the car and walk carefully. Even then, every other step prompted a controlled grimace, which I knew reflected just a fraction of the discomfort he was experiencing. To our dismay, we ended up at the wrong building, apparently having lost favor with the gods of directions. When we finally made it into the right building and up to the right office, we found it deserted. Not a soul was around the elevators, corridor, or in the large waiting room. Hearing a faint clicking noise, we followed it to a sizable office inhabited at the far end by a lone individual, the secretary of the renowned Dr. Galliano.

We exchanged greetings and I handed her the CD. Explaining that Dr. Galliano would review it and that I was to call on Monday, she wished us a *bonne journée*, replaced her earbuds, and resumed her typing. Ralph and I exchanged surprised looks.

In French, I said loudly, "Sorry to bother you. I understand my husband is to see Dr. Galliano."

She looked up and said, *"Non, ce n'est pas possible maintenant.* There was an *urgence.* Dr. Galliano is in surgery."

What? We'd driven all that way and no doctor was available to examine Ralph? The secretary repeated that the doctor would review the photos and we should call on Monday afternoon to make an appointment to see him. I had no idea how Ralph was going to make it through the weekend. But it seemed there was nothing to be done. Back to the car. Back on the highway. Back home. Ralph got himself positioned on the futon-sofa in a near fully prone position, and there he resided until Monday.

Early Monday morning, I made an appointment with Dr. Galliano for two days later. The second trip to Marseille was a snap—for me, anyway. Ralph still had to brace himself for the plentiful potholes. We made it without major trauma and even found a good parking space near the front door of the correct building. This time, the clinic waiting room was packed with nearly two dozen patients. Ralph found a seat, but I stood. Every quarter of an hour or so, the venerable doctor himself appeared, looked down at his folder, and called a name. That person would obediently rise and disappear with the doctor down the hall.

Finally, when the room was nearly empty, it was our turn. The *docteur* ushered us into his huge office. He walked around his impressively large desk and sank into his swivel chair to study Ralph's photos. After he recorded all his comments into a little device, he turned to us and described the situation to us in English. The issue was located between C-6 and C-7. The doctor picked up a plastic spine facsimile and proceeded to describe how he would fix Ralph's problem. He explained that he'd go in through the front, around Ralph's throat, because it was easier and safer than entering through the back. He could perform the surgery the following Wednesday. If Ralph wanted to return to the United States, he'd give him a cortisone shot to get him through a flight home. We had a day to decide.

That night, overwhelmed with the severity of the situation, we considered options. Surgery in France. This was not in our retirement plan. But neither was Ralph writhing on the living room couch. One thing was certain—something had to be done, and quick. This surgeon seemed completely confident, and France usually takes top prize for the world's best health care. But this was a neck we were talking about, and you don't mess with a neck. Would this be the same surgery they would perform in the United States? Would they perform it in exactly the same way? Did they have all the latest equipment? Were they trained in the most current techniques? What if it went wrong? But if we got on a plane to California, we'd have to start the process all over again, and any remedy would be delayed for who knows how long.

We needed a second professional opinion. I found the prettiest photo showing off Ralph's disk in all its burst glory and emailed it to my niece, who just happened to have a good friend who was a neurosurgeon. That supportive buddy had agreed to review the MRI photo. The reply came back the next day—go ahead now. It's a straightforward procedure, the neurosurgeon wrote, and trust me, *they know what they are doing in France!*

The decision was made. Ralph would have surgery *en France*. I called the surgeon's office to confirm the date for the operation. The secretary emailed us all the information on the cost and payment procedure. We were to settle the bill at the hospital when Ralph checked in. Our insurance company would reimburse us. At least we hoped they would. Seven and a half thousand euros was nothing to sneeze at. We called our insurance representative in the US to explain the situation and got the go-ahead—no special authorization was necessary. That was really good news—one less hassle! (We realized later that this was probably because surgery here in France costs a fraction of what it does in the US.) Ralph just had to tough it out a few more days. Relief was in sight. He was to check in during the afternoon, have the surgery the next morning, and most likely could be home by the weekend.

Knowing the surgery was set lifted some weight from our shoulders. Some. Ralph was in such agony that he just wanted it over; he had no interest in worrying. That was my job, which I took to heart. Not surprisingly, repercussions followed. While Ralph was napping, I popped briefly into the end-of-term luncheon for my French class, which was taking place in the backyard of our dedicated teacher, Sylvie. Halfway through the garden party, I found myself in the kitchen, crying in convulsing bursts over a plate of petite toasts spread with black olive tapenade, which were salty enough already without my tears sprinkled over them. Sweet Sylvie gave me a hug while reassuring me that Ralph's surgeon was most excellent. "Don't forget what my son the doctor said," Sylvie reminded me, "Ralph's surgeon is *formi-DAAble*."

What more could you ask for than a doc who was *formi-DAAble*? We had found one, so I tried to dial back the worry and focus on the money. I was to get sufficient euros to pay for the surgery into our euro chequing account—a simple but time-consuming undertaking. I would go to the French sister bank of our US bank where I'd withdraw funds from our US account—in the form of euros. I would then deposit those euros directly into our euro account right there at our French sister bank. Easy peasy. We did this all the time to pay our rent in Aix. The only caveat was a daily maximum amount of dollars Ralph and I each could withdraw, so I had to repeat the process each day over the next few days, using both our bank cards, until I reached the required amount. All set.

Or so I thought.

On the big day, we drove back down to the Marseille clinic by way of Cassis. By then I could almost enjoy the gorgeous Mediterranean views without panic. Even the hairpin turns dipping down into Marseille didn't bother me that much. But the roads were often uneven and every time there was a bump, it caused Ralph to cringe with pain. We arrived at the clinic without any major traffic issues. I dropped him off right in front of the lobby and went in search of a parking spot. After a smooth check-in, Ralph tried to relax in his room, which, though minimalist in its furnishings, included a surprise upgrade—a distant view of the Mediterranean. As mesmerizing as it was, I couldn't dawdle. I had to scurry down to the clinic's accounting office to pay for Ralph's neck repair. When the accountant gave me the sign, I slid my bank card into the debit machine. It cranked along for a few moments and then stopped, and the little screen read, *Refusée*. The transaction hadn't gone through. I showed the machine to the accountant. Maybe she hadn't punched in the correct code. She asked me to try again, which I did. Again, *Refusée*. I explained I had all the money in there. Over ten thousand euros, as a matter of fact. She said to give it another try. The third time was not a charm. *Refusée*, again.

What the heck was going on? Then it struck me. Not only was there a limit on the dollar cost of euros I could withdraw from my US account on any given day, but there was also a limit on how many of those euros I could use from my euro account. Dang! "The daily amount I can spend is limited," I muttered to myself and then in French to the accountant. "All the money is there—I just can't get at it," I explained. "There is a limit."

"Mais oui, c'est ça," she said, nodding. She understood but didn't seem overly concerned. My worry machine, on the other hand, kicked into overdrive. Ralph was having surgery in the morning; it was all arranged. But I was to pay for that surgery beforehand. That was the deal, which had been explained to me very carefully. What if I couldn't pay? What were the implications? Would they postpone the surgery? Oh, my goodness, I couldn't bear to think that thought. It was too painful for me and would be a disaster for Ralph. He had been hanging on by a thread the last week, waiting to get to this point. My mind raced in panic. And then ... I jerked up out of my chair and stared at the accountant with eyes wide as if I'd just discovered electricity or stuck my finger into a live socket and said, "I can write a cheque!"

She smiled as she shook her head. No, the cheques had to be received by the hospital a week ahead so they would have time to clear.

"Wait! I know—I can go to the bank and tell them about the problem face to face and they'll give me the money." I felt frantic by now. Surely that would work?

"Oh, *madame*, this is not a good idea. To walk around a big city like Marseille with seventy-five hundred euros in your pocket ... well, this is crazy," she said gravely.

Good point. What was I thinking? There had to be a way. Then I said, "Maybe you can call my bank and explain the situation?" And she did. But she needed to connect with our personal counselor, and he was unavailable just then. She promised to try again later, which led me to hope she could work it out and wouldn't kick Ralph out.

Feeling a bit less distressed, I went upstairs to check on Ralph. At least he wasn't at home slumped on the living room sofa trying to find a position that didn't cause him to yelp. Instead, he was in the care of a team of superb—I hoped—medical professionals and had a private room with an electric bed next to a big picture window with sweeping views over clay-tiled rooftops out to the Med. As a bonus, there was a foldable bed for me, so I could spend the night beside him. It would have been counterproductive to tell my hurting pup of a hubby the full story of the nonpayment debacle. Staying positive was the name of the game right then, and besides, at this point, I felt certain that the accountant was certain of payment. So I got out the TV remote and tried to find something entertaining to distract him. I found just the thing.

"Hey, honey, look, it's *The Simpsons!*"

"In French?"

"Well, yes. It's good it's in French, really. If you understood it all, you'd laugh too hard and that might hurt too much. Here, you take the remote, but be careful. Safety first!" I gave him a little peck on the cheek and went back down to the accountant.

Luckily, she'd finally been able to speak to our bank counselor. He confirmed the funds were in the account and said he'd transfer them directly from our euro account to the hospital's account. My job was to email him my request, along with the hospital's proper account number. Thank goodness, the hospital had WiFi, so I was able to quickly take care of business right then and there on my laptop and make it back to the hospital room in time to join Ralph for the earlybird dinner special. While he had a mostly liquid repast, I enjoyed a tasty plate of pasta, accompanied by a stemmed glass generously topped off with a spicy Côtes du Rhône. Not. But some rich *vin rouge*, or any color, was going to be in order once Ralph was fixed up. When that was accomplished, yes indeed, we would celebrate. But in the meantime, there in the hospital, our task was to keep calm and carry on, as the Brits say.

During the next few hours, one by one, several doctors and specialists filed through, each making sure all was in order for surgery the following day. They answered any questions we had with utmost professionalism and kindness. Each one was exemplary. Our confidence in the success of the mission was sky-high. I also knew for sure that when we had to vacate the room, we were going to miss that stunning view.

Early the next morning, a couple of nurses arrived. Showtime. While they prepared the bed to roll, I gave Ralph a big kiss and said, "Sweetie, you're going to be good as new very soon. I'll be right here waiting for you. Love you bunches." Ralph grinned and told me to behave. I passed the time channel-clicking, web-surfing, magazine-flipping, and Med-gazing, but mostly pacing. A few hours later, a nurse came in and told me the news: Ralph was doing great. It had all gone great. In short, it was a great day—the best day ever. They'd successfully patched up my love, and for that I gave France's medical establishment a huge virtual squeeze. And I hoped Dr. Galliano wouldn't mind getting a real one.

Amazingly, that very night Ralph got up, unassisted, still connected to his IV, and walked (well, shuffled) the few feet to the WC—without moaning! The following morning, he walked outside for some fresh air, and the day after that, he was ready to face the world. Dr. Galliano agreed. Glancing out the window, the good doctor pointed to the nearby woods and said encouragingly, "In fact, even today you can go walking up there if you want. Just stay on your feet." Then the tireless surgeon turned slightly for the door, my cue to deliver a gentle hug of gratitude. As I started to move forward, he smiled, nodded, and wished us a *bonne journée*. Convinced that he had fully read our hearts, I let him go, off to mend the next patient, who we hoped would be as appreciative of his expertise and kindness as we were.

The two of us sat on the edge of the hospital bed for a moment, took some deep breaths, and let it sink in that Ralph was patched up and we could move on.

"Okay," Ralph said, "we've satisfied my neck's demands for a personal investigation of the ins and outs of the French health-care system. So where were we exactly before we were so rudely interrupted?"

"We were in the middle of a tennis game," I answered, thinking back to that beautiful spring day a couple of months back.

"Yeah, I owe you a rematch. Well, after therapy and an all-clear sign from the doc, that is."

"That's right, you do. And I owe you a birthday celebration. You know," I added, "while you were getting a new neck nut, you missed a birthday."

"Yeah, that wasn't the best timing, was it?"

"No time is. But now, even more reason to do some celebrating. What are you up for—maybe a little skydiving or hang gliding, perhaps?"

"Ha! Let's not and say we did," he chuckled. "To tell you the truth, what sounds like an extreme sport to me at the moment is going home and sitting in a chair, totally upright."

"Now that's an idea I could get my arms around," I said, laughing as I slipped one of mine around his waist and rested my head on his shoulder.

After gathering our things, we bid *au revoir* to the glistening Mediterranean and headed toward the elevator. As we crossed the main foyer, sunshine was pouring in through the glass walls, lifting our already high spirits even higher. Ralph said, "By the way, does that chair I'm going to sit upright in come with *une bière*, preferably the chilled variety?"

After giving his request thoughtful consideration lasting a full nanosecond, I replied, "I'll have to check my schedule, *mon chéri*, but I'm pretty sure that can be arranged."

Cheer—hip, hip, hooray—for France's world-class health-care system.

You can tap into top-notch medical services— without selling the family *ferme*.

Chapter 8

Name Droppings

Saint-Rémy-de-Provence — Fall 2012

Sometimes the writing on the wall is carved in stone.

Villa des Lavandes, Les Oliviers, Mas de Pinet, Les Rosiers—all proud house names that conjure up dreamy dimensions of Provence, a region awash with fields of lavender, groves of olive and pine trees, and trellises enveloped in cascading roses. Typically, the *nom de maison* is etched into a pillar at the front gate, glazed onto a ceramic tile cemented into the wall, or forged in metal cursive letters bolted to a façade. However the name is presented, the proprietors are determined to make their mark endure for eternity. This wasn't the case, however, with *our* new home—it was nameless.

After Ralph's spine surgery and several weeks of physical therapy, his sojourn at the Marseille clinic faded to a fuzzy memory. A couple of months after that, he was moving boxes, albeit carefully, to our new address in our old stomping grounds of Saint-Rémy-de-Provence.

It was a move that surprised us. Our eighteen months in Aix had been terrific (except for that pesky operation), and we'd made wonderful connections, but finding a rental with a *piscine*—a swimming pool was one of our retirement must-haves—was proving impossible. We'd exhausted ourselves looking at dozens of properties in and round Aix, but none even came close to what we wanted. Realtors told us our budget was fine. The problem was the lack of inventory of small homes in good condition that had the all-important in-ground pool. If we'd been willing to compromise on an above-ground pool, chances for success would have been greatly increased. But at the time, we thought we had to hold firm. So, when we found the spanking new Saint-Rémy property with its small garden, pool, and short walk to the lively town center, the tug was so irresistible that we were powerless. We stopped dating Aix and fired up a relationship anew with Saint-Rémy, where the house was twice the size with half the security measures. Whenever an adventure beckoned, we could lock up and leave in no time. Our considerate landlord even offered to collect the mail and water the plants.

Our first trip from our Saint-Rémy house happened just two weeks after we moved in, but it wasn't exactly the kind of getaway of discovery we'd envisioned. We'd found the Saint-Rémy house unexpectedly, after we'd booked flights to California for a three-month stint, no less. The plan was to test the concept of staying in our Palm Springs condo for part of the year. Similar arrangements suited lots of people, and we wondered if it would work for us too. So we bid adieu to our new *maison* without complying with the custom of naming it.

During the three months in California, our thoughts were constantly shifting back to France. By Thanksgiving, we'd made the decision that once the winter renters vacated our condo, we'd put the property on the market.

∽

Back in the Saint-Rémy house, we ran around like crazy kids, kicking up our heels in all our new found spaces, delighting in the blank canvas that it was. We dug in the dirt, dipped into the pool, hung pictures, and positioned furniture we'd found at flea markets. But the process of making the house our own wouldn't be complete without choosing a name for it. Not that we'd decided to rock on the front porch together into our twilight years in Saint-Rémy or mount a permanent sign on our rental property, which would have mortified our landlord, but we did at least want to nurture a mind-set of commitment. Even if our house's name was known only to us, that would be sufficient. It was nesting with baby steps. And besides, playing the name game was festive, like naming our cars.

Our current compact Renault Modus we named Beau Mo. The pink-and-white tank of an Oldsmobile I used as a teenager had been called Grapefruit. The speedy white two-seater I'd had when I met Ralph was dubbed Snowball. The good-for-nothing green Mazda 626 that regularly broke down had been assigned Avocado Pit.

So what name for our Provençal *maison*, then? Mon Rêve? Mon Paradis? Indeed, Provence *was* a dream and a paradise for many, including us, yet we were searching for a more personalized house handle, one that symbolized our particular journey south. And one that had a soupçon of pizzazz. Then it struck us that we might find the answer in bird life. After all, it was the wild winged creatures of the Camargue that were responsible for bringing us to Provence in the first place.

Ralph got out his bird book and flipped through.

"You know, maybe we should name it after an American bird," he said.

"Terrific idea!"

"Maybe even use the Latin term to make it a bit more creative."

"Yes, that's the ticket," I said. Just then the mail delivery arrived, and Ralph turned to go out to the letter box to retrieve our six-times-a-week little treat, *The International Herald Tribune* or *The New York Times, International Edition*, as it is now called. On his way, he handed me his bird book.

Over his shoulder, he said, "Okay, how about the American robin?"

"Perfect." I opened the book to the index, found the page for the American robin, and ran my finger down to the entry where it was listed in English, French, and Latin.

"Honey," I shouted so he could hear me outside, "the American robin won't work. We definitely need another bird."

He came back into the house, unfolding the paper as he walked, then stopped and looked up at me. "How come?"

"Two words." I pointed to the entry: *Turdus migratorious.*

"You're kidding—the Traveling Turd?" he said.

"Catchy … as in you-caught-something-in-your-throat-and-started-to-choke catchy."

"Yeah, gagging isn't what we're going for here. We need a name that's upbeat and playful."

"Maybe we need to go somewhere inspiring. So how about a priceless picnic place?"

"Maybe a Roman one?"

"Perfect." I knew Ralph meant Les Antiques, the two grand monuments at the gateway to Glanum, Saint-Rémy's claims to Roman fame.

We put on our hiking boots, grabbed our water bottles, and tossed a few nibbles in a backpack. Instead of taking the most direct route, we opted for a slight detour through *centre ville* so we could pop into the mayor's office, the unlikely distribution center for rolls of yellow recycle sacks. Though each town has its own procedures, in Saint-Rémy, it's the mayor who stacks the sacks. We crossed the ring road in front of Église Saint-Martin, passed by the little street that leads to Nostradamus's birthplace, and went on to Place Pelissier, dominated by the striking Hôtel de Ville. After acquiring our plastic sacks from the accommodating civil servant at the front desk, we continued on up the rue de la Commune, through the arched Port Saint-Paul, and across the ring road on the south side of town. As we rounded the corner to head toward the tourist office and Les Antiques, I paused.

"Hey, honey, give me a moment, *s'il te plaît*," I said. "This little deli has really fresh and tasty takeout. I'll grab us something, okay?"

"Sure. I'll wait out here—surprise me."

I was back in a jiff, toting a pair of *pans bagnats*, large round buns stuffed with seasoned tuna, lettuce and tomato, black olives, and hard-boiled egg. The plump sandwiches were tucked into a tangerine-hued paper bag with matching napkins, design touches that instantly upgraded our impromptu *pique-nique* into more of a special event.

Fifteen minutes later, we reached Van Gogh's former residence, Saint-Paul-de-Mausole. There, we crossed the busy street that winds up the hill past Glanum, through the Alpilles, and down to Maussane, near Les Baux. Without passing through a turnstile or paying any fee, we stepped into the area of Les Antiques, composed of a multitiered mausoleum (40 BC) and triumphal arch (10–25 AD), a mighty symbol of Roman power. The wide-open space around the pair of stone masterpieces was ringed with huge, flat quarried stones, positioned several meters apart, providing perfect picnic seating. We plopped on the rocks, tucked into our tuna treats, and took in the striking view. Beyond the majestic Roman monuments stood the commanding Les Alpilles and, in between, the ubiquitous olive groves and cypresses that Van Gogh painted so often. The sun highlighted the pocked limestone arch, banded with an intricately carved cornucopia of the region's agricultural bounty—olive branches, apples, bunches of grapes. A mere two thousand years old and simply gorgeous.

"So, what about our house name?" I asked Ralph.

"I've been thinking, thinking … our neighborhood is Clos Mozart, so maybe something music related?" he suggested.

"Right, Wolfgang Amadeus Mozart. Or maybe Maison Mozart? Nah, I take it back. That doesn't quite do it. And Mas Mozart doesn't work either because a *mas* is a big ol' farmhouse and our house isn't that."

Ralph continued. "Let's see, some of his famous works are *The Magic Flute*, *Marriage of Figaro* and …"

"Wait a second," I said, sensing an idea taking root, "Figaro. Take off the *a-r-o* and you get fig. Our address is technically Chemin des Figuières Folles, pathway of the crazy fig trees."

"Or it could be pathway of the crazy fig-tree *farmers*," Ralph added.

"I know, it's crazy that we're hazy about the precise meaning of our own street name. Plus, it's plain cuckoo we're so close to town, yet nobody can find us. Well, except the postman," I conceded.

"It's totally *fou*. Completely crazy."

"And, crazy makes perfect sense when you're talking about us ending up here. So, we have *fou*. It pairs well with *chez*, don't you think? Chez Fou. I believe it works, *n'est-ce pas?*"

"It does," Ralph agreed. "Chez Fou. I like it. Has a witty ring to it."

We raised our water bottles for a bump.

"Okay, our *petite maison* has hereby been named. Our work is done here. *Merci*, priceless picnic place," I said, nodding to the monuments and their stunning setting. "Guess we can go now."

"Yep, back to Chez Fou," said Ralph. In that moment, I realized that our bond with Saint-Rémy was deepening. Was an engagement imminent? Did I hear wedding bells in the distance?

8

Cuddle up to local customs.
Although you'll never *be* a native,
you can *feel* like one.

Chapter 9

Zum Wohl, Santé, Cheers!

Saint-Rémy-de-Provence — Winter 2013

German beer. Nothing tops it, according to Ralph. If you're a beer aficionado like him, *bier aus* Deutschland is as good as it gets. During our fourteen years of living and working in Heidelberg, Germany, the pantry was always stocked with at least one twenty-bottle plastic case of the frothy brew. And those were half-liter bottles to boot. Here in France that kind of beer is hard to come by. Ralph has found some perfectly quaffable French *bières*, but in his beverage book, they don't hold a stein to German beer. So not surprisingly, on a trip back to Germany, he planned to stock up.

In addition to ending the *bier* drought at our home in Saint-Rémy, there was another pressing reason to drive up north that March of 2013. After over sixty years, our former employer, Headquarters, US Army, Europe, and Seventh Army—its origins dating back to the US liberation of Heidelberg from German occupation in 1945—would soon be relocating to

Wiesbaden, closing up shop in Heidelberg, the heartbreakingly beautiful city nestled in the lush Neckar Valley. Famous for its partially ruined pink sandstone castle, the oldest university in Germany (serving over thirty thousand bright minds), a fabulous Baroque Old Town, and Philosopher's Way with its magnificent view of the entire magnificent valley, Heidelberg steals hearts. Goethe, Mark Twain, and Marilyn Monroe fancied it. And so did we, and not just for its scintillating self but for its close neighbors, Belgium, Holland, Switzerland, and of course, La Belle France. While we were living in centrally located Heidelberg, Europe was our oyster. There was just one major hitch—work.

To enjoy a European lifestyle, we had to set an early alarm, five days a week. It wasn't total drudgery. Once, when I was the government liaison to the American schools, I got a call from Jane Goodall's office. The world-renowned primatologist would soon be in Heidelberg and was giving a presentation at the International School. She hoped to do the same at the American high school. Would that be possible?

I was ecstatic that the rock star of chimpanzee research was offering a visit to the American community. No question, after 9/11 some logistical hoops had to be jumped through, especially concerning security, but the undertaking was thoroughly thrilling. I even got to ride in the car with Dr. Goodall between the two schools, probably a whopping ten minutes at most, including the security check at the base where the American high school was located. I was in the passenger seat in front and she was in the back with one of her associates, deep in hushed discussion. Waiting anxiously for her to engage me in conversation, I wondered what topic she might choose. Possibly it would relate to her work in Tanzania or the

American school system or the presentation itself. I doubted she was a big carnivore or a party girl, so she probably wasn't going to ask me where to get the tastiest schnitzel or where to join frat boys singing drinking songs à la *The Student Prince*. (If she had, I would have advised her to forget the schnitzel and go for the large pan of zingy *nürnbergerwürsts* at Vetter's and hit Zum Roter Ochsen, Zum Sepp'l, and the Schnookerloch on her pub crawl.) The car pulled up to the high school auditorium behind schedule. Realizing there was no time for a casual, one-on-one conversation, I silently helped usher the world's premier chimpanzee expert inside and watched her walk down the center aisle to a thunderous standing ovation.

The Goodall experience was unforgettable, as were so many Heidelberg friends. Several were still working, but since their employer was moving, their positions were being dispersed in numerous directions. They had to either follow those jobs or make other career plans. Not an easy decision by any stretch, and on top of that, leaving glorious Heidelberg made it even tougher. We wanted to wish them well and say *auf wiedersehen*, so we planned a trip to Heidelberg.

Since settling in Provence, we hadn't driven up to Heidelberg for a couple of years. One thing we hadn't forgotten about the journey was how long it took—if we were lucky and didn't hit any *bouchons* in France or *staus* in Germany, we might be able to do it in eight hours. But we're not all-day-in-the-car kind of drivers and are retired with time to spare, so we planned to stop over in Beaune. Not only was it a convenient midway point, but it was also a gratifying treat with its impressive Burgundy architecture, vineyard setting, hearty cuisine, and of course, spectacular wines.

We made the trek to Beaune in record time, so we squeezed in a power walk around the town's ramparts before a casual meal at a buzzing brasserie in the town center. After a good night's sleep, we set off on the second leg of our journey. Luckily, the traffic cooperated and by early afternoon we checked into our well-located hotel in Heidelberg near bustling Bismarckplatz, where the city trams converge. In one direction, it was an easy drive to our former offices, and in the other, a quick walk over the Theodor-Heuss-Brücke, down the riverside path to Neuenheim, the heart of our old stomping grounds. Also, the hotel was practically next door to Café Rossi, one of our favorite rendezvous addresses, which was convenient if, on the off chance, Ralph got a hankering for a real German beer.

During the next couple of days, we consumed a number of *biers*, not to mention a variety of dry German Reislings, some with distinctive pucker power. We meandered down memory lane with our former colleagues, bosses, and neighbors. Pretty much everybody was struggling to put on happy, brave faces, trying to look on the bright side about their jobs moving. At least they still had jobs. The only ones who weren't sad were our neighbors because they weren't going anywhere. Their lives remained in the remarkable city where they would continue to enjoy all its delights, not the least of which was the vibrant Hauptstrasse, the main pedestrian shopping street, and the exceptional Jugendstil (art nouveau) architecture that typifies Neuenheim. Let's not forget the constantly entertaining river traffic, including ferries, scullers, kayaks, and geese. And in the grassy, park-like area that runs along the river, you can always join power walkers, cyclists, and joggers—with and without baby buggies and canines. Weather permitting, you can watch Frisbee players, beach volleyballers, soccer matches, and bikini-clad sunbathers freshening up under the outdoor showers.

There's always action down at the "beach," as locals call the riverside park.

We were reminded of Heidelberg's many charms and how fortunate we were to have lived there for so much of our careers. We had almost too many exceptional memories to count, from the spectacular summertime fireworks over the castle to the mundane, scrap-metal barges that slowly chugged up and down the muddy Neckar waters. We loved them all. But our most cherished memory was in a category all by itself— Heidelberg by night. From the vantage point of the riverside path by the Old Bridge, looking back at the graceful arches channeling the shimmering river and the illuminated castle towering over the storybook Altstadt (Old Town), romance came to mind. Even on a brutally wicked winter's evening when we were anxious to get home to warmth, we'd turn around to marvel at the mesmerizing vision. Every single time, despite losing feeling in our extremities, we'd remark what a picturesque, world-class vista it was—and then we'd seal it with a kiss. We never took the view for granted. In retirement, part of us wanted to remain in Heidelberg just so we could stare at that dazzling nighttime scene. Alas, the siren call of sunny Provence beckoned.

After a couple of days of reminiscing, it was time to head back home to Provence. Our compact Renault Modus was stuffed with a jumble of too many suitcases, totes, and travel gear. When we're on a driving holiday, I tend to overpack, and this trip was no exception. In my defense, it's always harder to pack light in winter. But even I'm not sure why I felt compelled to throw in such a vast array of boots, puffy vests, jackets, and coats. Among all the paraphernalia, there also was a special treasure—a whole case of zingy American dill-pickle relish, a thoughtful present from our cleverly creative, long-time American friends who were still working and had access to the US commissary. It was a great gift, not only because it was sure to crack us up, but also because dill relish is one of those uniquely American products that we get homesick for and simply can't find in France. A little bit of home, chopped up, and squeezed into a jar.

Since we were anxious to get started on our long drive, we didn't take great care to neatly rearrange all our—okay, mostly *my*—bulky stuff. We crammed it here and there, wherever an opening was spotted, trying to pack down the heap enough so as not to obscure visibility. Also, there had to be enough room for the all-important case of beer that we'd pick up at our last stop before heading south to France.

Our French-tagged, middle-aged auto, with its scraped and slightly dented right back bumper, chugged along dutifully. We proceeded cautiously, as it was well known that Heidelberg was fond of permanent *and* temporary speed-trap cameras. The latter used to crop up periodically and where you least expected them. In fact, years ago I'd had an unhappy encounter with one. It was after work and I was late for a much-needed hair appointment. Surely everyone would understand that I needed to drive at top speed to get there. But not the heartless, mechanized flasher. It didn't care one bit that attention to my roots was long overdue. An extremely high-resolution photo of me in my trusty little Honda CRX arrived in the mail one day, along with a healthy fine. I couldn't believe the impressive quality of the photograph or the stated maximum speed limit for that stretch of street. My recollection was that the posted maximum speed was higher than the ticket stated. If I was right, it would mean I hadn't been speeding after all, so I returned to the scene of the alleged crime. I was going well under the speed limit. Skateboarders were passing me on the sidewalk. Glancing from side to side, trying to spot the speed limit sign, I failed to notice I'd inadvertently slipped into a special zone with a stricter speed limit—only to get flashed yet again. Soon afterward, another high-rez photo arrived in the mail, along with another fine that was even heftier. That was one dismal day way back when, one that my husband enjoys reminding me of more frequently than is necessary.

But on this day, we were already on a sweet-sorrow-in-our-parting farewell tour of Heidelberg, and we certainly didn't need any additional reason to be melancholy. We repeated our go-slow mantra on the way to the beer store and Autobahn 5, which would take us south. We'd decided on the *getränkemarkt*, a beverage-only store with a super selection, near Campbell Barracks, the military base where our former offices were located. We could wave goodbye one last time. When we worked there, we normally would have rushed to make the last light just before the right-hand turn leading to the side entrance of the base, in the hopes of getting to work on time. But today we weren't in a hurry—we wanted to absorb it all, and we weren't going to take any unnecessary speeding risks.

As we approached the last stretch before the complex, some of the challenges we had faced during our working years bubbled to the surface. I let them drift by, wanting to focus on positive things like walking in the hills during our lunch hour. In the depth of winter and the heat of the summer, several times a week we'd pry ourselves out of our cubicles and into the dense woods across from the base—it was the break in the day that got us through the day. Since the car was moving slowly, it wasn't surprising that before we got to the crosswalk, the light changed to red. Not a problem. I wasn't anxious to pass the historic site for the last time before it closed, returned to the Germans and repurposed for civilian use. Just around the corner, I could see the guards standing watch at the gate to the commander's house, multiple lines of barbed wire above the surrounding walls, and towers with cameras. On the sidewalk next to us was a big sign pointing the way to the base: "Campbell Barracks, Headquarters, US Army, Europe." Ralph saw me fiddling with my camera and reminded me about photos of military bases—*verboten*.

"Oh, come on," I said, "it's just a directional sign," and I held up the camera to focus the shot. "For old time's sake."

"Yeah, but you're also going to get the base in the background and probably the guards too. A really bad idea," he grumbled.

It was in my nature to be somewhat of a smart-ass, and I was also experiencing a strong nostalgic moment, so my finger pressed the button—*click*.

"Can't believe you did that. Don't expect me to visit you in jail," Ralph said with exasperation.

The light turned green and off we went. I waved goodbye as we passed the main entrance to the base, the one the high-ranking officials were allowed to use, right across from the compact, American convenience store where we used to rent the latest blockbuster videos for the weekend. It was the store where in the early '90s on a Sunday morning I'd taken my visiting girlfriend, who had overdone it at a wine fest the night before and was in desperate need of some Pepto-Bismol. The same store where you could get a variety of American beers. But Ralph never bought it there when he could get his favorite

German beer from a *getränkemarkt* like the one we were heading for just now.

A long block after we passed Campbell Barracks, we made a right turn and cruised by the former American housing section, which we noted, sadly, was in a state of dismal disrepair, completely overgrown. We pondered how it would be used in the future—university student or social housing, perhaps? The city had a permanent shortage of both. We were then just a few blocks from the beverage store.

As we continued a bit farther, Ralph said, "That *polizei* car that was parked to the side of the road by the housing area ... it's just pulled in behind us."

"Not to worry," I said, "you're going under the speed limit. They're probably just responding to a call." We followed the priority road as it swung around to the left. A couple of blocks later, we turned into the *getränkemarkt* parking lot. One case of half-liter bottles of Deutsche *bier* and we'd be heading home.

In the parking lot, Ralph and I opened our doors simultaneously. I bounced out and headed toward the trolleys by the entrance. At the front door, I realized Ralph wasn't with me. I turned back and spotted him, still next to the car. He was not alone. Uh-oh, this wasn't good. Two German police officers—with serious faces—were talking to Ralph. I assumed the guys were the same ones who had been parked by the housing area. As I walked back to the car, my heart started racing. Geez, what could they possibly want? Ralph nodded at them, opened the car door, and reached for the glove compartment. Yikes, he was retrieving the car insurance documents. I sure hoped they were all there and in good order. I joined Ralph and said *guten tag* to the officers, but their expressions remained stern. Saying nothing more, I tried not to look nervous as Ralph handed over the passports, the French *cartes de séjour* (the documents allowing us to live in France), and his driver's license—a German one that was valid in France. Mine was French, but they didn't ask for that. While one *polizei* examined the documents, Ralph explained in German that we were Americans. He switched to English to describe how we had worked at Campbell Barracks for a long time, and now we were retired and lived in France but had returned to visit friends. They kept flipping through the documents but didn't say anything. Why had they pulled us over? Had the guard at the military base seen me snap a photo and alerted the Germans about suspicious characters in a French auto? It seemed we were not going to get *bier* after all but an escort to a gloomy military interrogation room with peeling paint and the proverbial two-way mirror.

Or had they noticed our French license plate and our Beverly Hillbillies car untidily crammed to the gills and wondered what contraband might be inside? Oh, no, I thought, remembering the case of American dill-pickle relish. I sure didn't want to have to open the trunk. The *polizei* might take exception to our not-so-little stash of an American product. Holy cow, a whole flat of relish jars. Would they want to know where we got so much of it and think it strange it was a gift? Well, of course they would. What normal couple could eat that many chopped pickles before the expiration date anyway? What if they thought we intended to mobilize a dill-pickle relish black market? We could have some serious 'splaining to do. A worst-case scenario formed in my head. That dreary interrogation room in my imagination grew grittier.

I considered making a cheerful comment to ease the tension, but reconsidered. *Polizei* weren't known for their sense of humor—at least that was my impression. Neither one of us had ever been stopped before. They might have thought I was forcing perkiness and had something to hide. In truth, I did— my nervousness that they might find us or our relish suspicious and exercise their authority in the name of thoroughness. I glanced at Ralph. He might have been paddling like crazy inside, but on the outside he looked calm and unruffled. After all, he had routinely briefed multiple-starred generals at the Pentagon, I reminded myself.

The pair of *polizei* exchanged a few words and glanced at the car. Were they about to ask for a look-see? I recoiled. And then jumped when the police van radio erupted. One officer answered the call, paused, and yelled to the other who hollered back, *"Jawohl!"* He handed Ralph the paperwork, said, *"Danke,"* and hopped in the van which screeched out of the parking lot, leaving Ralph and me with pounding hearts and at a loss for words. Trying to process what had just happened, Ralph and I robotically entered the beverage store for the all-important beer. Still in a daze, we didn't utter a word to each other as we passed through checkout. With some difficulty, we got the case of beer arranged in our overstuffed car and drove off. Once we merged onto the A5 heading south and our blood pressure was approaching normal levels, the silence was broken.

"What was that all about?" I said.

"I really don't know," answered Ralph.

"Was it the photo?"

"I kind of doubt it, but it still wasn't a good idea." Ralph gave me that disapproving, I-told-you-so-and-don't-ever-think-about-doing-that-again look.

"Yeah, that wasn't such an ingenious idea," I admitted. "Sorrrrry."

"Well, at least we know our French documents pass muster. But that was an encounter I could have done without. And all because of buying beer."

"Technically, you almost got busted *before* buying beer."

"Well, we managed to get it, and man, how I'm going to appreciate it now."

"As well you should ... it was no small effort becoming legal aliens."

I thought back on all the hassle, cost, and fraying of nerves to get our first *cartes de séjour* from the French consulate in Los Angeles. Since then, the drill has been to submit updated dossiers each year to the local *sous-préfecture*—the county government branch office—which for us, living in Saint-Rémy, meant driving to Arles, about twenty-five minutes away. But luckily, the process doesn't require a trip back to the US. Temporary visas arrive by mail in about a month to six weeks, and after another month to six weeks, the permanent ones are available for pickup at the sous-préfecture. By that time, there are about eight months and change left to relax and enjoy not having to take a number at a French government office before it's time to begin the whole process over. But we've taken the procedure in stride, and it has become routine, like filing taxes, except the grumbling is punctuated with markedly more *"merde"* outbursts.

And it's all worth it. No question about it. It's all worth it only for that single unpredictable moment when you need that documentation. An American friend of a friend who lived in France for most of the year for over a decade and regularly flew between the US and France with only a passport, minus a *carte de séjour*, eventually was stopped at immigration at Charles de Gaulle Airport in Paris. The official simply instructed her to go get legal and sent on her way. She was lucky, but had it been us, would we have been? Maybe. Or maybe not.

For Ralph and me, getting busted would likely not involve dramatic fanfare like missing a flight. I imagine it'd be an ordinary day and would go something like this. I'm in the kitchen about to whip up a quiche to enjoy on our sun-drenched terrace, under blue skies, a balmy breeze blowing, when I realize I'm an egg short. So I hop in the car to buzz over to the market. Just as I'm coasting around the last roundabout, two blocks from home, an observant gendarme pulls me over to inform me one of my taillights has failed. Protocol dictates she (or he) must request my official papers— only to discover I haven't done my homework. Ouch. What follows? Detainment? Fines? Deportation? No idea if any of that is involved, and I don't want to know. No good news there. And no quiche either.

9

Walk the extra kilometers to legal land.
Tempting shortcuts may leave you stranded.

Chapter 10

Missing the Boat

Saint-Rémy-de-Provence — Fall 2013

"Ahoy, matey! Fancy a ferry ride?" I asked Ralph one lazy Sunday morning. Wearing faded jeans and a long-sleeved navy polo, he was slouched comfortably in an oversized chair, socked feet up on the coffee table, perusing a British newspaper, mug of dark espresso in one hand. I loved looking at him like that, completely relaxed, his bod trim, his thick head of curls now steely gray. A real-life magazine ad for the hot-diggy-dog mature set. Yeah, baby, that's my baby, I mused.

"Always. Where to, my saucy wench?" he replied as he looked up to see me waving a worn manila folder in front of him.

"Well," I said, bringing my wandering thoughts back to the matter at hand, "guess what I just stumbled across? It's an old article I'd stashed away about that little island just off the Côte d'Azur where you bike everywhere. Wanna go?"

"Absolutely. How about we make a plan and get ourselves there this time?"

"I know. We've wanted to get to Porquerolles for a while now and there's always been some obstacle. It's going to happen this time—timing is good," I said, grinning and giving him a big squeeze.

∽

Several years earlier, when I'd first read the article about cool, under-the-radar experiences in Provence, I'd sat up and taken notes. One appealing tidbit highlighted the Monday market in Forcalquier, located in the Alpes-de-Haute-Provence, the eastern part of the Luberon. While visiting friends nearby, we'd checked it out and deemed it definitely worth a detour.

So it was with high hopes that I focused on another topic that caught my eye. It was a nugget about the sun-kissed Île de Porquerolles, just a short ferry ride from Giens, south of Hyères, on the edge of the Côte d'Azur. The article quoted an expat who had settled on the island and considered it paradise. Friends who had come to visit hadn't wanted to leave. There were acclaimed vineyards, gorgeous horseshoe beaches, bustling harbors, forested walking and biking trails, charming cafés, and no cars. In short, idyllic.

Had we visited enchanting Porquerolles while living in Aix, we could have buzzed over and back in a day—easy peasy. But that was the time when Ralph had felt compelled to test the French medical system—followed by the recuperation period. Then we'd found our house to rent in St.-Rémy-de-Provence. We'd already bought tickets to Palm Springs to test our part-of-the-year-in-the-US theory, so we took off for a few months. And after we returned to La Belle France, winter was looming—not prime time for ferrying or bicycling. Porquerolles had been moved to the back burner. And then spring hadn't been able to make up its mind about gracing Provence in 2013—we were still burning logs in our potbellied stove into May. But when warm weather finally arrived, so did all the Europeans on vacation. Making the trip in high season made little sense. Better to wait till the mad crush was over, we decided. And so Porquerolles had stayed on the back burner.

Finally, the *rentrée* happened. This is that delightful time of year in early September when the kiddies return to school, moms and dads go back to work, and retirees hit the road. It was the right time to make the Porquerolles trip happen. Of course, now that we were in Saint-Rémy, it would be tricky to visit Porquerolles in a day unless we departed at the crack o' dawn, a timeframe not listed in our *Retirees' Handbook*. Since we would have to spend the night somewhere anyway, why not make a bigger trip out of it and take in a few other sights in the neighborhood? I reasoned. Maybe La Ciotat, Hyères, or Bormes-les-Mimosas? And heck, we had to at least take a peek at St. Tropez, right? It was not far from Giens, just a small smidgen to the east. A four-day excursion emerged.

So where to stay? Ideally, it would have an outdoor space. And a sea view. And updated furniture. And be private. And walking distance to charming bistros for dinner. And have a safe place for the car. And not break the bank. Plus, we wanted to be near the ferry, but also didn't want to spend eons getting to the other places we wanted to visit. And we didn't want to have to pick up and move to a second hotel in just three nights. And there was that cute little lunch place in Hyères I wanted to try coming or going. Hmm. Too much to ask for? After half a day of internet surfing and more hours leafing through a stack of guidebooks and articles, my brain was half melted and I still had zilch. Wrong location, wrong price, wrong features, or wrong availability. I went downstairs and broke the bad news to Ralph that we had to bag the trip—it was squarely in the too-hard-to-do box.

In the middle of the night, a specific photo from a guidebook kept popping up on my sleep screen. It was a view through a window, beyond a terrace, over a small village, and out to a beautiful yacht harbor. This was what we really wanted—the expansive sea view. The next morning, I dug through our guidebooks again and found that photo. It belonged to a lovely little bed and breakfast in Le Lavandou and was reasonably priced to boot. We'd have to backtrack thirty minutes to the ferry in Giens, but it was an easy drive and would save us from having to move twice.

I emailed the owner, and she promptly responded that she couldn't accommodate us until later in the week unless the current guests decided to leave earlier than expected—she'd let me know the next day. Well, the later timeframe wouldn't work too well for us, as then it would be the dreaded weekend. That's exactly when you most definitely want to avoid visiting St. Tropez and squishing onto a crowded ferry, not to mention the daunting traffic on the autoroute returning home to Saint-Rémy. The next day came and went with no word from the B&B owner. We resigned ourselves to going another time, because now that we'd found the B&B that ticked all the boxes, no other place measured up. We'd just go to Porquerolles *plus tard.*

Woo-hoo! A day later, I received an email from the owner that the room would indeed be available for the period we wanted. On departure day, we left on time (a miracle for us), got caught in traffic in Toulon, but still made it to Hyères in plenty of time for lunch at the sweet little bistro I'd read about. We arrived in Le Lavandou by 4:00 p.m. and tried valiantly to follow the owner's directions, plus the ones from Google maps, but to no avail. We looped back around and through the hills above the town but finally gave up and called the owner. "We're totally *perdus!*" I lamented.

"Don't worry," she said, "I'll come get you—on my scooter. Where are you?"

"By the *boules* court, near the Office de Tourisme."

Before hanging up, she added, "Blah-blah-blah-blah-blah-*casque blanche.*"

"Okay!" I chirped. *"À tout à l'heure."* Turning to Ralph, I said, "She said something about a white *casque*. What's a *casque* anyway?"

"Probably a cape, à la Wonder Woman, swooping down to save the day," he quipped.

We stared intently into the traffic, jerking our heads this way and that whenever we saw a flash of *blanche*. No white cape, but a few minutes later, Madame pulled up beside us. She was probably in her seventies, dressed in a fitted Chanel-like jacket with shiny gold buttons and matching earrings, and sitting ramrod straight on her little scooter—wearing a white helmet. (Ah, *casque* is "helmet"—good to know.)

"Bonjour, Monsieur et Madame Padgett!" she exclaimed with a wide smile.

In unison we said, *"Enchantés, madame!"*

En français, she explained slowly and carefully that we would pass the driveway to the house but then loop back around to approach it from another angle to make it easier to enter. Very thoughtful of her to take such care about a small detail, I noted.

Not such a small detail, as it turned out. The driveway dove sharply downward and then disappeared around a bend. "No way, José—we can't go down that," I said, shaking my head. But we were following a demure septuagenarian who did this routinely—on a scooter, no less. Could we bear admitting that we weren't as fearless as she? Maybe we should just park on the street? But pride propelled us down the skinny twisty-turny, gravelly drive to the parking area, positioned, thankfully, next to the mountainside and not by a sheer drop-off.

Once I was safely ensconced in the gorgeous view-with-a-room and I could breathe again, it occurred to me that leaving the car parked where it was and skipping the Porquerolles altogether had a lot of merit. Just kidding! The defeatist thought was only fleeting, thank goodness. We'd come so far that we just *had* to make it the rest of the way. But we did leave the car there. It turned out there was a ferry to the Île de Porquerolles right there from Le Lavandou. Though the journey was a bit longer than from Giens, we thought it would be fun, and we could walk to the dock, leaving the car safely at the house and our nerves calm. The next day, we found the ferry terminal and reserved our places for the Porquerolles crossing. On the big day, we trotted down the hill and paid for our reserved tickets direct from Le Lavandou to Porquerolles.

Surprisingly, we found long lines in the staging area even though we had arrived ahead of schedule with lots of time to spare. When we were herded onto the Porquerolles ferry, it was a madhouse to find seats. By the time we made it to the upper deck, it was jammed—none of the benches had room for two people to sit together. Luckily, Ralph found a full human-sized space on one side of the aisle, just opposite a half human-sized space. I sized up the small expanse and concluded there was room for at least one cheek if the large man sitting there could slide over just a wee bit—this would beat a standing voyage. So with a bright smile and a cheery tone, I got the man's attention and asked ever so politely if he could *bouger juste un peu.* He frowned, paused to consider the request, and finally nodded as he managed a slight scoot-over. I positioned myself carefully on the exposed space as the ship heaved ho.

While the sun gleamed and a breeze whipped our faces, we were treated to a running commentary in French, 95.7 percent of which we didn't get. There most certainly was something about some pirates and World War II, or maybe it concerned the damage of climate change. At any rate, the natural scenery was striking, including the bronzed young sailor-commentator right out of a Harlequin Romance bodice-ripper, replete with sun-streaked shoulder-length curls that bounced freely as he ran back and forth taking care of sailor stuff and attending to customer needs, particularly those of the skimpily clad young Brigitte Bardot wannabes. Bet he'd had a busy summer.

But I digress. As we approached the picturesque harbor, I popped up eagerly from my seat and prepared to disembark onto the charming island from the magazine article that had captured my imagination several years before. Finally, after all the fantasizing, planning, health issues, moving house, more planning, driving, walking, and ferry crossing, we were arriving for our day in the sun, tooling around a gorgeous island on bicycles, picnicking, following our noses, free as birds. We had arrived!

We bounced down the gangplank like kids running to Santa with their Christmas wish lists. Scanning, scanning, scanning— we were eagerly taking it all in. Big blue sky, bobbing boats, shimmering harbor, outdoor cafés, and a quaint hotel. Now, where were all these bike rental places I'd read about? Not a one in sight. They had to be tucked in on a backstreet, I reasoned. Not a moment to lose—off we marched at a brisk pace to the tourist office to ask for directions to the bike rentals. As we entered, a perky woman greeted us, a big smile breaking across her face.

"Bonjour, monsieur, madame."

"Bonjour, madame," we responded. Then I continued, "A simple question, madame—where are the bicycle rentals?"

"I am so very sorry, but there are no bike rentals on the island. People here walk everywhere," she said.

"But this is the Île de Vélos," I replied, recalling the island's nickname—the Island of Bicycles.

"Oh, madame, that's Porquerolles."

"Oui, Porquerolles, here in Porquerolles," I confirmed, nodding.

"But this is Port Cros," she corrected me.

"This is where?" Ralph and I both said in simultaneous disbelief. Very slowly, she repeated the island's name. "It's a wonderful island too," she added proudly.

She went on to itemize the delights of Port Cros, but I couldn't hear her over the banging of my head on the counter and the voices in my head screaming. After all these long years of anticipation of and yearning for your fantasy island paradise getaway, you ain't gonna get it today because *you are an idiot!* On this day, the Île of Porquerolles is close but no baguette.

Ralph pulled me gently back off the counter, we thanked the upbeat, patient woman, and with heads hanging, consumed with disappointment, not to mention humiliation, we went back outside, muttering to ourselves. How considerate it would be, we grumbled, if the citizens of the fair isle of Port Cros could take mercy on clueless foreigners by posting any kind of a city sign. No, wait—what Ralph and I needed were gargantuan banners posted at every gangplank, reading PORT CROS ≠ PORQUEROLLES. Of course, maybe no signage was their business model. And where had this island come from anyway? I thought we'd bought a direct ticket from A to B! Oh, wait a sec. Direct isn't necessarily nonstop. Darn. Okay, time to stop the whining, I scolded myself. Get over the pity party.

Truth be told, there were, in fact, more than a couple of tip-offs that the first ferry stop wasn't *the* ferry stop. Not to be uncharitable to our fellow ferry travelers, but that bunch had made a remarkable improvement in the courtesy department during the brief voyage from Le Lavandou to Port Cros. When we'd arrived at the island, there had been an absence of pushing and shoving that had ensued when we had boarded, and many passengers had stepped aside to let us go first during the disembarkation process. Even that unchivalrous guy who had begrudgingly budged a whopping 0.5 centimeters so I could sit down hadn't been clamoring to get going. But at the time, consumed with delight, I hadn't paused to consider the reasons—I was simply grateful.

Yet another clue surfaced when we were stepping off the boat. Mr. Harlequin Romance had repeated the destination directly to us, but when I'd replied so confidently, *"Oui,"* his surprised look swiftly morphed into a smile, followed by a *"Bonne journée."* For the record, in our defense, if you say "Port Cros" fast and you say "Porquerolles" fast and swallow the double *l*, they really do sound the same. Really, they do—to non-French ears.

While we were busy beating ourselves up, we happened to look up and notice there was a boat at the dock and a sailor out front. Not a Harlequin Romance-type guy but another more commanding, serious, I'm-in-charge kinda guy, dressed all in white with a ship-shape, tidy haircut. We took off running toward him, and as I drew close, I blurted, *"Monsieur, monsieur, je suis idiote, je suis idiote, je suis idiote!"* My right arm extended straight up, frantically waving my flimsy ferry ticket.

With both arms held out in front of him, the fingers of his hands spread wide, he pumped the air, indicating I should slow down. *"Madame, s'il vous plaît, s'il vous plaît, anglais, s'il vous plaît."*

"I'm an idiot, I'm an idiot," I kept repeating like the moron that I was.

"What is the matter?" he asked.

I pointed at the destination on my tiny ticket: Porquerolles. The power of the written word—too bad we hadn't shared that little treasure with Monsieur Harlequin Romance.

"Aaaaah, oui," he said, sighing. "You are not the first and you are not the last. But do not worry, madame. I go Porquerolles! I take you both Porquerolles—on my boat." He gestured to a fancy ferry behind him. "You arrive 12:20. I take you on my boat, *n'est-ce pas?* I take you Porquerolles."

"Really?" I said.

"Absolument!" he replied.

"Magnifique! Très gentil, très gentil. We'll be here!" I squealed. I was so excited, I didn't even ask what the cost would be.

We had about ninety minutes to fritter away, so we decided to check out some views from our bonus island, while not straying far from the dock. Erring on the side of let's not screw this up a second-time, we returned to the harbor area in a half hour. In one of the little cafés, we saw our new best friend, the ferry captain, seated at a small bistro table. We ambled nonchalantly in and found seats in the back, keeping a close eye on him. He ordered a coffee. We ordered a coffee. He sipped. We sipped. He read a newspaper. We read a newspaper. Correction, we *pretended* to read a newspaper—our French literacy skills were less than fully developed. As soon as he paid his bill, we paid ours and trotted after him. He sure as heck wasn't leaving without us.

True to his word, Monsieur Capitan welcomed us aboard his impressive ferry, which was much grander than the one we'd come over on—and at no extra cost. Thirty minutes later, we landed at the Île de Porquerolles. Not only did a big sign greet us at the entrance to the port, but before vacating the vessel, I showed my ticket to two sailors and everybody else in a white outfit.

As originally planned, we rented bicycles from one of at least ten bike rental outfits that encircled the port. The happy-go-lucky bicycle guy handed us helmets and, as an afterthought, a small folded map of bike paths. With a chuckle, he said we wouldn't need it—the island was quite small and there were many signs. To get lost, he said, you'd have to be an idiot. Our eyes opened wide, and we simultaneously shot each other a look of instant mutual understanding. We asked Bicycle Guy for backup maps. Missing two boats in one day was simply not going to happen.

With our helmets snug on our heads, sunglasses positioned, we hit the road. Soon, our shoulders relaxed, and we settled in to enjoy the ride around the fantasy island. On wide, hard-packed dirt trails, we cycled through thick pine forests, a gentle breeze blowing on our faces, stopping every little while to take in the magnificent sea views and to consult our trail map, making sure we were still on track. Just above some craggy cliffs overlooking an impossibly pretty beach, hemmed in only by low-slung pines with not a snack shack in sight, we plunked down on a big log. There, we munched through our simple *pique-nique* of goat cheese, olives spiced with herbes de Provence, *saucisson*, and a crusty baguette. Below, families with little kids and both young and mature couples dotted the pristine, sandy arc. We locked up the bikes, meandered down the path that led to the beach, and slipped off our shoes. The hard-packed sand felt deliciously warm, encouraging us to linger; alas, we had no time for a dip except for our toes.

Back on the bikes, we cruised by vast expanses of leafy vineyards, a fort, a windmill, and an early-nineteenth-century lighthouse perched on a hill that, according to a tourist brochure, promised stellar sea views. We had to take their word for that, as some renovating looked to be in full swing. Continuing on, Ralph was delighted to spot some entertaining birds—coots, moorhens, and gray herons were of particular note—from attractive and well-positioned bird blinds. At yet another ridiculously perfect beach, we witnessed a tanned and buff movie crew filming a scene involving a half-capsized sailboat, its colorful sails dipping into the shimmering blue water and a pair of nubile, bikini-clad starlets frolicking in the surf. The area within fifty meters of the action was cordoned off from the public, so getting close enough to appreciate all the fun and excitement was challenging—until Ralph's birding binoculars were pressed into action.

After we turned in our bikes and thanked Bicycle Guy for the excellent maps, we were feeling pretty pleased with ourselves. We had experienced a hiccup, or more accurately, a belching burp, but we'd managed a recovery. I've read somewhere that if you've never been lost, you haven't really traveled. Though we'd undoubtedly earned a pat on the back from the travel gods, at that point we hoped we were done with "traveling" for the day. Now all we had to do was relax and enjoy the voyage home. How better to do that than with a bit of local rosé? After all, by then it was officially happy hour. Since there was no bar on board the ferry, what to do? We found a little market, acquired a bottle of rosé, let our precious Swiss Army knife take care of the cork, decanted the "pink" into our plastic water bottles, and voilà, *apéro* time!

We returned to the dock at the right time, boarded the right boat—the one covered by our original ticket—and headed in the right direction. Though I didn't see a sign, when we pulled into the first harbor, I figured it was Port Cros, the port with no name. Feeling sassy after "hydrating" from my "water" bottle, I rose and started gathering my things. Ralph, obviously not paying attention, did the same and headed to the exit. I hustled along after him, wondering how long I should let the ruse continue. While the boat positioned itself alongside the dock, we stood at the exit, as if to disembark. When the roar of the engines hushed, and Mr. Harlequin Romance dropped the rope across the opening to the gangplank, Ralph turned to step off the boat. Enough was enough. I grabbed his wrist. "No, no, honey—we don't get off here—this is not Le Lavandou."

Pivoting around, he said, "Gotcha!" with a wide, sly smile, wagging his finger at me.

"Touché. You *totally* had me!"

"I *know*. Now you be*have*, lil' missy—time to focus," ushering us back to our seats.

Before long, another harbor—hopefully Le Lavandou—came into sight. Soon our eventful day-tripping adventure would be behind us—unless they added another stop just to see if we were paying attention, which, of course, we weren't. I consulted with Ralph. "Honey, this is *it*, right?"

He sat up, scanning the docks to the right and left. "Not sure where the city sign went, but that Ferris wheel looks familiar."

"Yeah, I remember that. Or was it a merry-go-round I'm thinking of?" No, I decided, this was it. Our two "yea" votes made it unanimous—we were home. So despite our onboard *apéro*, we did recognize where we were, and where we were was where we were supposed to be—back where we started—which was ideal for a round-trip journey.

"Okey-dokey," Ralph said. "*On y va*. Let's go." Like we had a choice. It was the end of the line.

10

Find the fine print.
Wishful thinking does not a plan make.

Chapter 11

Wheels of Misfortune

Saint-Rémy-de-Provence — Spring 2014

Rafael Nadal wasn't to blame. It wasn't Novak Djokovic's or Roger Federer's fault either. I couldn't pin it on Andy Murray—he wasn't even there.

It had started with a phone call from my energetic, proactive, doesn't-miss-a-beat girlfriend, Ellen, in Aix. "How does this sound?" she'd said. "April. Monte Carlo. World-class tennis championship—you guys want to meet us there?"

I'd found Ralph outside, next to the pool, staring intently at the bottom, which was covered in muck. I knew that look. He was thinking about vacuuming it but wondering whether, if he stirred up the muck with the broom, it would maybe float out through the filter and he wouldn't have to stick his arm in the freezing water to plug in the vacuum hose. At least not today.

"Honey," I'd said, staring at the dank pool, "it doesn't look too good. What are you thinking?"

"I was wondering—if I stir up the muck with the broom, maybe it'll float out through the filter and I won't have to stick my arm in that freezing water. At least not today," he added, his brows knitted with concern.

"Hey, worth a try!" I offered hopefully. "But before you do that ... I just got a call from Ellen. They've got tickets to the Monaco Masters in April—all guy players but lots of big hitters—and she's wondering if we want to go. They've got tickets for the beginning of the tournament, so they aren't very pricey. Wouldn't that be cool to go with Ellen and Rick and the girls to watch some of the top men tennis players in that beautiful small venue overlooking the Med?"

"Very cool. Hey, going and seeing and doing, that's what we're here for. Yeah, let's do it," he said with conviction.

I made a beeline for my laptop to seal the deal. It didn't take long to select seats and pay with a credit card. Bingo, we were on our way to Monaco, the glitzy principality with boatloads of "wow" factor.

⁓

During our first visit to the glamorous, pint-sized city-state, a few years before, we'd spent the day wandering around the less than two square kilometers of dense poshness that is Monte Carlo, the business and entertainment district of Monaco. Of course, we'd taken the quintessential photo on the steps of the stunning Belle Époque Casino, but passed on trying our luck inside—we needed to hang on to our lunch money. Instead, we strolled through the adjacent meticulously maintained park and gazed, mesmerized, at the gleaming harbor crammed with gabillion-dollar mega yachts. It had been a delightful Monaco familiarization day.

⁓

The Monte Carlo tennis tournament, on the other hand, we knew nothing about. Thanks to online research, I quickly discovered the tournament is technically called the Monte-Carlo Masters or, more specifically for the last few years, the Monte-Carlo Rolex Masters, though it's been going on for even longer than Rolex. Professional male tennis players have been duking it out each spring near Monte Carlo since 1897, eight years before Rolex started ticking.

That fun fact reminded me of my own "Rolex." It would be fitting, I mused, to wear it to this venerable event; alas, it had stopped ticking one day, and I hadn't thought it prudent to have it repaired. Years ago, in the dark of night on a backstreet of Seoul, a friend had selected it from an assortment of exquisite timepieces attached to the lining of a long black coat worn by a guy with wraparound shades (no doubt "Ray-Bans"). For longer than you'd think, my "Rolex" looked quite impressive, though not the same could be said of my wrist, which eventually turned a dull grayish-green. So, better to polish up my very genuine Swiss Army watch, in honor of Mr. Federer. Who knew, maybe we'd even run into him! Or more realistically, catch a glimpse of him and probably a distant one at that.

Now that we had tennis tickets for the Monte Carlo tourney, I just had to figure out logistics. The wheels began to turn. Soon, the one-day event morphed into a full four-day excursion. A few days before the championship, we would hop the high-speed train called the TGV (*train à grande vitesse*) in Avignon, which was just twenty minutes north of Saint-Rémy. Three relaxing hours later, we'd transfer in Nice to a local train called the TER (*transport express régional*) for our final leg to the precious little town of Beaulieu-sur-Mer. One of our favorite flicks, *Dirty Rotten Scoundrels*, starring Michael Caine and Steve Martin, was filmed there. We hoped to track down locations where some of the hilarious scenes had been shot. Then, on the day of the tournament, we'd be just a quick train ride away from Monaco. Lo and behold, Monaco being Monaco, a special train stop would be opened for tournament ticket holders—just a few hundred meters from the country club. I felt pampered already.

The forces were with me when I was researching hotels in Beaulieu-sur-Mer. Within minutes, one with very good online reviews grabbed my attention. It overlooked the harbor, and since it was April and off-season, the rate was very reasonable. Another plus was its location, a couple of blocks from the train station. There was availability, so I booked a room without hesitation. My good friend Lila was back home in nearby Vence after a visit to California, so we agreed to meet for lunch in enchanting Villefranche-sur-Mer, adjacent to Beaulieu-sur-Mer. In addition to that enjoyable outing, we could visit Eze, the medieval village perched 1,400 feet above sea level with stupendous views of the Mediterranean and reachable by bus. Except for the short drive to the Avignon TGV station, our Monaco getaway would be a carefree, leave-the-driving-to-somebody-else kind of escape.

❧

On the day of departure, we went through the usual routine, which we now had down to a science—secure all the window *volets*, give the plants a healthy drink, and review our travel checklist. Train tickets? Check. Tennis tourney tickets? Check. Healthy sandwiches for lunch on the train? Check. And so on. As we started to drive away, Ralph said, "Did you lock the front door?"

"Oops, I'd better double-check." He stopped the car and I hopped out. I tried the door handle—it didn't budge. "We're good," I yelled. Off we went in plenty of time to park and make our way into the TGV terminal, where we had to trade our e-ticket forms for the actual tickets. Since we didn't know how long that would take, we allowed some wiggle room. The last time we'd gone to the TGV station four months before, we'd become stuck in the morning *bouchon* and just barely made our train. We sure didn't want to go through that again—much too exciting.

Luckily, after rush hour, traffic moved fluidly. As expected, the *gratuit* parking lot (more of a dirt field hemmed in by tall trees) was packed to the gills with about eighty cars. "Oh well, it was worth a cruise around," I said to Ralph.

"Yeah, you never know," he said, "and we're ahead of schedule."

A string of cars slowly followed us, the drivers' heads swiveling from side to side, searching for an empty slot.

"Whoa, honey. There's a guy back there walking this way with keys in his hand. Wonder if he's leaving?" Ralph slowed to let the fellow catch up to us.

"Excusez-moi, monsieur, vous partez?" he asked hopefully.

"Oui," the man said as he pointed to his car just up a few cars on the left. Woo-hoo—our lucky day! Coincidentally, it looked like the same spot where we'd parked Beau Mo, our trusty ten-year-old Renault Modus, when we'd gone to Nice the previous December.

"We should go buy a Lotto ticket," I joked.

In short order, we exchanged our voucher for the real tickets, then browsed the expansive bookstore and enjoyed a relaxing coffee in the spick-and-span café. We wandered up to the train platform and sat on a bench in the sunshine, people watching. There was just a sprinkling of tourists, business folks, and train employees. No crowds. No mad crush of humanity. Nobody rushing. All was calm. Only the catchy xylophone-sounding jingle announcing the train arrival disturbed the hush.

The train swooshed up and the doors slid open, inviting us aboard. Now our only job was to relax and enjoy the lovely landscapes. About three hours later, we arrived at the regally beautiful Nice train station. How easy it was to while away twenty minutes admiring it before our follow-on train pulled up. From Nice proper, the TER regional train took us through the charming village of Villefranche-sur-Mer just a few minutes before arriving at the seaside gem of Beaulieu-sur-Mer. After we stepped off the train, we put our bags down and inspected our surroundings. Yes, this was it, the train station from our beloved *Dirty Rotten Scoundrels* movie. We were sure of it; it looked almost exactly as we remembered it. The only difference was that the Beaulieu-sur-Mer sign of today had been changed to Beaumont-sur-Mer, the name of the town from the film. Right or wrong, we gave ourselves credit and snapped a few photos to document the result of our keen investigative skills.

Just around the corner from the train station and down a few short blocks stood our stylish multistory hotel, right across from the yacht harbor. The online photos hadn't stretched the truth at all; in fact, the view was even better in real life. I had feared that the street in front of the hotel would be a crazy-busy thoroughfare, but the traffic seemed leisurely and nothing to be concerned about. The chilly but efficient clerk at the front desk showed us two rooms, but the choice was not difficult. The one in the middle of the hall seemed dim and snug, whereas the other was a large corner room with a spacious bathroom with floor-to-ceiling tiling, a sparkling two-person tub, and high a transom window that framed the arched supports for the corniche mountain road.

And then there was the glamorous yacht harbor view—seductively superb. As if that wasn't enough, our end unit offered a panoramic vista of the dramatic mountains towering over the village. And neatly positioned on the roomy balcony was not the flimsy plastic outdoor furniture typical of beach resorts. Instead, we found a sturdy contemporary table and a pair of comfortable armchairs, all necessary components for fully enjoying our sea view. Off to a stellar start!

After collecting a few supplies at a local grocery store, we kicked back on our comfy balcony chairs for our first Beaulieu-sur-Mer *apéro*—divine. For dinner, we opted for a quick bite at a casual bistro so we could get back to our view. We lingered in our outdoor space, mesmerized by the dazzling lights dancing around the yacht harbor and scattered across the majestic mountainside—a memorable, blissful experience.

The next morning, we set off on foot for Villefranche-sur-Mer to meet our Vence friends, Lila and Mario, for lunch. We decided not to walk the shore route but to hike up to the Belle Époque Anglican church in Beaulieu and through the attractive residential neighborhoods over to Villefranche. At times, it was a hard push straight up, but gleaming Mediterranean views rewarded us. Arriving early in Villefranche-sur-Mer, we had time before our lunch rendezvous to explore the maze of streets in the charming village and admire the exquisitely restored façade of the Chapelle St. Pierre, where fishermen used to store their nets and equipment. We learned that it housed some notable Jean Cocteau murals, but alas, our visit didn't coincide with opening hours, so we had to put off becoming "culturized" until another time.

We strolled down to the shore and plunked down on a bench to admire the Mediterranean. A couple of women of a certain age were just finishing a late-morning swim and began walking toward us. About halfway, they bid each other adieu and one strode off across the sand toward town. The other made her way to her towel, which was spread out just below the elevated walkway where we were perched, and proceeded to casually change into her street clothes. No big deal—at the *plage* in La Belle France, no prudish attitudes need apply.

Ralph's mobile phone chirped. "Must be Lila and Mario," I said. It was, and after a quick chat, we set off to meet our friends at the agreed upon beach-shack café, so close to the water that we nearly had *les pieds dans l'eau*, feet in the water. After hugs all around, we caught up over a carafe of chilled rosé and simple but delicious *salades de chèvre chaud*. Although humongous cruise ships often anchor in Villefranche's deep harbor, on this gloriously sunny day with our friends, we had the idyllic place almost to ourselves.

After goodbyes and promises to meet again soon, Ralph and I turned back toward Beaulieu-sur-Mer. We took the route that cuts right across Saint-Jean-Cap-Ferrat, home to the famously ravishing Villa Ephrussi de Rothschild with its magnificent gardens. But instead of making the detour, we allowed the allure of a *sieste* to trump the opportunity to visit the much-heralded property. Besides, it was always a good idea to leave something special for next time.

That night in Beaulieu we saw a newly released George Clooney flick in *version originale* in a spiffy art house-type theater with low ceilings and plush seats. As it was late when the movie finished, we grabbed a pizza to go. I felt slightly embarrassed at the thought of walking through our tastefully decorated hotel lobby with a pizza, so we folded it into a calzone and then did the same with the box and bundled it into Ralph's backpack. If the night desk clerk caught a whiff, he graciously didn't let on. In an attempt to keep up the ruse that we were above taking in takeout, the next morning I stomped the cardboard container into submission and deposited it in a city trash can. What pizza?

The next day, we took a local bus up to the dizzyingly high Eze. Yikes! I'd never want to drive up there on my own with all those sharp hairpin turns the entire way. We made a point of finding seats on the right side of the bus so we'd be on the mountainside. Neither one of us was a fan of heights, but the ride was worth it to experience quaint Eze, which gives new meaning to the term *village perché*. Despite the high altitude, traffic was furiously robust in both directions. Undoubtedly, the locals had nerves of steel to face that road day in and day out.

Keeping true to our movie buff selves, it was de rigueur to find the Eze hotel where the Jack Nicholson character took the Morgan Freeman character in *The Bucket List*. It was a luxury hotel with a glorious view overlooking the Golfe de Saint-Hospice toward the Saint-Jean-Cap-Ferrat peninsula. I couldn't remember the hotel name but figured in such a small village, we'd sniff it out. Our first stop was La Chèvre d'Or, where we chatted with the doorman. *"Oui, madame*—this is the one!" he said proudly.

Then the diplomatic, mind-reading chap saved me the trouble of delivering my next question—perhaps a quick peek was possible? "Madame," he added, "we would be delighted for you to take in the view while you enjoy a drink at the bar. May I show you the way?"

"*Ah, merci beaucoup, très gentil.* But no time for a drink now—we're on our way to the Jardin Exotique. Perhaps the next time," I said.

As much as we would have enjoyed an adult beverage in the fabulous bar, which I'm sure came at a price in keeping with the road leading to the vertiginous town, we were in picnic mode, so we continued on to the view from the Exotic Garden. Up, up, and farther up we trudged, where we paid the entry fee of six euros each, a bargain for the million-dollar view. In the distance, the Saint-Jean-Cap-Ferrat peninsula curled out into the vast, silvery Mediterranean waters that sparkled under brilliant blue skies. It was a gorgeous but not stagnant movie set—it was alive with movement. Birds crisscrossed the lush landscape, autos zipped along the corniche road, and a cruise ship cut a curvy path out to sea. What a delightful spot to eat our gourmet sandwiches, bought that morning at a terrific bakery in Beaulieu. The oversized ovals of hearty multigrain bread hugged creamy rounds of *chèvre*, tomatoes, lettuce, honey, and walnuts, plus a dash of balsamic vinegar for a slightly sweet tang—a tasty repast to accompany a delicious view. Heavenly.

Instead of returning to Beaulieu by bus, we opted to hike off our sandwiches by following the footpath down to the seaside enclave of Eze-bord-de-Mer and follow the shoreline back to town. I was grateful for my industrial-strength hiking boots, as it was extremely rocky. And not as easy to descend as you'd think, according to my knees. Our hiking poles would have come in very handy. We stopped to catch our breath many times. Every now and then I heard rustling in the bushes and hoped no reptiles would cross our path—I was hopelessly freaked out by the long, slithery types. I can't even say their names; I refer to them as the S-word. My irrational fear probably dates back to when I was a little kid and my older brother placed a rubber version in my bed. In any case, I told myself the sounds I was hearing in the underbrush were most likely birds or bunnies. We weren't exactly in the wild. Families with small tykes were pounding up and down the slope. If they weren't afraid, I shouldn't be, I reasoned.

≪⧁

On the day of the big tennis tournament, we arrived at the little train station right on time. The train not so; it was running twenty minutes behind schedule, according to the electronic sign. I commented to Ralph, "Bummer. Looks like we're gonna be a bit late. I'm surprised tardiness is allowed in Monaco."

"You know," he said smugly, "the country club is located in France, not Monaco—Roquebrune-Cap-Martin, to be exact."

"Right! I forgot that fun fact to know and tell. Well, slowing down could be a good thing. Gives us a chance to soak up the ambience," I said, trying to be positive.

From the special train stop, it was only *deux pas* (two steps) to the tennis club. Our Aix buddies, Ellen and Rick, called to let us know their exact location, so we found our fun family without a hitch. As planned, we all got to sit together on the main court where the tennis players were duking it out fast and furiously, but those screaming aces and unexpected drop shots had to compete with the magnetic Mediterranean view. Many of the big tennis guns weren't on center court during our timeframe, but it was a pleasure wandering around the practice courts where Tsonga and Ferrer were impressing the crowd. Erin and Rick's two girls, Caitlin and Cameron, were excited about the activity tents for kids. They won lots of treats and gifts, including a beautiful French designer handbag that sweet, thoughtful Caitlin presented to her mother. "Thanks so much, Mom, for bringing us. I love it here. It's just great," she said as she wrapped her arms around her mom. We couldn't have agreed more.

Our last night in Beaulieu-sur-Mer was a beauty. After a plate of veal piccata with a velvety lemon caper sauce at a bustling Italian bistro, we ambled around town, slowing to admire the elegant casino—just maybe the one from our treasured Steve Martin flick—and of course, the exclusive La Réserve de Beaulieu luxury hotel. That evening, back at our slightly less *oh là là* but very comfortable digs, we climbed to the observation deck to soak up the enchanting Med view, alive with a million twinkly moonbeams bouncing off the water. Then came the icing on the cake—fireworks illuminating the sky. The next day we learned the spectacle had been part of a private party, Beaulieu-sur-Mer style. Even if they hadn't been farewell fireworks in our honor, it certainly made for a spectacular grand finale to our visit.

Departing Beaulieu was a sweet-sorrow scenario. We hated leaving but knew we'd be back. We were captivated by the town's gorgeous natural setting, tidiness, charming architecture, and compact dimensions. Within walking distance were a pretty beach, bistros, boutiques, a cinema, and tennis courts—in the middle of town! And there was a basic hardware/all-purpose store (a big hit with Ralph), plus a train station from which we could easily scoot off to other destinations when impulse struck. Did it have to end? Not surprisingly, the perennial question surfaced—could we live in Beaulieu?

Checking out of the hotel, we bumped into the owner. "I'm a Jersey boy," he told us. "My name is Swiss, my family is Swiss, but I was born in New Jersey. Just decided to come back here to settle down and bought this hotel."

"A pleasure to meet you, Jersey boy," I said, shaking his hand and feeling even more at home in Beaulieu, where we hoped we'd return soon.

The train practially flew back to Avignon, arriving at 3:30 p.m. As we rolled our suitcases to our car, we chatted about the supplies we needed to pick up on the way home—some fresh fruit, veggies, eggs, and yogurt. And some *bière* and *vin*, of course. And then silence fell as our thoughts turned back to our dreamy life-in-Beaulieu fantasy. Would be rather stellar, wouldn't it? As we approached Beau Mo, we stopped dead in our tracks. Our eyes bulged out of our heads like a couple of cartoon characters when they realize they've lost their brakes as they're blasting down an alpine mountain road with sheer drop-offs and no guardrails, careening through hairpin turns on two wheels. What the … ? It couldn't be!

Instead of sitting comfortably on its tires, the front end of Beau Mo was resting on two large square rocks. It was a bizarre sight. Why on earth would someone tamper with our modest car? I wondered, stupefied. It was nearly a decade old. And no one would mistake it for a Porsche. It had to be one of the most basic, common cars around. And with local French license plates, it was obviously not a rental. It had nothing to indicate we were foreigners or from elsewhere. On the other hand, I reasoned, maybe being so average made it A-list in terms of practical desirability? Were market forces such that high demand for and low supply of wheels from a lowly, aging Renault Modus inspired a creative entrepreneur to develop that rarely found empty market niche—the after-hours auto parts supplier whose business model featured midnight deliveries?

117

I could imagine a typical business transaction:

"*Bonsoir,*" the shifty night-shift entrepreneur says to the anonymous caller on his mobile phone.

"*Bonsoir.* Is this Prêt-à-Porter Auto Parts?"

"Maybe. Who wants to know?"

"*Un bon client.*"

"Good customers know the password."

"Wheels-to-go."

"*Bon.* Whaddaya need?"

"A pair of tires for a ten-year-old Renault Modus."

"You and everybody else and his *frère, mon ami.* They literally fly off the axles, uh, I mean, shelves. I can hardly keep those babies in the field, uh, I mean, stock. But, your timing is most excellent. A good pair was just parked in, uh, I mean, delivered to my 'warehouse' this morning."

"*Parfait.*"

"Don't forget, monsieur, Prêt-à-Porter Auto Parts is a cash-only operation."

"*Pas de problème.* I'll stick up someone, uh, I mean, *pick* up some on the way over."

I guess we were lucky the "order" wasn't for *four* wheels. But the hubcap from the rear right tire was missing too. So maybe the culprits had intended to lift four and were ready to start on number three when someone interrupted them? In my stupor, I gazed out at the grassy field by the front end of the car. There I spotted all three hubcaps scattered in the weeds. I gathered them and returned to Ralph. Holding them out to him, I said, "Well, honey, it's something—at least we don't need to replace the hubcaps."

After walking around the car like dazed zombies, berating ourselves for not paying to park in the secure lot, we settled down and called the insurance company. They called their tow-truck guy, who arrived on site quite quickly. When he saw the car, he eloquently summed up the situation: *"Merde!"* My sentiments exactly.

But Tow-Truck Guy hadn't brought any tires with him because he'd been told by the insurance company that our tires were merely flat, not completely AWOL. (Probably a direct result of my refined French skills.) Though not a professional mechanic, I was fairly certain that four tires were needed to roll a car onto a flatbed, and two plus one spare didn't quite do the trick. Though a rush hour *bouchon* delayed Tire Guy with the critical fourth wheel, once at the scene, he and Tow-Truck Guy wasted no time positioning Beau Mo on the truck bed.

As Ralph and I crammed ourselves in the front seat with Tow-Truck Guy, we thanked him for coming to our rescue. No problem, he said—he'd known exactly where we were because he came to that particular lot often. "But look there," he added, pointing to an area adjacent to the TGV station. "This is where you can park. No trees. It's safe, though no security cameras. I am never called here." Ralph and I looked at each other and, without saying a word, deleted that information. Why clog memory banks with details never to be used? Ever. We silently vowed to be "pay lot" people.

En route back to Saint-Rémy, we called ahead to our Renault garage to relay our dilemma and make sure they'd stay open for us. They did, and the considerate garage owner even offered us a lift home though we lived just around the corner and could have wheeled our small suitcases. He had sold us these tires just a few thousand kilometers earlier, so he felt our pain. At our house, we thanked Garage Guy profusely and arranged to check in with him the following morning to confirm when the new tires would arrive.

The next day, we made an official declaration to a polite and efficient gendarme at the local Gendarmerie Nationale, conveniently located a five-minute walk from our house. We explained that only the wheels and tires were missing, that the hubcaps had been left behind. *"Très bien,"* he said, handing us a copy of the report, which we needed to send to the insurance company. A couple of days later, the insurance inspector evaluated the car at the mechanic's garage and issued the go-ahead to restore its wheels. Soon afterward, Beau Mo was back on all fours, ready to roll.

But that was not the moment to rush anywhere. It was a time to pause and reflect on our sad saga, learn from it, and acknowledge the upside. The main thing was, of course, that everyone was all right. And, we didn't have to replace four new sets of wheels and tires but only two. Also, we'd learned to pass on the pay-nothing-now-pay-a-lot-later lot. Plus, for toppers, our French automotive lexicon had been enhanced. We'd learned the pretty word for hubcap—*enjoliveur.*

Pop for the pay lot.
The investment pays dividends in peace of mind.

Chapter 12

Carotte to Crudité

"What do you *do* all day, anyway? I mean, all those touristy things have got to get boring after a while, right?" wrote my doctor friend, toiling away in the United States.

"Vacuuming," I could have replied, because cleaning, dishwashing, laundry, and all that mundane maintenance stuff doesn't miraculously take care of itself in households planted in Provence. *Bien sûr*, boring chores still need doing, yet I opted to discuss an activity reflecting the freedom to expand our horizons, a precious gift of retirement.

"I'm putting *crudités* on the table, baby—that's what I'm *dooo*-ing," I replied. "In fact, just the other day, from my very own *jardin*, I harvested my very first French *carotte*, and she was a beauty!" I added proudly.

That day of revelation had been the Fourth of July. I'd gone out to the garden plot to check on my crop. The bushy green

121

carrot tops were flopping all over the ground, and when I flicked the dirt away from the top of one, some orange color was revealed. Woo-hoo, the real deal! But when to harvest it? I'd wondered. I had had no earthly idea. What experience did I have with growing foodstuffs?

Once, when I was a kid in science class, we'd stuck celery stalks in blue-tinted water and watched the inky hue rise up the stalk. In college, there was my Avocado Period. I used to stick toothpicks in fat avocado pits and rest them in tall glasses of water on the windowsill above the sink. Eventually, loops of green vine, resembling a tangled, withered mess, would overcome the kitchen counter, prompting my roommate to toss it. But witnessing osmosis and neglecting houseplants wouldn't win me any Green Thumb awards.

Zut, I should have written down the date when Ralph—who'd grown up wielding a trowel—had decided it was time to kick-start my garden education program. It had been a sunny day sometime in the spring, and now it was summer. Back then, he had led me out to our compact backyard to a slender strip of plain dirt, just thirty centimeters wide, that ran along the slatted wood fence. That three-meter-long patch that divided the grassy area from the gravely area didn't qualify as a proper *jardin*, but at least it was free of concrete. After waxing poetic about the wonder of the cycle of seasons, Ralph had presented me with a pack of carrot seeds.

"Ready?" he said.

"Sure. So what do I do—dig a hole?"

"No, just sprinkle them on the dirt," he answered with conviction.

"That's it?"

"Yep."

I ripped open the packet and with one flick of my wrist, flung the contents on the ground. "Now what?" I asked.

"Nothing. Just wait and you'll see," he said knowingly.

That seemed so long ago—had it been early or late spring? Ralph knew, of course, but his lips were sealed—he wanted this project to be all mine—learning by doing and all that.

I went back outside to examine the carrot patch more thoroughly. Where I'd seen a bit of orange below a frilly plume, there was now quite a lot of orange showing. It was America's birthday, I realized, a fitting date for a grand entrance into La Belle France for a baby *carotte*, cultivated by *une américaine*. I deemed it time.

My husband got the camera to document the sacred event. He focused on the bushy top while I took hold of the bit of visible orange. The little guy didn't want to come out at first, so I wiggled it gently around and around and then some more. I sure didn't want to traumatize my first *carotte*—I was hoping for a natural birth. Labor went on for a while and then finally, with a bit of extra help from my mini spade and some more wiggling, the infant *légume* started to release its grip from its dark, dirt womb and ease up toward the sunlight. Voilà—there, before our eyes, was one fine, bona fide *carotte*!

I scurried to the kitchen to rinse the mud off the long, slender stalk and placed it delicately on a soft cloth on the dining room table. Rest was in order after that ordeal. I sank into a chair while admiring my handiwork. How sweet it looked! It had to be *the* most precious of *carottes* ever, I mused. I snapped more photos from different angles for the baby veggie album and to send to friends and family, especially those who wondered what I could possibly be *dooo*-ing with my time in La

Belle France. But now that I had an actual carrot, what to do with it? I hadn't given that any thought at all.

"Make a salad," Ralph said.

"Salad—gah! I can't bring myself to *eat* it—not my infant veggie!" I answered, aghast.

"Well, that's really the point, you know," he said matter-of-factly.

As I patted my *carotte* affectionately, I decided to put it in a carafe of water, admire it as I would a tall posy, and ponder the dilemma. If you grow a veggie, the idea is you are to eat the veggie, not use it as decoration, just like Ralph said. Certainly my Kansas friend, Brian, would know what to do—he'd grown up on a farm and occasionally still helped his father plow the back forty. I emailed him a *carotte* photo and asked him for advice, encouraging accolades. He said it was the most beautiful first French *carotte* he'd ever seen and would definitely be voted Most Likely to Succeed by its high school senior class. He suggested I preserve it in a shadow box. Or perma-plaque it.

Too funny for his own overalls, I thought, but a snappy comeback eluded me—my mind skipped over to my *crise végétale*. My *carotte* wasn't getting any younger, and it was looking pale. I reasoned I could buy some time by removing it from the vase where it had been soaking and losing its vibrancy. I wrapped it in a paper towel and placed it in the fridge's crisper drawer. I checked it the next day, and though it still looked like a sturdy *carotte*, its radiant shade of orange lacked its previous luster. No question about it, my *carotte* had peaked. I manned up and took out the peeler and knife—which I handed over to Ralph. He did the dirty work. Peel gone. Frilly green top gone. Now we stared at the smooth, gleaming, edible progeny, which although completely abandoned in the ground for a few months, had turned out to be a perfectly lovely, fresh consumable. All bonding aside, consume it we did and *bien sûr*, delectable it was. Nothing like doing nothing and getting not only a product, but a perfect product in return. That's a gardening concept I could wrap my wellies around. Perhaps my exemplary *carotte* was beginner's luck. Or maybe a hands-off approach was exactly what Mother Nature intended.

The coming season I planned to test that theory—but the next time 'round it would be radishes that I'd ignore.

Play in the dirt.
Expanding your horizons produces joy—
and sometimes a vegetable.

Chapter 13

Say Bye, Sky

Saint-Rémy-de-Provence — Summer 2014

"*Eeek*, naked men … in … my … bedroom!" I squealed.

It was 7:30 a.m., and I'd just wandered bleary-eyed into my second floor office/walk-in closet/atelier combo with a view of a once-vacant lot bordered by a thick row of gently waving bamboo and distant layers of terra-cotta rooftops marching up to the stony peaks of Les Alpilles. But this morning, as I gazed out at the morning light, still in a half-dream state, two shirtless guys topped with red hard hats loomed large. They were standing on the concrete-block shell of the half-built house next door—less than eight meters from our terrace—and appeared to be heading directly for my private space. With the curtains in my room pulled back, we both had a direct line of sight of each other—yikes. Though not in my birthday suit, I wasn't dressed for company. Fully awake now, I instinctively jerked back and crouched down. Crawling to my dresser, I reached up, yanked open a drawer, grabbed a T-shirt and yoga pants, and backed out the door. Geez, what a rude awakening.

∽

It had all started with a woman clutching a clipboard. One afternoon, several months earlier, I'd spotted a lady wearing a suit taking notes as she wandered around the property. She snapped photos from each of the five points of the small, pentagon-shaped lot. A chill ran through me. We had always feared that a building would come between us and our Alpilles view one day. Was that day coming soon? I ran downstairs and hustled next door to inquire. The woman was sure new construction would happen eventually, but she didn't know about the timing. We clung to the hope that the photos were for long-term planning purposes and not for any building activity during the last year of our three-year rental agreement. That hope vanished a couple of weeks later when a young man pulled up in a van marked SOIL TESTING.

When we had first rented our house, the owner, Monsieur Gilbert, had informed us that he intended to build on the empty lot to the north, but that didn't bother us. It was the lot to the south with the view of mountains that was a concern. We were told it was indeed "constructible," but the owner, one Monsieur Frédéric, a local vintner and, incidentally, a neighbor of our landlord, didn't have a permit or plans to build on the small, irregularly-shaped plot. We reasoned that the winemaker was already over-programmed and would never have time to think about building a house. Turned out he wasn't and he did.

It was going to be a single-level, energy-efficient house. Our upbeat neighbor Didier told me to look on the bright side. After all, he reminded me, it's not a forty-story apartment building. From our point of view, however, it was one story too many, even if it was to be carbon-neutral. That house, no matter how "green," would block our blue.

Construction moved ahead with alarming speed. The new garage was attached to our two-meter-high wall, which ran the length of our property a mere half meter from the side of our pool. Consequently, the hard hats spent a lot of time on our wall—if not technically in our yard, definitely in our face. Despite some advantages of lean, tanned pecs parading around, our privacy was compromised and the construction concert disrupted the peace—and very early too. The cacophony began around 7:00 a.m. with the tap-tap-tap of the hammer, backed up by the churning of the cement mixer, punctuated by the wood planks meeting the buzz saw. This kept up until close to 4:00 p.m., with a short break for lunch. But that wasn't the end of the building day. Often diligent Frédéric would show up after hours to unload rebar, dump gravel, or drill something. No matter what primary activity he engaged in, his routine typically included a promenade on our now communal wall. As an adept multitasker, he could evaluate recent construction work, check on how we were coping with the heat, and practice his balance—all in one brief stroll.

If we were on the patio, however, we could avoid seeing the builders during the day and Frédéric in the evenings. This was due to the large triangular sails we'd strung over the terrace. While sitting under the crisscrossing sails, we were mostly protected. But we could hear every word the builders were saying, like the instance one of them muttered, "A little piece of metal just fell into the pool." We peeked out from behind our sails to see the guys standing on our wall and pointing at the *piscine*.

"I'll get it," Ralph said. He didn't need to yell, because he could practically shake hands with the guys. He tried to nudge the sunken metal piece into the netted leaf skimmer, but it wouldn't cooperate. Then the doorbell rang. It was one of the hard hats who'd come to help retrieve the escaped chunk of building material. He'd already taken off his shoes, so it seemed he was a considerate builder, or maybe he had a refreshing swim in mind. Wanting to dispel the idea that anytime they wanted to take a dip they could simply toss something into the pool, my husband hopped in himself and fished out the metal chunk.

One day several months into the build, Ralph came downstairs and asked me if I'd heard the mailman yet. On a normal day—before the construction had begun—hearing the mailman wasn't difficult even if I'd been whizzing ice in the blender. Our youthful mailman arrived via a bright yellow La Poste scooter, which screeched to an abrupt halt at each mailbox before revving up to warp speed to travel the twenty meters to the next *boîte aux lettres*. But that day the workers had started installing rafters, and the horrendous drilling was less than thrilling. I shouted back to Ralph, pausing between each word, "How—could—I—possibly—hear—him?"

"My, my, aren't we the cheery one."

"Yeah, just call me Little Miss Sunshine," I grumbled.

As the summer rolled along, more construction surprises came our way. At six o'clock one night, Frédéric came by, intent on educating me on an aspect of the construction. His enthusiasm was not infectious. All I wanted was a magic wand to transform the new house into a supremely eco-friendly structure—a transparent one. Frédéric plowed ahead with his lecture, none of which I comprehended. I should have nodded and bobbed my head as I've learned to do to avoid complicated and usually fruitless explanations. But my blank stare betrayed my ignorance, so he asked me to follow him. Grudgingly, I did.

We tramped over to the construction site, through the mud, and up the wooden plank to the interior of the house. When he pointed to the holes in the Swiss cheese-like terra-cotta blocks, his face lit up. Ho-hum, to my eyes. Could I go home now? He picked up a plunger-type thingie that you'd use to apply caulking. Again he pointed to the gaps in the blocks, where there was much oozing of goo, bright orange like my lovely *carotte* harvest.

"Oh," I said, trying to look interested although I had no idea what he was going on about. "Is that a special material?"

"Yes," he said, "very, very special," his face beaming.

With some effort, I forced out a weak smile and thanked him for the information. His grin revealed one proud builder. On the way back to my house, we made small talk. He asked if the workers were making noise. Inwardly, I flew into a rage at the mere thought of the hour upon hour of jackhammering—it wasn't noise but the stuff of insanity. Outwardly, I reacted calmly. I was resigned to the fact that building a house, even a commendable zero-emissions house, was not a quiet endeavor. As deafening as the process was from time to time, the real disappointment was the loss of our view, as slender as it was. Our sweet little view of blue was a casualty of his green dream, and we had to accept that. Still, I wasn't overjoyed about it. Scrunching up my face and plugging my ears, I told him the noise was impossibly loud, but that I knew it was impossible to avoid. I followed up with the all-purpose, *"C'est la vie."* He nodded and asked me to notify him if anything else bothersome came up. He was probably alluding to a builder blocking our driveway or drilling at dawn. Sadly, giving our sky back he was powerless to do.

≪≶

A few days before Bastille Day, it was terribly windy. It was one time that I felt more sorry for the builders than for myself. They were trying to crisscross wood strips over a green tarp attached to the rafters. Fierce gusts of wind were whipping up the corners of the covering as fast as they could strap them down. I stared at the struggle for a while from my upstairs window, but it was too scary to watch for long. It wouldn't have taken much for one of the workers to have lost his footing, and that made me nervous, like watching a tightrope walker.

When Bastille Day arrived, no builders did—yay! We took advantage of the peace to read quietly under our big umbrella on our little grassy patch. A little after 7:00 p.m., we strolled into town to check out a musical event featuring a group called Surprise de Minuit. We could hear the band before we got halfway to town and they sounded good. We stepped up the pace. Four guys were singing convincingly in French, Italian, and English. Soon a shapely young female singer materialized— she had a cream-colored minidress painted on. She wore sparkly stilettos secured with elastic bands over her feet, clearly an important safety feature considering her rapid-fire movements. A cadre of dancing gals joined her, and together they executed some complicated choreography and multiple costume changes. Ralph was particularly taken with the military "nurse" outfits. They included high-heeled white ankle boots, thigh-high lace-topped hose, ivory satin hot pants revealing some derrières that were no strangers to the gym, silver vests with wide lapels and hefty shoulder pads, and military-style hats with sparkles around the rims. The stage, constructed in front of Saint-Rémy's Église Saint-Martin, had a steep staircase leading down to the main stage with a level in between. The dancers covered all the territory with impressive agility and creativity. Occasionally, the lead gal mistook the lead male singer for a pole, which she slid up and down with grace and athleticism, reflecting an obvious dedication to a rigorous practice regimen. Move over, Las Vegas!

It had been a relief to be spared all the banging and sawing and nail gunning on Bastille Day, but the next day the boys were back, walking the wall. There were two of them. One was pointing at the roof tiles and the gutter running along the new garage. Their backs—and their backsides—were to our side. When they both stopped and crouched on the wall, their derrières, with big pockets filled with tools, hung over the wall into our space, which coincidentally involved Ralph. Not seeing any builders initially, he had placed his chair in the morning shade by the bamboo next to the new garage. There he'd settled in to have his first cup of coffee and read the paper. Now, unbeknownst to Ralph, a pair of builders with impeccable timing were crouched on the wall directly above his head. If a tool had fallen from one of their pockets, it wouldn't have been pretty. Silently, I motioned Ralph away from a potential headache but not before clicking a photo. He'd owe me one for saving his scalp, literally.

As luck would have it, the builders had seriously messed up the tiles at the edge of the garage on our side, so they had to rip them out along with the gutter, which meant the pleasure of their company was extended. Then they readjusted the sheet-metal drainage apparatus so when it rained, water wouldn't gush directly into our pool. *Merci!*

The building of the house, as green as it was to be, was too much. On our standard walking loop that day, we had a curmudgeonly conversation about the unhappy development. Building permits happen. *Hmmph.* When we got home and found the builders weren't on the roof, we took advantage of the opportunity and took a dip in the pool. Five minutes later, they were back. Then I heard a ding-dong. It was a builder. This time he'd dropped his measuring tape into the bamboo and had come to retrieve it. I found it quickly and when I handed it over to him, he offered multiple sincere thanks. With complete resignation I followed up with, *"A bientôt."* See you soon. That I knew was inevitable.

Finally, they packed and drove off for the day. Wonderful silence. At 6:15, we were standing out on the grass ready to clink wineglasses. I was wearing one of my least modest bikinis, wide-rimmed, floppy hat, and sunglasses. Before taking a sip, my lips parted, preparing to say, "Alone at last," when out of my peripheral vision to my left on top of the two-meter-high wall I saw moving human legs. It was Frédéric. Responsible supervisor that he was, he'd probably come to check the tiles and the gutter.

"Bonsoir," he said brightly, looking down on us.

Tilting our chins skyward, we replied dutifully, "Oh, Frédèric, *bonsoir.* How are you?"

"Ça va, ça va. Et vous?"

Ralph answered all was fine. Just barely fine. Thank goodness, before I'd returned to the *jardin* with the drinks, I'd thrown on a long tank top over my skimpy bathing suit. Otherwise, there would have been no *ça va* coming from *moi.*

⤾

Gayle Smith Padgett

Other than hearing loss, and near insanity, the construction hadn't posed any real threat to our well-being—until the humongous, red cement machine arrived. The new house was built by then, but the wall on the west side wasn't. The machine had an impressive four-part arm that spiked high enough to soar over the new house and drop down the other side in order to spit cement into the wall trough. Sometimes it passed over our yard. The droning and loud coughing of cement was deafening and maddening. Ralph had agreed to a trek to Ikea, so we hurried to get out of the house and away from the racket. When we returned late in the afternoon, there was not a soul or machine in sight—yay! We changed for a relaxing swim.

Then the doorbell rang. It was Frédéric, and he looked worried. He'd left a message on Ralph's cell phone and wanted to know if Ralph had received it? No, he hadn't. He'd inadvertently left the phone in the car while at Ikea, so he hadn't heard Frédéric's frantic voice. The cement machine had hiccupped and spewed some of its product over our property and into the pool. Frédéric hadn't known if we had been outside then. Frédéric said he was scared! Unable to locate us, he'd called our landlord, who had rushed over and verified there were no casualties. When I heard we could have been perma-plaqued while milling around our own backyard, I shook in my flip-flops. Frédéric wanted us to go with him out to our yard, so he could explain what had happened. I half expected a Pompeii scenario, but the cleaning crew had done a good job removing the evidence. A small portion of cement dust, which had settled at the bottom of the pool, was the only remnant of the eventful day.

When Frédéric finally left, Ralph and I stared at each other in disbelief.

I said, "Man, so glad we got out of here today."

"Yeah, that didn't sound good at all."

"So, surprising as it is, retail therapy saved the day," I replied with an impish smile.

"I'll give you that one." Before we could revel in not having been attacked by the big, red cement spewer, the doorbell rang again. It was Frédéric once more. He volunteered to vacuum the pool. Ralph convinced him not to worry—he was happy to take care of it. And he was extremely happy he was *able* to take care of it.

✺

After all that excitement, we were especially looking forward to an upcoming peaceful kayaking trek on the Gardon River by the fabulous Roman aqueduct, Pont du Gard, built 40–60 AD. We left the house by 9:00 a.m. and reached the kayak outfitters in Remoulins before ten. There, a chipper young English-speaking woman with "Camille" on her name tag asked if we wanted one kayak for two or two one-man kayaks.

"Well, what do you recommend? Which is easier?" I asked. Camille suggested it was more fun if you had your own, and we agreed. Ralph handed over forty euros in cash.

"Merci beaucoup, Camille," I said.

"It's Cam*eee*," she said, correcting my pronunciation.

"Oh, I'm sorry. *Merci beaucoup,* Cam*eee.*"

"Yes, like Cam*eee*-la in your country."

It took me a second before I realized she must have thought we were British and was referring to Prince Charles's wife, Camilla. There wasn't time to explain that we were American, because a family of kayakers was already in the van, anxious to get to the drop-off point upriver. We hustled over to the vehicle and hopped in. The driver was a talkative guy named Thomas, an architectural landscape student on his summer job. He was eager to practice his English and visit the US national parks. We assured him that our parks were indeed magnificent and hoped he'd get the opportunity to go one day.

Ten minutes later, Thomas let us out at a campground and instructed us to follow the trail down to the water, where the kayaks were lined up in a neat row. With our life vests strapped on, we hopped in our slender boats, took up our paddles, and away we went. Immediately, I headed toward a massive tree trunk in the middle of the river. *BAM!* Though I might have incurred minor whiplash, I was more concerned that I might have sprung a leak in my vessel. I kept paddling and nothing happened, so I figured I had an intact kayak. For a few minutes after the incident, I cruised merrily along, but I still had zero control. Not only was it frustrating but also humiliating, because we were still in sight of the departure point and loads of people were watching. Some colorful words slipped from my lips, but hopefully they didn't reach shore.

My poor technique hadn't been improved by the extensive in-house instruction, which consisted of, "Have you and your wife done this before?" a question Camille had asked Ralph while I was in the loo one last time before embarkation.

"Once, about ten years ago."

"Wonderful—you're all set then!"

As we continued on our paddle, from time to time some strong eddies spun me around, but I pulled through each time to catch up with Ralph. Just before sailing under the majestic Pont du Gard aqueduct, we took photos of each other but thought better of attempting a double selfie. That effort would most assuredly have landed us in the drink. A little ways farther down, we maneuvered our kayaks up onto a private sandy beach, where we enjoyed our *pique-nique* in full view of the remarkable World Heritage Site. Composed of three tiers of arches and soaring to a height of almost forty-nine meters, it made for one magnificent vision.

After two and a half hours, we were nearing the end point of our cruise. We were given the option of docking before or after a whopping one-meter drop—did we dare take on the challenge? Two professionals were standing off to the side to position the kayaks and give them a little push so they'd slide diagonally over the drop. Ralph was ahead and easily slipped over and floated toward the official end point. I hesitated. Despite the mini-whiplash, I'd had fun so far and didn't want to finish the day by capsizing, especially in front of so many spectators. That would have been embarrassing. I waved to the guys that I'd paddle to shore *before* the drop. I hesitated again. Upon further inspection, and witnessing several young children scooting over the drop, I deemed myself up to the task. I waved to the guys that I'd go forward. Paddle-paddle-paddle and *wheeeeee*! Piece o' cake. And a thrill to boot.

And speaking of boots, on the drive back home, I was plotting how to give a swift one to the builders if I found them meandering around on our wall. We'd had such a delightful, carefree day, and I hoped we could continue the peaceful glow in the backyard. I envisioned lounge chairs in our immediate future. Upon return, much to our relief, we found we were home alone.

❧

While summer marched on, the builders finished the exterior and then devoted the bulk of their time to the interior of the new house. Eventually, they disappeared altogether. They weren't invited, but we had a farewell party in their honor. Though they were no longer in our face, the house they left behind most definitely was. If the roof had been flat, we could have retained a good portion of our sky view. Alas, the roof was the pitched, pointy type, capped with rows of terra-cotta tiles, which effectively stretched our two-meter-high wall to double that. Toodle-loo *vue*.

We lamented bidding our view adieu, and we were determined to find another one. In the meantime, we thought about faking a view by painting a mountain-vista mural on the wall, or setting up a pair of tennis umpire chairs, or erecting permanent scaffolding, or installing a trampoline. With each bounce, we could peer over the west wall to the peaceful olive grove beyond. We would burn some calories, but fully enjoying our leisurely morning cappuccinos would prove tricky. Thus, a plan for a new home for our hammock was hatched. We called it Operation View-Finder. Although we'd been going steady with our Saint-Rémy neighborhood for two years, the loss of our blue view looked like an irreconcilable difference.

13

**Expect vacant lots to attract
clipboards and construction crews.**
You can only hope to control what you own.

Chapter 14

Where's Hoo?

Clandestine operation essentials vary according to the target. In this case, they included a pair of folding mesh lawn chairs, *apéro* staples—chilled rosé, a round of *chèvre*, sliced *saucisson*, a crusty baguette, and lavender-print napkins for a dash of Provençal flair—and a scope. But this outing wouldn't be confused with a carefree *apéro pique-nique*. Instead, it was a time-sensitive, top-secret stakeout deep in Les Alpilles. Dusk was approaching, so time was short to complete our mission—to capture a glimpse of an elusive night crawler known in these parts as the Grand Duc d'Europe, aka the Eagle Owl.

As a passionate birdwatcher, Ralph takes his hobby very seriously. For his birthday years ago, some good friends had given him a slim tome, *What Bird Did That?* which matched images of dark splats with photos of classic birds. When he had unwrapped the gift, the rest of us burst out laughing. Good

139

sport that he was, Ralph responded with good humor. "You guys are simply hi*lar*ious."

British folks call avid birdwatchers "twitchers" and often assume he is one. When they ask, Ralph always gives an emphatic no, and not because he doesn't chase rare birds. It's just that twitchers tend to twitch together, and Ralph is primarily a lone birdwatcher; he doesn't often go with the flock to bird. And he sets a very high standard for himself. If he's in a bird blind and someone points out a particular bird to him, he won't let himself count it. If another birder divulges a bird's location but no other details (such as the species), when Ralph identifies it, he allows himself only half a point. That's how he chalked up five and a half new birds during a week in the Orkneys. Hopefully, for the Grand Duc, he'd score full marks.

That night was our sixth formal owl stakeout. The first few times we'd chosen sites close to Les Baux that had promise but hadn't worked out. This was our third time to test out an area to the east, close to Eygalières, about twenty minutes from our house in Saint-Rémy. We parked under a massive pine tree in a level area just off the road in a remote sector of Les Alpilles. Based on a reliable bird-sighting hotline—permitted according to Ralph's book of bird-spotting ethics—this was where the Grand Duc was soaring these days, or technically, nights. With his binoculars looped around his neck, Ralph positioned his spotting scope on the tripod while I set out the *apéro* goodies on a flattened backpack next to the slingback chairs. We eased ourselves down into them, from where we had an unobstructed view across the low brush and up into the hills. The sky was turning a soft cotton-candy pink and the roughly notched limestone Alpilles peaks were beginning to take on a sharp delineation. Occasionally a car whizzed by, but other than that it was a serene scene. I poured some rosé into a pair of short plastic stems and handed one to Ralph. "To the Grand Duc!"

"To the Grand Duc!" echoed Ralph, as we clinked glasses. Plastic on plastic sounded dull compared to the energetic clink of crystal, but toasting was a reminder that the stakeout was to be enjoyed, whatever the outcome. Easy for me to say, though. I wasn't the real birder here. It was Ralph who was anxious to put another notch in his birding belt. He took a small sip of wine and put down his glass, swiveling it in the loose dirt so it would stay put. The window of opportunity to owl spot was narrowing rapidly. He scanned the rocky outcroppings where the elusive owl liked to hang out, stilling his binoculars for a second while he studied a tree limb, and then letting them fall back onto his chest. He tore off a piece of baguette, topped it with a gooey blob of *chèvre*, and popped it in his mouth.

"This is really good cheese—where's it from?"

"Remember the cute cheese shop on the square where we stopped to listen to that terrific combo playing on market day?"

"Oh, yeah, yeah, I remember that place. They must have a million cheeses in there—man, this is really creamy." Ralph picked up his binoculars again. With a sigh, back they went to resting position. "Well, think it's time to explore a bit," he said.

"Not too far, okay?" I knew from numerous birding outings that, like me searching for treasures at a *brocante*, my favorite birder could easily get stuck in search mode and lose track of time and place. In the twilight, in the semi-outback, this most certainly was *not* an advantageous occasion to lose focus.

"No, no, not too far," he yelled, disappearing around a bend.

With a glass of rosé in one hand and Ralph's hand-me-down binoculars in the other, I marveled at the gentle, balmy breeze and clean pine scents. Periodically, I set down my glass and pressed the binocs to my eyes. It was a perfect setting for Your Lordship, the Grand Duc, to drift by. But would he?

Owl-spotting is a very tricky business because owls typically mobilize at night. Darkness is their friend, but not ours. Using a spotlight to locate them is tempting but not effective. Usually. But one night we had done just that while living in our third-floor apartment in Aix-en-Provence. We'd been sitting by the open French doors admiring the colorful illuminated clock tower on the Place de l'Hôtel de Ville when something extraordinary happened. Had it been a hot summer's afternoon a couple of weeks prior, our attention would have been drawn to the resident of the property on the hill below our building—the shapely, rakin' naked gal. Even though her appearance in the open had been brief (like her "outfit"), there was no question about it—she had been raking her garden leaves completely au naturel. No, that's a lie. Ms. Bashful had been wearing a wide-brimmed straw hat, sunglasses, and a red scarf around her neck, and hopefully sunscreen.

On the evening of the winged creature event, it was around 9:30 and nearly dark. Other than the muffled *thwop-thwop-thwop* of a helicopter taking off or landing on the distant hospital roof, it had been peaceful. Suddenly, a black shadow swooped down, landing on the utility pole about fifty meters from us. Ralph scrambled for his binoculars. "It's an owl!" he whispered. He handed me the binoculars, so I could see the grand bird clearly. Wow, what a majestic sight. A tawny owl, Ralph told me. Something about its rigid posture made it seem utterly

142

monumental, although, as I later learned, it was, at most, forty-five centimeters long. And it just sat there with its head slowly pivoting, seemingly 359.5 degrees in one direction and then in the other. While Monsieur Owl stayed put, Ralph quickly set up his spotting scope on the tripod. He brought the magnificent bird into focus and let me have a peek. Up close, it appeared almost human-like with its round head and big eyes set close together. When the last wisp of natural light was on the verge of disappearing, so was the bird's shape. What to do? But without a pair of military-strength night-vision goggles handy, there was only one possibility—a flashlight. That was risky because the light could startle the owl and that would be it. But Ralph said seeing it fly away would be a sight to behold since the wingspan measured a whopping meter.

Off to the kitchen I scurried. I pawed through the oddball collection of miscellany in the junk drawer until I felt the old flashlight. Miracle of miracles, the batteries still had some juice in them, so when I slid the button forward, a faint beam came on. The next surprise was that the light reached the utility pole. With Ralph behind the scope, I aimed the light on the bottom of the pole and then inched the pale ray upward. We fully expected the bird to take off—but it didn't. We switched places so I could see the bird while Ralph illuminated it. When the light met its penetrating eyes, the reflection lit them up bright, blazing scarlet. We knew the owl would soon spot a snack and the show would be over, but until then we were glued to the mesmerizing vision. Mealtime came quickly enough and then it was liftoff—the owl's massive wings outstretched as he dove for his take-out dinner.

Each night after that, we sat and waited. Waited and sat. We were not rewarded most nights but occasionally we were, and those nights were extra-special. It was as if we had a silent neighborhood-watch protector who was making the rounds and reassuring us all was well. After a few encounters, we felt it was appropriate to move to a first-name basis with our raptor friend. We decided on Orville because in Wright-brother fashion, he flew "o'er-the-ville."

Orville was a majestic bird, not whimsically cute like the owl logo for the ubiquitous American sports-bar chain, Hooters. That pub would normally be light years from my radar except for our recent trip to Prague, a magnificent city rich with spectacular cultural venues, none of which was Hooters. Our holiday apartment entry was off a passageway just opposite the watering hole, encased in vast glass windows. On the interior brick walls, I could see a variety of spirited Hooters T-shirts and tank tops for sale, which made me think of our great friend Dan and his famously wicked sense of punny humor. He was having a worrisome surgery soon, and I thought an irreverent T-shirt would cheer him up. With that humanitarian thought in mind, I put my feelings of inadequacy aside, and fearlessly propelled myself into a bar where the servers are fit, attractive, young gals dressed in hot pants and tank tops revealing formidable décolletage. As it turned out, the server who helped me delivered flawless English as well as impeccable customer service. With polished ease and composure, she guided me to the shirt that read, "Hooters makes you happy," adorned with that adorable owl logo I mentioned. (Dan got a big kick out of it, by the way, and on cue he said, "It's a hoot.")

The real-life bird of prey I saw through the spotting scope that night outside our Aix apartment didn't look fanciful at all; it had a soulful, enigmatic presence. Consequently, it was easy to succumb to its mysterious allure even if it meant losing sleep.

Sometimes I'd get up in the middle of the night to answer a nature call and feel compelled to detour out to the living room to see if the utility pole was occupied. There I'd be at three o'clock in the morning, in my jammies, squinting steadily at the top of the pole, trying to focus. Every now and then, instead of the sharply cut pole top, I'd see Orville's rounded shape and rush to the bedroom to update Ralph with the exciting news. He would mumble something about obsessive behavior and roll over. That was annoying because hey, he'd gotten me hooked on the owl-watch thing in the first place and now he wouldn't even come out to play. Apparently, he was a fair-weather birder—*hmmph*. I never did break my middle-of-the-night habit, and when we moved from Aix to Saint-Rémy, it meant saying adieu to my favorite utility pole and Orville. Boo-hoo, bye, hoo.

≈

Happily, there were more hoo-birds in Saint-Rémy. The tourist office that gave regular owl tours promised a Grand Duc sighting; some friends had participated in one of the tours and they did, in fact, observe the creature—pointed out by the guide. Of course, that would not work for Ralph. It simply wouldn't count unless he found the Grand Duc himself, and that was the reason for our trek deep into the Alpilles this night. When barely any light was left in the sky and Ralph was still off wandering around, I started to get a little antsy. As gratifying as it would have been to spot the Grand Duc, safety came first. I picked up my cell phone and gave him a jingle.

"Hi, honey. Just thought I'd check in. It's getting a bit darkish."

"Yeah, that it is. No action out here so time to abandon our posts, I guess. I'll be there in two seconds," he said, not entirely masking his disappointment.

"Nothing going on over here either. Okay, *à très bientôt.*"

When Ralph reached our makeshift campsite, I gave him a squeeze. "Sorry, honey. But we tried."

"Yes, we did. And I did get a good look at some blue tits and a robin," he said, with an almost upbeat lilt to his voice.

"Well, that's something," I said supportively.

For a birder, patience is first and foremost. Keeping at it is the name of the game. Even if this particular stakeout hadn't been productive, hope sprang eternal that the next one would be. It was like combing thrift shops for that pristine Burberry trench coat. Lofty goal, I know, but not impossible. In fact, a friend found a new Burberry shirt in a charity shop in Florida and, generous chum that she is, passed it on to me. Normally, I'd only wear it on special occasions like when we were flying long haul. It was probably my imagination, but that shirt seemed to work miracles on some airline staff, resulting in a variety of perks. So, I'd make an exception for the Grand Duc. Yes, I believed he was worth my lucky shirt, even if he was powerless to upgrade us to business class.

In the deepening shadows, we broke camp. It took just a few minutes—we had the drill down well. As we headed down the winding road back home, I wondered if perhaps we were trying too hard. Maybe we'd catch up with Orville's cousin when we least expected it—say, during a break after nailing the Texas two-step at twilight during Saint-Rémy's country-western festival or pausing to stargaze during a concert intermission in the courtyard of a vineyard snuggled into the Alpilles foothills. Or maybe we needed to look no further than our very own backyard? Perhaps the Grand Duc made forays beyond his typical stomping grounds and was right around the corner in the field by our house? In fact, periodically at dusk, we'd heard a hoo, and tantalizingly close too. But it wasn't *the* hoo we were looking for—Ralph knows his hoos and was pretty sure it was just a tawny owl and not the Grand Duc. Just the same, it was encouraging to know that members of this bird family were out and about, making themselves known, if only by song. Ralph says some birders consider a *contact auditif* equal to an actual sighting. Well, that's some birders. Ralph wasn't one of them.

And I liked the idea he needed to see the real deal. I wanted to see the real deal too. I'd come to find *chouettes* and *hiboux*, as the French refer to owls, adorable and enchanting. I even checked out the difference between the two. The *hiboux* were the ones with tufted feathers that looked like pointy ears on top of their heads, like the Grand Duc (and the Hooters owl, as a matter of fact). But I doubted my limited research qualified me as a budding birder. I looked for the commanding nocturnal creature while chilling in a lawn chair in wildly pretty settings without doing any of the real investigative work. So, the search continues. We are committed to tailing "our" hoo until he makes his move in our full view. When that dusk comes, when the Grand Duc finally makes his debut for us, it will be an event to remember. And *that* hooter will make us happy.

14

Get a kick out of each quest.
There's no weight limit on the
fun packed in your bags.

Chapter 15

Life of Pee

With one disgruntled tiger topping the list, the challenges faced by the boy on the boat in Yann Martel's *Life of Pi* were numerous. A place to pee wasn't one of them. It can be an issue, however, for landlubber adventurers. When you need a restroom, it behooves you to know how to ask for one. In France, the correct phrasing implies you are asking for *two* of them, as in, *"S'il vous plaît, où sont les toilettes?"* In cafés and lots of restaurants, typically the restroom is a mere "uni," so it's very optimistic to expect a pair, though it can happen. But better to err on the side of too many than too few.

And there always seem to be too few, especially when you're a female in an urban environment. If you're near a big department store or hotel, you're in luck. Otherwise, you're left with primarily four choices. Lots of cities have free WCs available, but often they are tricky to find. They may not be available in obvious places such as next to the tourist office.

148

More often than not, wherever you are, they aren't. If you do find one, it's unlikely it will resemble a buzzing, cheery welcome center but rather a dim, deserted dungeon. Don't rule them out, though. Although basic, sometimes they are spotless and don't house remains of former inmates or small animals. But just in case, it's a good idea to exercise caution. Use your phone to light the way or better yet, send in an advance team for a quick sweep. My accommodating (and practical) hubby prefers that over hearing me yelp, in which case he'll be rushing in anyway to calm his squeamish, distressed damsel.

The public restrooms that are guaranteed to be in fine shape typically charge a fee—at least fifty cents. But they're found at airports or train stations, not in town where you're likely to be. Alternatively, some cities and towns have metal container-like WC stations plunked in the middle of parking lots. Some cost and some don't. You might have correct change or not. Either way, I'm not a fan—I've always found them suspect. What if you get in there and lock the door, but there's a malfunction? That happened to me once, and when the door suddenly whipped open and a man was standing there, it nearly scared the pants off me, which were already at half-mast. So unless there's a buddy at hand who can stand guard, it's best to buck up and keep looking.

That's when you decide to dash into a café, but don't even think about heading straight to the facilities. As I discovered on our first trip to Arles, if one of the staff notices you, that sighting might spark a tutorial on café etiquette, which will probably prove embarrassing and not enhance international relations. Also, the public admonition will take longer than ordering a coffee, but once drunk, that option defeats the purpose. As soon as the beverage filters through, you're back at square one. When I'm in that squirmy state, my distress can often be temporarily relieved by running into a promising clothing sale. Then miraculously, the urge to go is forgotten, and the only urgency becomes finding a little treasure in the right size and color.

But rarely is any of this is a pressing issue for guys. If nature calls on them in desperation, they can answer with minimal fuss. Consequently, their WC standards are fairly flexible, resulting in greater options. Granted, in crowded cities, they face pretty much the same challenges as us females, but in Provençal towns and villages, the way of life is much more relaxed. Here, guys attending to nature "off to the side" isn't so unusual. This behavior is particularly prevalent during festivals involving beer and wine. And there are a lot of festivals here, and they all involve beer and wine. And many involve four-legged creatures too. During the 428 (at least) annual events in Saint-Rémy that feature herds of horses, bulls, donkeys, goats, and sheep, believe me, there is a lot of peeing going on. And that's just the cowboys. While the four-legged creatures aren't bashful about peeing as they mosey down main street, their masters retreat to shadowed walls outside the historic center. Whichever wall it is, it's undoubtedly along your route home. So during *ville en fête*, expect to witness nature taking its course. And have a Gallic shrug ready.

That shrug will come in handy again when you're on a national highway, particularly on the vacant stretches between towns. You pass a car parked on the shoulder and to the side of the vehicle is a guy with his back to the road executing the classic let-'er-rip stance—elbows pressed against his sides, head tilted down slightly. A question springs to mind. Why did he choose *not* to go behind the big bush? Two reasons. One, the front of the bush is closer, and two, the back of the bush isn't. As admirable as the lack of puritanical prudishness is, the level of uninhibitedness is notably curious. After polling the local male population (Ralph), I discovered it's not an issue of exhibitionism or laziness or that the guy turning his back to the road had already depleted his daily reserve of discretion, but rather something simpler—it's the "who cares?" attitude in motion. Guys peeing in the open air isn't considered heathen behavior—it's just matter-of-factly natural. Though it used to be a pet peeve of mine, I'm getting used to it. Truth be told, I'm just jealous that women need more room to work.

My envy extends to museum and concert halls. Often the bathrooms for men and women have the same number of stalls, plus guys get the extra *pissoirs*. Sometimes, ladies miss the curtain going up because they're shifting from one foot to the other in a long restroom line while the guys blithely stream in and out with no delays. The fabulous Musée Picasso, situated smack-dab on the glorious Mediterranean in Antibes, is an exception. That place endeared itself to me on my first visit and not just for Pablo's fabulous works of art. The multistall restroom is unisex—there's a single queue, so guys stand in line along with moms with their kids. It's not often that you find a level peeing field.

Except in nature. When we're out in the countryside with lots of bushes and trees, women's freedom to pee reigns. It's so very liberating. Since Provence is a magnet for hikers and bicyclists, women popping out from behind a shrub while adjusting their outfits is a rather common occurrence and doesn't turn heads. Out in nature, a girl can duck behind a tree any ol' time she feels the urge, fret-free. Some have perfected the procedure, like a clever friend of mine who lives about an hour's walk from central Saint-Rémy. Once, she mentioned she had designated pit stops along her route. She didn't volunteer any details and I didn't ask. Some things in life you must discover for yourself.

And I did, and perhaps surprisingly, in Aix-en-Provence. While we lived in that vibrant, cultural hub, I had my preferred pee stations—on the periphery of town, in *plein air*. One of our favorite walking circuits wound by the little terraced park where Cezanne used to paint "Vicky," as my husband dubbed Mont Sainte-Victoire. After admiring the view that the master painted over and over and then repeated a few thousand times, we'd walk through open fields, up a very long, steep road, and past some impressive estates. Though the villas were not positioned cheek by jowl, the area didn't qualify as genuine countryside. The foliage in the open fields was too exposed for my comfort level. Consequently, I knew I had to hold my drink on that walk.

It was a pretty promenade but with no obvious solution to the pee problem, or so we thought. Then one day, quite by accident, we made a discovery. We found a skinny path sandwiched between two estates that led back down into the valley. This meant we didn't have to retrace our steps but could loop around back to our starting point, which was much more gratifying. Also, the road that led to our "secret" passageway was a dead end, so traffic was minimal—another plus for a walker seeking a private pee place. In addition, lining the road were some lovely mature trees with thick low branches that formed accessible, inviting pee spots. After a few walks, I became especially partial to one particular canopied pine tree. It was well-designed with a broken but sturdy branch about ten centimeters long positioned about a meter from the base—

perfect height to hold a roll of toilet paper. Yes, I did give it more than a passing thought. In moist months, I could have wrapped it in a zippered plastic bag to protect it from the elements.

We left Aix for Saint-Rémy before drizzly weather set in, so I didn't get a chance to winterize my pee place. But I did feel compelled to recognize its many fine attributes through the application of the Padgett Pee Places (PPP) scale. Whereas Michelin awards stars, my triple "P" system assigns TP rolls—one roll for privacy (good vegetation coverage), one roll for access (easy in and out), and one roll for conditions—nettle-free with loose dirt and stones to discreetly restore the terrain. At an invitation-only event, the selection committee (*moi*) awarded it top marks—*trois* rollers.

At least in private homes, you would think that finding a convenient pee spot would be straightforward. But even for adults, sometimes potty training is required. In France, you need to reprogram your system to forget the association between bathroom and toilet. The former doesn't necessarily include the latter. The toilet is often in a separate enclosure, usually but not always next door to the bathroom. During one getaway weekend outside quaint Lourmarin at the beautifully renovated farmhouse of some friends, our tastefully decorated bedroom had a spacious en suite bathroom, including double sinks and a large tub. Reaching the WC, however, required a trot down the hall, followed by a right-hand turn past another bedroom. In sophisticated Aix-en-Provence, some buddies moved into a gorgeous brand-new 230-square-meter state-of-the-art house with floor heating, a custom kitchen, a second-floor mezzanine, and floor-to-ceiling glass windows with silent, automated shutters. Upstairs, there was a lovely guest suite with a full bathroom, including a shower and toilet. The two other bedrooms shared a big bathroom with a tub and a toilet. The master bedroom, however, with its beautifully tiled bathroom, including an impressive Italian rain shower, offered no toilet. That was installed in the guest powder room by the front door. But there was no sink. For that you retraced your steps back to the master bathroom. Or you visited the utility room where you could wash your hands in an oversized industrial sink next to the washer and dryer. My friend said that finding herself by the laundry facilities at 3:00 a.m., wide awake after her middle-of-the-night ramble, was a terrific opportunity to throw in a load. And bonus—electricity is cheaper in the wee hours.

Even during the first few months in our Saint-Rémy home, finding a potty presented a challenge. When we first saw the place, the builder-owner was putting the finishing touches on it. After our pint-sized apartment in Aix with its toilet squeezed into a windowless space beneath the water heater, behind a pocket door that sometimes stuck in locked position, it was delightful to find a spanking new house with two bright bathrooms—hooray! On our initial walk-through, I was thrilled to discover, not only a guest WC by the front entry, but also a spacious en suite guest bathroom with double glass sinks and glassed-in shower, and an upstairs master bathroom with a large bathtub, two windows, and sink. The toilet was located in an adjacent room with a window and standard hinged door.

Soon after our first viewing, the excitement of the new house receded, and I started to think about its practicalities. I couldn't visualize the toilet in the guest bathroom. I studied the photos, but not all angles were available. Uh-oh. Please don't tell me there's no WC in there, I prayed. That would be sheer craziness, wouldn't it? And besides, having two full bathrooms was one of our must-haves. On our next visit to the house, I made a beeline for the guest bath. Just as I feared. *Pas de toilette.* I couldn't believe it. There was an empty space between the sink console and the shower. I wanted to hold out hope one would be installed, yet the tile floor had been completed. I called the owner over and stated the obvious: "There's no toilet in here."

Without missing a beat, he answered, "Correct."

"Why?" I asked.

"Because it's by the front door."

Disheartened, all I could manage was, *"Ah, oui."* Not only did that discovery compromise my excitement over the house, but it was also a tip-off that while some cultural differences like long rosé-marinated lunches were easy to embrace, others, like bathroom design, would prove more challenging.

We'd decided to accept the compromise and went ahead with the rental despite the less-than-adequate toilet facilities. There was a learning curve to conquer, however. Since the guest bedroom also did duty as an office, music, exercise, and laundry-drying room, I had a lot of opportunities to be in there. So unsurprisingly, sometimes I'd be in the guest bedroom when the call of nature rang out. In the early days of living in the house, I'd step into the bathroom at hand and be about to close the door behind me when I'd realize the key architectural feature I needed was located elsewhere.

With time, however, we've adjusted. Now it's just our guests I worry about. If, after getting snuggled into bed for the night, they'd like to pop by the loo, first they'd need to get presentable (hopefully) and walk into the main living area, navigate around the dining room table, proceed past the open kitchen (prepared not to be alarmed by someone rummaging around for a snack or a nightcap), pass through a door to the main foyer (and avoid accidentally opening the door on the right, which would land them on the front steps, or the one straight ahead, which would put them in the garage), and make a left, which leads to the WC. Ralph has suggested we install ribbons of floor lighting to illuminate the path to the WC, just like those emergency lights on an airplane that guide passengers to the nearest exit. Or perhaps our guests would prefer to step outside the French doors that open from the guest bedroom directly onto the enclosed garden? Far less risk of injury. And they wouldn't even have to bother with a robe.

15

Stock up on Gallic shrugs.
They pair perfectly with cultural curiosities.

Chapter 16

Stamps of Approval

"Bravo! Braaa-*vo*! *Braaa-vo*!" exclaimed the official, increasing the intensity of each accolade. The praise was music to my ears. I could hardly believe it—my achievement, at long last, had been duly recognized! I stood motionless before the crowd, beaming with pride, sensing my feathers fluffing. Granted, there was no marathon trophy, no Lotto winnings, no country fair blue ribbon. But it felt like it. I had just triumphed over the town's new stamp machine, and the post office employee was ecstatic, like a parent witnessing her firstborn's first steps.

It was my second try at the spiffy, newly renovated *poste* to mail our dossiers to the sous-préfecture for our fifth *cartes de séjour*, the document that would allow us to legally remain in La Belle France for another year. The first time I'd shown up at the Saint-Rémy post office to mail our thick, legal-sized envelope, I was expecting the usual drill. That meant I'd wait my turn in line, then once up at the counter, I'd pass over whatever I had to mail to the clerk, who would ask me a couple of questions, quickly interpret my confused expression, smile knowingly, and proceed to efficiently do whatever had to be done to get me and my package gone. However, this time 'round, I was out of luck. Along with the new paint and design, automated machines had been installed and apparently the procedural manual rewritten.

Now, much to my dismay, customers were expected to engage in a self-checkout. As I fumbled around, pushing this button and that on the stamp machine and getting increasingly frustrated, a clerk miraculously materialized at my side. *Merci beaucoup*, postal people, for having troubleshooters at the ready. The clerk took my too-large-for-the-machine hundred-euro note out of my hand and went for change. She returned with smaller bills, weighed my packet, inserted the proper amount of payment, gave me a tutorial on filling out the return receipt form, ripped off my copy, stuck one on my packet, and reminded me to write my return address on the back—all without an obvious hint of condescension or exasperation, though I wouldn't have blamed her. Maybe she'd relate the story of the clueless foreigner who was chewed up and spat out by the stamp machine to her co-workers for a knee-slappin' hoot during their coffee break. At that point, I didn't care. Gratitude trumped humiliation. I thanked the lady from the bottom of my heart. Our important packet was signed, sealed, and hopefully en route to being successfully delivered.

The dossier did make it to the sous-préfecture in Arles but was rejected for lack of proof of residence. Monsieur Sous-préfecture (Mr. SP) considered the bank statement and mobile phone bill—both showing our current address—unworthy. According to the letter, he was expecting something directly connected to the house like a utility bill issued in the last three months. However, the water and electricity bills are only issued every six months and we were in a "tweener" time. The landline telephone bill didn't list both our names (to be rectified forthwith!), and the rental agreement, topping seven pages, would have unnecessarily bulked up our packet. And that is why we used the mobile phone bill. I wouldn't dare mention it to Mr. SP, but monsieur knew where we lived because he mailed the failed dossiers back to us. Nonetheless, Mr. SP needed what he needed, so one more time with feeling.

Back at the *poste* with the much heftier dossier—this one included the lengthy rental agreement—I marched confidently to the machine, grabbed a *recommandé avec avis de réception* (return receipt request) form, filled that baby out, weighed the goods, punched the right buttons, inserted the proper amount, got the stamp, and retrieved the receipt. I turned to find my postal protector so I could present my latest work for evaluation. It wasn't lost on me that she'd been right there behind the nearest counter, observing my machinations from afar, prepared to intervene if I started to teeter on my trike. She inspected the packet, checked the return address, reviewed my return receipt form, and ensured the stamp reflected the correct amount, while issuing an increasingly hearty "bravo" after each checkpoint.

A hush did not fall over the post office crowd at my breakthrough. The customers continued milling about, greeting friends and neighbors, all in a nonchalant, everyday, manner. Oblivious to my triumph, no one stopped to congratulate me. But no matter. I was gleefully jumping up and down on the inside. This was a private victory—I had passed Postal 101. If France issued merit badges, I felt I'd earned one.

It was a no-news-is-good-news situation that we didn't hear anything from Mr. SP in the following couple of weeks. That, we surmised, meant he was a happy camper with our dossier. It was nearly a couple of months later when we received our interim *cartes de séjour* and yet another month before we got our hands on the crucial letter inviting us to the sous-préfecture for the real *cartes*. And oh, by the way, we were to bring along 106 euros each in the form of stamps. Not postal stamps (no stressful trip to the *poste*) but *timbres fiscaux*, which were like money. They're available online now but weren't then. So where would we acquire such precious fiscal stamps? At a bank? Don't be silly. Crazy as it may seem, *timbres fiscaux* were sold only at bars, honest-to-goodness bars, which makes sense in a way. Though a village may not have a bank or a post office, chances are good there's a bar, the lifeblood of any respectable French enclave. And that was very convenient because we couldn't get an adult beverage at a bank or a post office, and we were definitely going to want one to block out the fact that we'd just spent well over US$200 for a few tidbits of sticky-backed paper. And then we were going to follow up with a refill to celebrate that same fact. Because that meant we'd still be legal, baby!

∽

The excursion to the sous-préfecture in Arles was surprisingly painless. Instead of the usual two-hour wait, we were in and out in minutes. In a sense, it was a bit disappointing. I'd had the foresight to assemble a life-support duffle bag to see us through an extended stay at Hotel Bureaucracy—liters of water, a vitamin-rich fruit basket, a packet of nuts, unread newspapers, and greeting cards I hadn't gotten around to writing yet. At the last minute, I'd even stuffed my yoga stretchy bands into the pack. I was prepared for meals, entertainment, writing chores, and a workout. I was worried about finding a loo during the long wait, however. Each year, impressive new "improvements" had been made, but they had yet to install what topped my wish list for government office upgrades—a public WC. We'd plucked a numbered ticket from the customer service machine inside the front door and prepared to settle in and wait.

Typically, there was a large crowd, including a few strollers. But before we'd even decided where to plop, a strident buzz sounded as our number popped onto the electronic screen bolted high on the wall of the general waiting room. Hardly believing we were next, we raced up the stone steps to the visa waiting room, where, amazingly, we were alone—something that had never happened before. We headed to the door that leads to the offices of the government officials, but this year it was locked. New security procedures were in place, it seemed. A voice erupted through an intercom asking for our number before we were let in.

We walked down a long corridor and into a large room to meet with one of Monsieur SP's assistants, seated behind a contemporary desk in an open cubicle. We'd had the same guy the past couple of years, and although he was efficient and knowledgeable, he wasn't what you'd call a Chatty Cathy type. We exchanged greetings—briefly, as usual—and handed over our letter, passports, current *cartes de séjour*, and the pile of precious fiscal stamps. After scrutinizing all of the documents, positioning the stamps in descending order of value, and double-checking the total amount, he gave a slight nod but uttered not a single "bravo." A wee voice inside my head wanted to object to the lack of fanfare, not even the slightest acknowledgment that all of our duckies were neatly in a row,

161

but wisely I opted to silently accept the fact that we were in the big leagues now. No gold stars for foreheads. Then he flipped open the lid of a large black ink pad, picked up a mammoth rubber stamp, pounded it on the pad, and slammed it down on our documents a few times, as if to say, "Monsieur, Madame Padgett, consider yourselves stamped and approved." After the official handed over the precious little cards, we offered our heartfelt *merci beaucoups* and skedaddled.

Delighted it had gone so well but also dazed at the unexpected swiftness of the process, we thought a jolt of java was in order, preferably on a sunny square where we could relax and take a slow, deep breath. We headed to Place du Forum, the pretty square flanked on one side by the legendary Grand Hôtel Nord-Pinus—former patrons include Pablo Picasso and Yves Montand—and on another side by a charming café immortalized in Van Gogh's oil, *Café Terrace at Night*. I love that painting with the indigo sky punctuated with enormous twinkly stars that look like mini bursts of fireworks, suggesting a celebration in progress. How fitting that we were sitting on the very same terrace, beaming with pride over our newly renewed, legal alien status, an accomplishment that merited kicking up our heels. But first the espressos. No question, doubles were in order.

16

Celebrate cracking codes.
Small triumphs build confidence, a helpful tool for shaping a life in a foreign land.

Chapter 17

French Fried

Blasting through the French language barrier like an *escargot*, I was. But times they were a-changin'. The new motivator came in the form of a piece of paper called the DILF—*Diplôme Initial de Langue Française*. That official document verified a basic level of French language competency, and it looked as if acquiring a DILF was soon going to be necessary for Ralph and me.

Before dwelling too much on that unwelcome idea, we reveled in receiving our fifth *cartes de séjour*. It meant that the following year, we'd be eligible to apply for a ten-year residency card, which was hop-up-and-down exciting. It was akin to being told you had to submit a tax return only every decade—a very big deal. We were proud of our good progress and beamed brightly for a day. Then we turned our attention to the dilemma at hand—French proficiency. Conflicting guidelines abounded, but the sixth dossier *probably* needed to include written proof that Ralph and I could *parler* some *français*, which brought us to the DILF. It appeared that France, like your mom, expected you to eat your *carottes*. Okay, half your *carottes*. A passing grade on the DILF exam was 50 percent.

That's right, 50 percent. Now, that paltry percentage had a reassuring ring to it, as passing scores went. Yet as user-friendly as that number sounded, a lot was riding on this *Diplôme Initial de Langue Française*, and we had no idea what it entailed. It was listed specifically on the official website of our *departement*, Bouches-du-Rhône, as an option for proving language proficiency. While at the sous-préfecture to pick up our latest *cartes de séjour*, I'd asked the official to clarify the situation. Would the DILF be required for the following year?

The official read the printout I'd handed him, then shook his head. "Non, ce n'est pas nécessaire. C'est blah blah blah." Oh crud, what was that last part about? He added, "You have your *blah-blah-blah, n'est-ce pas?*" Simultaneously, Ralph said, *"Oui,"* and I said, *"Non."* In the face of the blatant disconnect, I switched my answer to *"Aaah, oui, oui."* I gave Ralph a sidelong glance, nodding knowingly though I hadn't a clue what the guy had said. One thing was for sure, this was *not* the time to request an explanation—our weak language skills would have been laid bare. Say something—anything, my head yelled. I repeated back to the official exactly what he'd just said about the DILF not being necessary and he nodded. We were good.

As we maneuvered down the uneven stone steps to the ground floor, we discussed the shaky ground we were on in terms of our French language skills. No question, they needed improvement and maybe not just for us personnally. An official website indicated proof of language proficiency was required. Yet, our government guy had said the opposite. But what if he forgot what he'd told us or changed his opinion? What if the rules changed? We agreed we could do only one thing to mitigate all the potential what-ifs—buckle down and prepare for the test. How hard could it be? Maybe all we'd have to do was pair a photo of a plate of French fries with the word *frites*. But what if we had to debate the merits of Camus versus those of Sartre with a panel of Sorbonne professors? Knowing precisely what we needed to know was a very big need-to-know. We didn't want to take any chances, and goodness knows, we'd been, shall we say, less than diligent in our pursuit of French fluency.

For my own part, the reason my French wasn't better could be traced back to my linguistic hubris when we were living in dreary, cloud-covered Germany. Pretending to be French, I would wear a black beret to my work cubicle every day and fantasize about living in sunny France. I used to say, "Six months. Just get me to France, and I'll be speaking French in six months." And amazingly, I discovered I wasn't lying. In fact, it didn't even take that long. As soon as we hit the proverbial *terre*, I was running off at the mouth *en français*. It was nothing short of a linguistic miracle. The power of place, maybe. Then my pragmatic hubby, who was on the verge of venturing into French language territory, helpfully suggested I try conversing with an actual French person.

As tough as that reality pill was to swallow, I had to concede that merely *speaking* French wasn't going to get me very far. *Understanding* what people were saying back to me was key. It wasn't about being able to babble a bunch of words; it was about engaging in communication. The best-defense-is-a-good-offense approach—where I ramble without coming up for air so the other person has no opportunity to speak, and then I say, "Adieu," wave, and get the heck out of there pronto—could work for only so long. Nor could I present a sheet of preferred vocabulary and grammatical structures to people I wanted to communicate with and expect them to stay at my level. It would give new meaning to "being on the same page."

࿇

When we first settled in Aix-en-Provence, a university town that has no shortage of language schools, I opted *not* to step into one. The fees were formidable, and back then our budget was tight, and yes, I was basking in the newbie glow, thinking I would miraculously absorb the language. But there was something else. You would think that I, as a former language teacher, would naturally make tracks for a bona fide language program. But as a former language teacher, after too many years of hard time in the classroom, I couldn't bear the thought. First, I'd taught Spanish to public schoolkids and community college adults; later on, English to peewees and teenagers; and finally, composition to international grad students. No matter what the level, there was no shortage of blood, sweat, and tears—and that was just from me.

The structured, formal way of learning French was clearly the hard way; in retirement, I wanted to play hooky. Despite this, I knew I needed to get on a dedicated language track, listening, speaking, reading, and writing my way through the equivalent of the French educational system, no doubt repeating a level here and there. As appealing as skipping class was, I wanted to make *some* language progress—just progress in a kinder, gentler way. The international group we joined while living in Aix-en-Provence offered a terrific solution—a French conversation class once a week for two hours. It was casual and easygoing. No homework. No tests. No grades. No pressure. *Parfait*. We'd meet at a little café where we'd order coffee and share what had happened to us the previous week. I'd practice my little presentation before class in the hopes my delivery wouldn't be entirely incomprehensible and listen intently to the others. Some spoke even less French than me, which was hard to believe, but that gave me hope. Other participants were nearly fluent and just wanted to polish their already impressive language skills. That gave me hope too.

Sylvie, our tireless, retired science teacher-cum-volunteer French teacher, would correct us with great wit and kindness. Occasionally, she would write brief explanations of important grammatical phrasings on a piece of paper and pass it around, each student copying the golden nuggets into their notebook. Typically, those practical terms slipped through my sieve of a brain, but some fun phrases stuck like glue. Now, if I need a scrape repaired, I can impress a French doctor by referring to my English "boo-boo" as a *bo-bo*, just as a five-year-old would, an age group with a linguistic skill level I aspired to achieve.

Embracing less-than-swift progress up the steep language curve was a new experience for me. As far as my US education went, I fell into the achiever category from an early age. When I was in the fifth grade, my older brother challenged me to match the nine out of twelve top marks he'd earned when *he* was in the fifth grade. He pledged to give me one dollar for each one I received. I'm sure he never imagined he'd have to fork over ten bucks from his paper route earnings, but he did—Mom made him.

My first year at university, my mother "encouraged" me to join a sorority, so I'd be supervised—that's what the brochure claimed. While many of my sorority sisters were memorizing secret songs, playing bridge, and attending beer busts, I was studying. College wasn't carefree for me. Staying out late wasn't my thing. By ten o'clock, I was asleep. Oh, wait—there was that one time in grad school when I shared an apartment with two other girlfriends, one of whom was having a birthday. To celebrate, I treated her to a movie. While walking back to my 1964 Mustang (wish I'd kept that!), we happened to run into some Latin-lover types from my Spanish class, and they wanted to party. As native Spanish-speaking Spanish majors, they had plenty of time on their hands. I had an important presentation the next day and didn't want to stay out late, but the next thing I knew we were in a conga line, winding through a stranger's apartment. We eventually got home in what for me seemed like the wee hours but was probably before midnight. My roommate had graduated the year before and now worked at a bank, so she didn't have to rise at pre-dawn like I did to practice my presentation for the umpteenth time. I think I aced it but vowed never again to put my precious grade point average (GPA) in jeopardy. Even a single B grade would have put an unsightly dent in it.

My GPA did, in fact, include a few French courses that covered *Le Petit Prince* and some Molière, but not before some French grammar was hammered into me via a hefty French language textbook I affectionately named *Mon Petit Chou*—MPC, for short. I'd learned the term of endearment while working at a French pastry shop during high school. *Mon petit chou*—my little cabbage—was how the lovey-dovey owners typically addressed each other.

"*Mon petit chou*, when will the Napoleons be ready?" *Madame* would holler from her position by the cash register.

"Coming right up, *mon petit chou*," *Monsieur* would shout from the kitchen.

"And the croissants, *mon petit chou?*"

"*Oui, oui, mon petit chou, tout de suite!*"

But what a bummer that the primary French language morsel I'd retained after that summer gig was the name of a single vegetable. Now I really needed MPC to come to my rescue. Maybe it could reactivate some of that French it had taught me years ago. I started with the introduction. In short, the book was a first-year course introducing a hundred basic language structures and thousands of words. Each of the multiple *échelons*, was accompanied by numerous lessons, followed by pages of exercises. But that wasn't all. In addition to answering all the questions—without exception!—the authors added yet more helpful tips, the gist of which follows here:

❖ Live and breathe French.

❖ Live and breathe French some more.

❖ Dream in French.

❖ Dream in French some more.

❖ Welcome confusion.

❖ Welcome more confusion.

After reviewing the text's ground rules, there was one thing I was absolutely *not* confused about, and that was that MPC meant business. As my thoughts drifted back to my university days, I recalled how strict the French professors had been. Not one I could remember took a laissez-faire approach—even remotely—to teaching their mother tongue. But that's what I needed now, a proverbial kick in the derrière. I continued reading. MPC practically guaranteed that by the end of the first year, students could visit Paris and manage to effectively communicate. That sounded like a reasonable goal. In one year, ostensibly, I'd be able to hold my own, linguistically speaking. Hopefully, that meant being able to do more than select a robust cabbage.

My custom-made, self-guided language plan was born. In addition to the once-a-week French conversation class, I vowed to get cozy with MPC each day. Easier said than done. I started at the beginning and whizzed through multiple chapters, cutting a few corners here and there but writing out a sampling of the exercises. It was comforting that so much seemed familiar, and I was making such good progress. But then came some speed bumps like the pesky *passé composé* (simple past), one of two past tenses, consisting of a two-part verb comprising one of two auxiliary verbs, *être* (to be) or *avoir* (to have) in the present tense, followed by the past participle of the primary verb.

Obviously, I'd arrived in new language territory. I wasn't just reviewing anymore, but learning new stuff and on my own without a teacher. As I neared the end of the chapter, things became even tougher. A review of the grammatical explanation helped, and I moved on to the second past tense called the *imparfait* or the imperfect. Both tenses take place in the past, but one occurs quickly and the other continues to roll on and on. That little gem I had committed to memory but assimilating the long list of verbs forms was a different matter. I hit the proverbial wall and had to call it a day. My poor brain was fried, French fried, to a crisp.

The next day, I was just beginning *Leçon 22* when the phone rang. Instead of screening, I foolishly answered, *"Allô, oui?"* with smug confidence. My *"Allô, oui?"* is pretty good, but the problem is callers don't know that phrase forms the bulk of my linguistic arsenal.

"*Allô. Blah-blah? Blah-blah-blah-blah-blah?*" said the caller.

"Can you speak a bit slower, please?" I asked *en français.*

Just as rapidly, the caller repeated, "*Blah-blah-blah-blah-blah?*"

Geez, it sounded like someone who knew me. Who could it be? I had absolutely no clue. Someone from the tennis club? Oh, wait a nano-second. Did I hear a "*pas-que*-something-something?" Maybe it was Pascale, the downstairs neighbor. She had sent an email recently about a rendezvous, and I hadn't written back yet. I took a deep breath and asked, "Pascale, *comment allez-vous?*" Had I just made a fool of myself yet again? Was it somebody I knew well, someone whose voice I should recognize? "Oh, you're well—great!" I said in French when Pascale replied. What a relief. I continued in my baby French, "Yes, I did receive your email. *Désolée*, I am so late to reply. We'd be happy to join you and Alex for an *apéro* tomorrow." The conversation with Pascale went fine after that because it was brief—I only needed to understand one word—the number six. The *apéro* was at *six*, pronounced "cease," as in "cease and desist," which all French people needed to do if they were considering calling me on the phone anytime in the next few years.

But since getting that message out across France was tricky, French people kept ringing, and I continued to automatically reach for the phone when it jingled. Force of habit, I guess. On another memorable telephonic occasion, I cheerfully picked up the phone with my refined, "*Allô, oui?*" A friendly female voice fired off a big bunch of *français.* As usual, I struggled to comprehend even the tiniest tidbit of information so I could quickly formulate some sort of logical answer followed by stalling until I heard more comprehensible nuggets. Failing that, I went for my fallback position, which was, *"Comment?"* What? She repeated the whole thing again at the same high velocity. Still with no luck, I went to fallback position number two, which was to say in French, "Sorry, but I think the number you have is not correct." Then she asked if I was Madame Pah-*ZHETT* (the real pronunciation is *PA*-jet). That, unfortunately, I understood. A chill ran through me—busted! But for what? I couldn't think of anything. I relaxed my clenched body a tad, figuring it was maybe a follow-up to a car insurance transaction or simply a cold call. But typically, with the cold call they don't want to deal with English, so they apologize for bothering me and politely hang up as fast as they can. Okay, so now I was into it—I'd owned up to being Madame Pah-*ZHETT* by replying weakly, *"Oui."*

The woman's tone continued to be upbeat, but then came more accelerated *français*. I divulged my lack of French telephonic skills while trying to retain a wee modicum of self-respect by qualifying my comment: *"La communication au téléphone est très difficile pour moi."* This way, theoretically, there was the chance I could still be literate but with a hearing issue. So she came at me again *en français*, only louder. Then I said in French, "Pleeeease, caaan yoooou speeeak veryyy slooowly?" She laughed (at my hilarious French?) and said sure, but was there someone else in the house who could speak more *français*, like a husband, perchance? Ha ha! My turn to chuckle. Emitting more of a spontaneous snort (sorry, honey), I explained that my husband spoke even less than I did. She laughed again and proceeded to rattle off a bunch of stuff, which I didn't understand except for *services sociaux*. And something about *santé*, health. I now surmised that I was speaking to a government official who was dealing with either tax (OMG!) or use of health services, a subject to be taken very seriously here. We were *visiteurs*, I explained, and we had our *cartes de séjour pour visiteurs* but not a *carte vitale* (which provides access to health services at a low or no cost). With that, she stopped and laughed some more and repeated in French, "You don't have a *carte vitale?*"

"*Non, non, non,*" I explained as definitively as I could, "we have private insurance from *les États Unis.*" She seemed satisfied and said, "*Très bien,*" followed by a lengthy pause, which I filled with asking whether she needed any other information. Yet again she laughed, which I was now taking in stride. But nothing more was necessary; she had all she needed and said au revoir.

She had all she needed for what? I wondered. To convict me of tax fraud? To haul me off to the clinker and throw away the *clé?* I imagined a courtroom and a voice in my head saying, "Judge, I know ignorance isn't an excuse, but mine certainly is immense. I honestly don't know what's going on most of the time."

To which Monsieur By-the-Book replies, "*Désolé,* take her away!"

On the bright side, if I did end up behind bars, I'd have more time to study French. Maybe then I'd make it to page 194 of my French textbook, where I'd master converting regular compound sentences to other more sophisticated ones by employing *après* + *avoir/être* + *l'infinitif passé* (after + to have/to be + the past participle). Then, when I related to other inmates how I ended up sharing their cell, instead of the banal, compound sentence, "The judge read the sentence and he sent me to jail," I could now provide an upgraded version with an impressive adverbial phrase lead: "After having read the sentence, the judge sent me to jail."

173

Vowing to let the phone ring and go to voice mail, I returned to *Mon Petit Chou*, plowing through the brain-numbing grammar section more quickly than I should have so I could get to the slice-of-life dialogues, which, by comparison, were positively riveting. One of the more compelling tales was a tragic cliffhanger about a university student who got sick, had no appetite, and couldn't eat his mom's delicious *boeuf bourguignon*. How and when he recovered were questions left unresolved!

Possible answers had to be put on hold while I faced the dreaded *exercices*, which required complete sentences and, therefore, focus. I answered them verbally to myself to save time though I should have written them out before delving into the next lesson. It took me two sessions to drag myself through the grammar segment. I cruised through the verb *pouvoir* (to be able) in the present, asking questions, answering positively and negatively. There was no problem with *vouloir* (to want), but I got stuck with the exercises where you had to respond negatively and with a pronoun replacing the noun. Pronouns are tricky little devils. For example:

- ❖ Do you still take tuba lessons? No, I don't still take them (tuba lessons).
- ❖ Are there any ripe rutabagas left at 3:00 p.m.? No, there aren't any (ripe rutabagas) left at 3:00 p.m.

After a dozen of those babies, I was able to create my own personalized applications of this structure:

- ❖ No, I don't want to do them (infuriatingly mind-numbing exercises) any longer.
- ❖ No, I don't need *one* (glass of rosé).
- ❖ Yes, I need *many* of them (bottles of rosé).

I turned the page to the next lesson, *Un weekend convivial.* But it struck me that even though it was Thursday, I wanted to indulge in one of those convivial weekends right then. French homework would wait. I bid MPC *bonne soirée.*

It turned out my language studies had to wait for more than a day. After we'd found the house to rent in Saint-Rémy, my attention had turned to organizing the move. That undertaking had presented all sorts of opportunities to avoid MPC and its laborious *leçons.* Then there was the trip to the US in the fall of 2011. When we got back to Saint-Rémy, there was the house to furnish, neighbors to meet, and a town to explore—yet more reasons to procrastinate hitting the books. Since we were then living an hour away from Aix, my once-a-week French conversation class became once every other month and then once a quarter, if I was lucky. Daryl and Elaine, our dedicated language-learning Irish friends in Saint-Rémy, had given me the phone number of their volunteer French teacher from a social services organization. I never called. Procrastination still trumped commitment.

I compensated by watching some French TV (love the commercials—context rich!) and engaging in experiential, extracurricular activities. I was a regular at the local fitness center, where I attempted to pump myself up and absorbed useful phrases such as *on y va*—let's get a move on! We also joined the tennis club, and I even slugged my way through a competition in winter, which I won't make the mistake of repeating. (Call me wimpy, but I lack the stamina to play tennis in a down-filled ski parka, which is absolutely necessary at night in February in Saint-Rémy. And yes, it can be brutally cold in winter, even in Provence.) And once a week there was tap class, called *claquettes,* under the direction of talented and enthusiastic

Suzanne, the dance studio owner. Most of the tap steps had English names, but Suzanne used French for all the directions and comments. And I had a chance to chat—or attempt to—with fun folks in the small dressing-room area, where both guys and gals nonchalantly changed. (Most of what I learned there didn't involve talking.) Together, we time-stepped and flap ball changed our way through to the end-of-year recital, which, if based on heart, should have been simulcast around the globe.

Also, the extra time I spent reading the *Farandole*, the free monthly newspaper listing local activities, and my *Côté Sud* design magazine, not to mention shopping, paid off to a degree. The saleslady at the curtain store said my French was much better. On a recent visit, I heard her comment to a colleague that when I arrived in Saint-Rémy, I didn't speak a word of French. "Now look at her—she's translating for visitors," she said with a hint of pride, which she deserved. She'd helped me a lot and always had been very patient. I wanted to object to the first part of her assessment but smiled and took the second part as a compliment, also with a hint of pride.

Still, the Most Improved Patron accolade issued by the kindly *vendeuse* probably wasn't going to impress the sous-préfecture folks who would decide my French fate. *Au contraire*—an actual test might be lurking in the near future. If we intended to be granted ten-year residence cards, we had to be prepared to conquer the *Diplôme Initial de Langue Française*. We still didn't know what it entailed, however. After quite a bit of digging, Ralph found a practice version online. It was a multipart test that included listening comprehension and speaking, possibly in front of a panel of judges. (Yikes!) One section of the practice test showed several pictures— a professor delivering a lecture, a woman shoe shopping (easy one!), and a thief lifting a wallet from a guy's back pocket. After listening to a message, you marked the number next to the corresponding photo. For example, *"Attention aux voleurs!"* (Watch out for pickpockets!) I got that one just from the excited tone of voice. In another scene, a fisherman dangles a lure over a lake filled with cute little fishies, all unaware that they may be hooked shortly.

As for the DILF, if we didn't want to meet with the same fate as the aquatic creatures featured in the test booklet, we had to find the best way to prepare. Ralph found an online course that was a possibility. Before signing up, we took a placement test. Ralph passed, much to his delight. I cruised through the beginner level, so I forged ahead with the intermediate, which I bombed. This was mostly due to not having memorized which vowels and consonants could take which diacritical marks (in academic parlance—tiny squiggles above or below certain letters) but also for failing to recognize some clothing items. This was embarrassing, considering all the time I spend in apparel shops. If I couldn't depend on wardrobe vocabulary, I really was in trouble. Anyway, it wasn't clear if that particular course was the type we needed to conquer the DILF, so we procrastinated on making a selection.

And besides, it was time for me to scamper off to the *coiffeur* for a hair repair. After tall, blonde Nicole applied the *couleur*, I flipped through fashion magazines to review clothing terminology. Thirty minutes later, during the shampoo, I explained to Nicole that I had to pass a language test and that on an evaluation quiz I'd missed *tailleur*, which I didn't know meant a women's suit in addition to a tailor. Nicole proceeded to fine-tune that information, explaining that a *tailleur* can be a jacket and skirt or jacket and matching pants, whereas a guy's suit is a *costume*. Right, I thought to myself, I gotta remember that a guy wears a *costume*, and not just to a Mardi Gras party. I thanked Nicole for the language assistance, wondering if she knew she was playing *It Takes a Village to Teach Me French* and then moved over to Lucas's hair-cutting chair for the all-important snip job. A few minutes later, Lucas passed me a hand mirror as he spun the chair so I could admire the rear view of his creation in the large mirror. With a big smile and a *merci beaucoup*, I thanked Lucas and headed for home under gray skies. Rain looked imminent and I was *sans* umbrella. Darn, had I forgotten *mon parapluie*, or was it *ma parapluie*? Right then, the heavens opened up and regardless whether *parapluie* was masculine or feminine, my just-done hair became swiftly undone.

After five years in France, with the DILF hovering ominously overhead like Pa Clampett waving a shotgun at Elly May's heartthrob suitor, there was no choice but to stop fooling around, and move this tentative relationship forward—a formal engagement was needed.

Dear family and friends,
The Padgetts are pleased to announce
their engagement to the langue française.
In lieu of cards and gifts, please send
grammar tips, particularly regarding the
subjunctive.

In all honesty, the subjunctive was probably the least of our worries. After reviewing the practice DILF test, we now needed a solid prep plan. So on our way back from one of our walks in Les Alpilles, we stopped in front of a private language school in the center of town. I took a deep breath and marched in. In the reception area, a woman told us their school could prepare us for the DILF, but they weren't an official test site. For that, we'd have to go to the Chamber of Commerce in Arles. Later at home, I found a phone number and spoke to a woman who transferred me to another woman who couldn't confirm that her department gave the test but suggested I call back in the afternoon to speak to a colleague.

We wanted to get the language test information from the primary source, and it was proving a challenge. Now that we were on a roll, we saddled up and drove to downtown Arles, about twenty-five minutes away. We didn't go directly to the Chamber of Commerce but first tried another office we'd read about online that mentioned the DILF. It was after the normal lunch period at this point, but I was still anxious about finding the office manned. As we drove by the building, I spotted an open door. So far so good. With no parking spots in sight, Ralph pulled in by a garage door around the corner from the office and waited in the car. Inside, I met a helpful receptionist who explained their office, in fact, was certified to administer the DILF but at another location. Getting closer now. She kindly gave me the address and detailed directions.

After some effort, we finally found the general area of the office, but again parking was impossible. Again Ralph stayed in the car in the middle of a full parking lot while I trotted down the street in search of the language test site. The building was clearly beyond its glory days, with its street number scrawled on the heavy wooden door in black marker. I proceeded through to an interior door that was closed and had no handle. The office seemed open, yet also *fermé*. Confused, I walked back outside and stared at the building, searching for opening hours. Through the tall windows I could see people inside, so I tried again. I tucked my fingers around the side of the wooden door with no handle and it opened. On my left was a classroom where a thirty-something guy and a mature woman were poring over some materials. Apologizing for bothering them, I told them of my quest for information on the DILF. The man led me down the hall to a desk, removed a book, and asked when I wanted to take the test. It was given the first Tuesday of every month and cost thirty-five euros. Would the first week in October work? Yikes, take the test so soon? No way, José!

Trying to compose myself as quickly as possible, I blurted in French, "No, no, first it's necessary to prepare for the test. Is there a booklet explaining the test or a practice test, perhaps?" He promised to email me some materials. I gave him my email address, thanked him, and let him get back to work. Making progress!

Still, we didn't have all we'd come for. We found the testing site but no guidance on the test itself. Since we were already in Arles, we decided we might as well follow up on the information the woman at the language school in Saint-Rémy had given us, so we drove to the Chamber of Commerce. Luckily, the large parking lot was nearly empty. I just hoped the inside wasn't empty too. After all, it was Friday afternoon and it was Provence. In the spacious entry hall was a high, curved reception desk behind which sat a helpful guy who said, "Yes, the Chamber of Commerce is involved with the DILF, but not in this building." I was getting used to this routine by now. He pulled out a piece of paper and proceeded to draw us a map. We found the address easily and, unlike the building in downtown Arles, this was a complex of buildings that looked quite spiffy. I explained to the person behind the fourth reception desk of the day that I was looking for information on the DILF, the *Diplôme Initial de Langue Française*.

She replied, "Oh you're the lady who called this morning." How could I have called her that morning when I hadn't even known she existed until that moment?

"Non, non," I said, "I didn't call you. The man at the Chamber of Commerce told us to come here." I held out the hand-drawn map for her to see.

She said, *"Oui,* you did call."

And I said, *"Non,* I didn't," and the conversation morphed into a French version of "Did too, did not, did too, did not." Then it hit me. I'd called the Chamber of Commerce that morning and had been transferred to someone. And now, there I was talking to that someone. *"Ah, oui, oui,"* I said. "I called the Chamber of Commerce and spoke to one lady and then another. You are lady number two!"

"Oui!" she said triumphantly, throwing her hands in the air. She then rapidly fired off a whole bunch of stuff in French, smiled politely, and bent her head back down to her work. I stood there for a moment, wondering what just happened. I didn't have a clue what she'd said. I didn't know if we were to leave or what. Trying to buy some time to figure out what was going on, we drifted over to a display filled with pamphlets. As we leafed through some, I whispered to Ralph, "Did you get any of that?"

"I think we're supposed to wait," he said.

"Do we know why?"

"Not really, but I think somebody's coming."

"Maybe I should confirm—otherwise, isn't she going to wonder what we're still doing here?"

"Yeah, probably a good idea," Ralph conceded. Feeling like my old friend, the Complete Idiot, I walked back to the receptionist and, apologizing for disturbing her, said I wanted to confirm that we were to wait a few minutes. I thought that phrasing it like that might save us a tad of humiliation by implying that we were in a time crunch and it wasn't a question of us floating in linguistic limbo. Though I doubt I fooled her, the kindly woman didn't let on or reveal her exasperation but smiled and said, yes, a colleague was arriving very soon. That time I understood and didn't need a repeat—what a relief.

And within a few minutes, another woman did come out to greet us. Friendly and welcoming, she explained she was a teacher and that one of her duties at the adult education training center was to help folks prepare for the DILF. She could offer some one-on-one assistance, but there was no course per se. And then, marvel of marvels, she asked whether we'd like to review a copy of the DILF course textbook. Eureka! We were finally getting to the heart of the matter. *"Absolument!"* we nodded enthusiastically.

Madame Professeur led us to a neatly arranged resource room, walls lined with full bookcases; it was open to the public during certain office hours several days a week. Computers, French books and magazines, and language assistance were available. She showed us the DILF textbook and let us sit down to review it. It was a practical, streamlined guide to basic French—just what we needed. With all due respect to my trusty MPC text, which could teach me (in due time, theoretically) to construct grammatically coherent (and no doubt, compelling) essays comparing surrealism and existentialism, the DILF text was going to train me to tie my linguistic shoelaces. We were happy to hear that we could order the book online. We thanked Madame Professeur profusely. Not only was she highly informative, but she also said I could easily pass the DILF right then. Hearing these welcome words from an experienced language teacher made me feel I could skip across the Mediterranean.

At the same time, as happy as I was to hear that positive assessment, we didn't want to take any chances with Mr. DILF. And besides, ego now fueled our newfound motivation—we sure intended to beat the 50 percent passing score. Ralph ordered the official textbook, CD and instructor's manual, which arrived in a couple of days. In short order, we made lots of progress on the real-life vocabulary such as airport and train station announcements and lesser known but, on occasion, highly important body parts vocabulary. For example, I discovered the word for eyebrow is *sourcil*. Now I could confidently instruct my sometimes overly zealous facial lady to leave me a full pair.

With our language goal neatly delineated and with proper preparation tools in hand, we felt we were going to be well prepared to carry out our DILF duel. And besides, improving our French was the thing to do. It was a win-win. Not only was it a humiliation/stress reduction program, but it also promised to maximize that undeniably alluring *joie de vivre* that flourishes in Provence—that magical je ne sais quoi that puts a smile on your face. And if we did our homework, we wouldn't trip up, because our "shoelaces" would be smartly tied and safely tucked into place.

Screwing up our courage, we committed to a test date after the New Year. That left a bit over six months to prepare—if we could maintain focus, a perennial challenge in a region full of seductive distractions.

Spend quality time with your new best friend, *la langue française.*

Osmosis lacks a lot as a
language acquisition program.

Chapter 18

Taken Aback on the Road Taken

Saint-Rémy-de-Provence — Fall 2015

Provence is for the birds. Flamingos, bee-eaters, glossy ibises, gray and night herons, egrets great and little, black-winged stints, cormorants, common terns, white storks, rollers, and many others. Like many Parisians and northern European folk who cherish warmth, bright skies, and good eats, numerous winged creatures also call Provence home or at least their *résidence secondaire* for part of the year. And for this my birder hubby is especially grateful.

Yes, birding in Provence can be spectacular—on days when the weather cooperates. When it doesn't, like the previous few days when the ferocious mistral steadily lashed out fifty-kilometer-per-hour winds with gusts up to double that, *les oiseaux*, like the rest of us, were hunkered down. Such conditions were not conducive to standing up straight outdoors, much less spotting birdlife cruising the vast Camargue skies. Even the thick forest of bamboo that hugged our backyard wall had spent most of those stormy days kissing the whitecaps on the pool.

Now all that hullabaloo had simmered down. Ralph had hustled off to go birding, and my plan was to walk a circuit we call the standard loop. It's not a huge workout, but it gets the heart pumping as it winds through town and up to the beginning of Les Alpilles, across the base of the mountain chain, and back down to the city center. The temperature hovered around an inviting twenty-five degrees 25°C (77°F), and there wasn't the slightest breeze. Not even the set of bed linens on a distant neighbor's clothesline wavered. The sheets were behaving admirably and were even color-coordinated with the French blue sky. It promised to be one of those perfectly luscious Provençal days.

My seventy-five-minute hike began with ensuring my backpack contained all the essentials—charged mobile phone, house key, bottle of water, tissues, euros, and of course the essential item in any outdoor survival kit, lip gloss. Satisfied that all was in order, I stepped outside and locked the door. The driveway across the street was empty—no sunflower-yellow Fiat 500. It wasn't because Didier and Jeanne had driven into town for their usual morning coffee with their buddies; it was too early for that. Our spirited Parisian neighbors were still at their main house up north, which explained the tightly shut *volets*. That wasn't the case at Violette and Samuel's house. All their shutters were wide open, which signaled they had arrived in Saint-Rémy from their primary residence near Antwerp. I could see the congenial couple through the oleanders that lined their expansive, neatly pruned backyard. The pair appeared to be in deep discussion, pointing and gesturing this way and that. I guessed they were planning the design of the new lawn area where their adorable pup would have more room to romp. I didn't disturb them with *bonjour-bonjour*.

Across the street, Antoine's shutters and windows were open. He was probably airing the place out after the big winds. Antoine himself wasn't to be seen, though, which was too bad. His big smile and unfailingly upbeat disposition always brightened my day. And not only *my* day; countless other neighbors counted on him too. In fact, we'd first met him while he was on a ladder fixing a neighbor's gutter. We had been in the middle of the street, trying to connect with a lost delivery van, when Antoine overheard me struggling to speak French into my cell phone. Soon he was standing at my side, my phone in his hand, asking the delivery guy for his location. Then he'd hopped on his bike to fetch the truck and lead it back to our house.

A few doors from Antoine lived Maserati Man. When powerfully built Maurice, who hailed from Marseille, fired up his magnificent silver auto, the whole neighborhood knew it. At first, I wondered whether it was missing the muffler, but I wasn't about to bother Maserati Man with intrusive questions about his pride and joy. In fact, the roar had grown on us, so not only did we find it comforting, but we also relied on it. During school holidays when Maurice wasn't taking his son to school, we missed the booming wake-up call. Maybe the intimidating beast of a car scared away sinister forces too. Once, when we were going to the US for an extended time, I mentioned our pending absence to Maurice. He said firmly not to worry about the house, and I took his words to heart. It wasn't so much his impressive ride but Maurice's commanding presence alone that radiated a protective aura. Each time we returned from a trip to find all was well, I sent him a silent thank-you.

Up the block and to the right, I headed toward the large trash containers, next to the space allocated for the yellow plastic sacks stuffed with recyclables. In Saint-Rémy, recyclables included only cardboard, newspapers, and plastics, but *verre* was a no-no. All things glass went in special rounded receptacles with rubberized holes for bottles and jars—minus lids, of course. Those, we learned, belonged in the recyclable bags, which were picked up every week. This trash can area also doubled as a neighborhood recycle center, and sometimes folks abandoned some nifty articles there. In fact, once we found a pair of barely used, blue-striped *chaise longue* cushions. More proud of our cool score than embarrassed, we trotted home through our neighborhood, each with a cushion folded over our heads. But on this day, there was nothing, *rien*.

Patrice and Marianne's open blue shutters indicated they were taking a break from Lille, where they lived most of the year. Remembering that Patrice had been lamenting an impending milestone birthday, I made a note to bake him some chocolate-chip cookies. They guaranteed smiles. On the other side of the street stood the *maison* of Philippe, the tall, lean builder with the perpetual mop of unruly blond hair who was constantly coming and going in his battered blue truck. We always exchanged waves and *bonne journées*. On the rare occasion he was on foot, Ralph would shake his hand, and he and I would exchange a trio of cheek kisses.

At the crazy little crossroads that marked the entrance to our *quartier*, I paused and looked both ways a couple of times. All too often cars came whizzing by at alarming speeds, probably late delivering their kids to or retrieving them from the nearby *école élémentaire.* Ahead of me was a two-way road barely wide enough for a dinky, classic Citroën Deux Chevaux, when cars were parked along one side, which they normally were, especially on market day and in summer. The cars driving in the skinny lane toward me couldn't see the traffic in front of them unless they pulled out halfway across the road, so I paused and took my time. I also had to check the traffic on my right, where a dead-end road sprouted off at a twenty-five-degree angle. Sometimes, a lost delivery truck could be seen driving uncertainly on it while the driver puzzled over his GPS, which didn't yet include our relatively new development.

All was clear, so up I pushed toward town, passing a large building with faded green letters: POMMES DE TERRE. The building used to store potatoes and other vegetables and now housed cars and an ornate, gilded gypsy wagon, straight off a movie set. A little farther along was a sign for *bail à louer,* a rental space. Our great hope was that one day it would be transformed into a Greek or Italian café that served authentic dishes at a *bon prix* with convivial service just a stone's throw from our *petite maison.* An ethnic neighborhood resto would be *formidable.*

Soon I entered the commercial zone. Straight ahead was the imposing Église Saint-Martin and on the right the distinguished pensioners' *maison de retraite.* There, a few years ago during a citywide music fest, we'd sat in the foyer along with the residents, many of whom were asleep despite the rousing jazz combo. Farther along toward *centre ville* was one of our favorite bakeries, which produced a deliciously chewy, rustic baguette called the Ancestrale. Just opposite stood our precious cinema, with its stadium auditorium and comfy velour seats. To our delight, it often played first-run flicks in the *version originale,* and

I attended at every opportunity. I also vowed to spend more time with French films. I'd be first in line for the coming blockbuster that'd be just at my level—*Blanche-Neige et les Sept Nains* (Snow White and the Seven Dwarfs).

Now I was on the main square, Place de la République. Kiddies squealed with delight on the little carousel next to the solemn monument to lost soldiers. Bright red and gun-metal gray metal bistro tables and *chaises* from the popular Café de la Place spilled out onto the blacktop. On market day, cars were banished from the area, but on this beautiful day with the tourist tide still high, the lot was jammed. While I dodged cars that were circling slowly, seeking an empty space, I wondered if I needed more euros. Our bank sat on the north side of the *place*, and I could have easily popped in. I decided I had plenty, so I headed up past the elementary school, where a daughter of new American friends was a student. She loved it, despite having a limited French vocabulary. Maybe I could audit her class?

My pace slowed to move around the handful of folks waiting at the bus stop for a thirty-minute ride to Avignon, Arles, or Cavaillon. Then past the ultra-contemporary, high-end home décor store that I kept meaning to investigate. As I crossed the street, toward the stone steps that lead to the Office de Tourisme, I noticed a familiar sight—a stooped, white-haired woman with her calves perpetually wrapped in bandages above fiery red, scabbed, and swollen ankles. She was shuffling along in black slippers and a printed housecoat, arm extended, hand tightly clasping a leash connected to a scruffy minuscule pooch. It was comforting to know she had the small companion, but I hoped there was a human watching over her.

Diagonally across the parking lot, a group of tourists was gathered in front of the tourist office, probably waiting for a Van Gogh tour. Just outside the entrance to the kiddie park, a forlorn golden labrador waited, its leash tethered to the fence, right next to the round red-and-white no-dogs-allowed sign. Sorry, gentle doggie, don't take it personally.

At this point, I could either head directly up the main drag to the Roman ruins of Les Antiques and Glanum and Van Gogh's hospital, Saint-Paul-de-Mausole, or continue by the back of the bullring and through a quiet *quartier*. I chose the less trafficked route, which included various plaques reflecting scenes Van Gogh painted in the late nineteenth century. Most of the reproductions were surrounded by mature bushes or walls, so the landscapes Van Gogh had seen were blocked, but on a bright sunny day like today, it was easy to free my imagination. Avenue Marie Gasquet petered out into a single-person-wide dirt path that followed the thick cement wall behind Saint-Paul-de-Mausole until it reached the Voie des Carrières, the highest point of my walk, at the base of Les Alpilles. Time for a water break.

Now I turned left onto the flat section of the Voie des Carrières lined with spectacular plane trees. When fully leafed, they formed a lush, green tunnel—so cool, refreshing, and beautiful. It was there that we often saw a group of residents from Van Gogh's hospital. There was usually a mix of about eight men and women accompanied by two or three caretakers. We made a point of greeting them with *bonjours* and *bonnes journées*, and many tried with great difficulty to respond. Their condition was saddening, yet I was comforted that the French health-care system provided for them in such a caring way.

On the right side about a kilometer back from the road, a flash of red caught my eye. Good grief, that was one tall crane. It must have been three stories high. And it was clasping a concrete pillar that looked to be four stories high. I couldn't imagine what kind of building would require equipment of that magnitude in such a densely forested neck of the woods. But "progress" was happening in a lot of surprising nooks and crannies, I'd noticed over the years.

Off to the left, I passed a two-story, golden-stoned farmhouse called a *mas* that had recently grown an extension. The gates were wide open to reveal how perfectly the addition blended in with the original house, encased in weathered, creamy stones. A battered open-bed truck with PORTES ANCIENNES in faded red letters stamped across the back was parked on the gravel drive. It was no surprise that the proprietors of that exclusive property with a big view over Saint-Rémy were sparing no costs. Once, I'd popped into the huge Portes Anciennes warehouse and found a virtual museum of doors. Aisle after aisle displayed intriguing *portes* from the most rustic to the most elegant. That was years ago when we were fantasizing about renovating or building ourselves. I wondered again if that could happen one day.

I continued along the road to the large, flat rock where Ralph and I usually take a short break to munch half the daily recommended portion of fruit. From here, the panoramic view extends over vineyards and all the way to Mount Ventoux. It was earlier than usual to be passing this spot, and since I didn't have a little snack with me, I marched on. I wanted to take advantage of being on my own and do a little shopping in town. When Ralph and I were together on a walk, any suggestion of me "popping" into a shop prompted an exasperated sigh and eye rolling. "Sweetie, you don't know how to 'pop' into a shop," my hubby would say. True. So today I could "pop" at my leisure.

I had a peppy pace going, nearly speed walking, and I became lost in thought. We'd been in Provence for over five years but had yet to feel completely settled. Lots of questions continued to dog us. Since the new house had gone up next door, blocking out our Alpilles view, as limited as it was, we'd felt hemmed in. Operation View-Finder had been in the works for ages but had yielded only disappointment. Of all the rentals we'd seen, there was always something wrong. If it had a view, there was something amiss with the general condition, layout, size, price tag, or some combination thereof. Admittedly, our list of demands was a tad high. Reality rarely delivers perfection. This we knew. And yet, the spirit of what we jokingly referred to as our "ski-to-the-beach" place, our perfect abode, continued to whisper in our ears, "Maybe, just maybe, I really do exist."

Would finding our view mean leaving Saint-Rémy? The village exuded an inviting blend of rustic charm and sophistication. It was possible to watch bulls charge through the streets—which they did frequently during the summer festivals—just steps from a five-star hotel serving gourmet meals in its serene *jardin*. Since our house was so conveniently located, in just a few minutes we could walk to the post office, market, bank, cafés, and shops—everything we needed. Sometimes, days went by without ever revving up the car. Even our dentist was only a short bike ride away.

And there were longer bike rides at our doorstop, as well. One crisp autumn Friday, we'd ridden past the glider field and on to the lively market in Eygalières where Hugh Grant now has a place and reportedly mingles with the locals. The outdoor cafés had been packed that day, but no celebrity sightings. Instead of retracing our steps home, we'd followed a small country road north toward Mollégès, which coincidentally passed by one of my favorite *dépôt-vente* (consignment) stores; naturally, I'd taken the opportunity to pause for a brief overview. Afterwards we'd headed east, straight back to Saint-Rémy. On the way, we'd passed a pair of black dogs and an old shepherd supervising his herd of sheep gobbling fallen apples. The old mustached guy, dressed in baggy dungarees and a hand-knitted sweater with bits of straw stuck to it, had given me a big smile. When I stopped to comment on his hungry flock and ask whether I could take a picture with my phone, he'd stood up straight and grinned. With a *merci beaucoup* to the kind man and a *bon appétit* to his charges, we'd pulled away thinking what an endearing corner of the globe this was.

Saint-Rémy's infrastructure was continuing to improve too, with the resurfacing of streets in the historic center and the installation of many sturdy, artfully designed bike racks. Many dilapidated buildings were being refurbished or remodeled, and more flowers were blooming in the roundabouts. New bistros, boutiques, wine shops, and bars were popping up regularly. The city now offered residents a heritage ambassador card that allowed entance into some of the historic sites and museums—*gratuit*.

And there was our marvelous landlord. If anything went amiss, our *propriétaire* was Johnny-on-the-spot. In fact, when a problem arose, we didn't call him unless the house was tidy because we knew he would appear in minutes. Late one Sunday morning, I'd texted him about a significant water leak in the garage. By the time I'd walked the few meters from the living room to the garage, he was there. On that occasion he had just happened to be passing by when he noticed the water surging across the driveway, but that level of responsiveness was typical for him. When we went away, he checked our mail and watered our plants. It would be tough to say goodbye to him, as it would be to bid adieu to our village tennis club. Even though it had only five hard courts, in September when it hosted an American Tennis Professional tournament, it was transformed into a mini-French Open with white, circus-like tents for vendors and cafés offering meals and refreshments. *Très* festive, and it was totally free too.

But regardless of whether we stayed in Saint-Rémy or whether our view quest forced a breakup, there was our storage unit in California to be sorted out. All our sentimental essentials were still stashed away there, years after selling our Palm Springs condo. What were we going to do with all that? Should we commit to France and ship our possessions over? But if we *were* going to move, shouldn't we wait to transport the household goods so we didn't have to move the stuff twice? Or did we need to find a bolt-hole in the US and stash our things there? How about winters spent snowbirding in the US? West Coast or East Coast? Should we sit tight in Saint-Rémy until our ten-year visas came through? If they did, maybe we would consider what we always thought we'd never do—buy. But that would require a serious commitment, and for perpetual rovers like us, it was sobering stuff. It sounded very much like an engagement, which was for grown-ups only. Were we even capable of settling down and being content in one spot—learning to accept some compromises? No place is perfect, after all, and every place has its challenges.

Whether it was our restless nature or a determined drive to discover that kept yelping for more, I felt a transition was imminent. But what was our next step? Certainly, it was a first-world dilemma, one we were grateful to have. We appreciated how precious time was and didn't want to squander it. We tried to act prudently and make thoughtful decisions to avoid known dangerous areas, but we weren't willing to stop exploring. Making the most of each day was a priority, though admittedly, I got sidetracked much too often. At the same time, we welcomed new paths, wherever they might lead. Who knew, maybe we'd reinvent ourselves completely—sell everything to barge the Canal du Midi or grow grapes or graze goats!

Holy crapola! What the ... ? There, outstretched halfway across the two-meter-wide road, a few centimeters from my left boot, was something too horrifying to name—the S-word. It was slithery and greenish-brown and glistening, and it looked very much alive. I swear it was eyeing me. The flight part of the fight-or-flight response kicked in to the tune of a hundred-kilometer-an-hour sprint to safety. I instantly transformed into a human Harrier Jump Jet, levitating skyward and then blasting forward. My heart didn't stop hammering until I was at least a soccer field's length down the Chemin de Valrugues. At a peaceful spot where Ralph and I regularly stopped, I rested on the small stone wall. While trying to catch my breath, I fumbled with my cell phone to text Ralph.

"S-word," I wrote, my hands shaking. "Survived." A few moments later my phone rang.

"I just got in the parking lot. You texted?" Ralph asked.

"Yes, did you read it?" I asked.

"I'm looking at it now. 'Sword. Survived.' What's that mean?"

"There was supposed to be a hyphen between the *S* and 'word,'" I said. Ralph was well aware that the S-word (along with earthquakes) terrified me. In fact, if there was a photo of an S-word in a newspaper or a magazine that I'd be reading, he'd cut it out—an effective scream-reduction measure.

"Oh, honey, I'm so sorry. Where did this happen?"

"Right before that pretty holiday villa on the corner where we stopped for the herd of sheep to come through, where you turn to go down to town toward the Croix Vertu."

"Yes, I know where you mean—where the renters invited us in for a drink."

"Exactly, that one. Don't worry, I'm okay, really. Just traumatized a bit. I just can't believe it. We've been down that road hundreds of times and there's never been anything scary."

"Do you feel safe now?"

"Yes, I'm on the Chemin de Valrugues. All downhill from here. And all paved. I'll walk in the middle."

"All right, but be careful. Maybe stop in town—go shopping. That'll calm you down."

I was so alarmed by the beastly animal encounter that I was unable to process Ralph's stunning suggestion that I indulge in some retail therapy. My heart was still pounding.

"Right, and honey, I need a hug," I said.

"There'll be lots when we're both back home."

In town, I cruised some boutiques, but my heart wasn't in it. I was thinking about nature versus the city—each one with its hazards. Neither was free of mishaps. I didn't want to avoid nature, but I'd just come very close to wrangling with a reptile. Nothing like a scary S-word to snap me out of my dreamy reverie, pondering how best to proceed with our retired lives in La Belle France. I had to pay attention and not only *look* but *see*. Perhaps I needed my vision checked, but not by an optometrist.

Maybe I needed to chill and view our situation from another perspective, a different angle. If I did, maybe the answer would reveal itself. When I'd come across the S-word, it wasn't moving. Maybe my pounding hiking boots had startled it to a halt. Or maybe it had paused for a moment of reflection, hoping to prevent a mis-slither. Maybe it had been questioning the wisdom of crossing *that* road at *that* time or in *that* manner or with *that* mind-set.

I knew the feeling.

Look and *see* both ways.
Just be careful where you step.

Chapter 19

Out to Lunch

Saint-Rémy-de-Provence — Winter 2016

"Nuts, the whole family is nuts," my dad used to say with a wide grin. As a kid, I thought it was funny and never took it to heart. He was an upbeat, look-on-the-bright-side, cup-half-full kind of guy, and that was his way of brushing off something goofy one of us four kids had just done, which happened frequently. Even when I was six and splashed pink paint on a bunch of large rocks that ran the full length of our property, my dad did not come unglued. Thanks to my effective defense of the home improvement project, I was grounded for only a day and avoided hard time.

Now, as a mature (but immature-for-my-age) adult, I realized it was possible my dad's off-the-cuff remark had merit. After all, there was a case to be made that more than a few screws were rattling around my brain. (My husband would not care to comment.) For one thing, since living in Provence, going to lunch has taken on a life of its own. Not lunch at just any old place but a midday meal at delightful venues to which I've awarded Destination Déjeuner status.

These restaurants shine on a multitude of levels—warm welcome, inviting interior, convivial ambience, engaged service, and tasty, often inspired, cuisine. And they offer a heartwarming *bon rapport qualité prix* (good value) for a multicourse meal, a French noontime tradition available during the week and sometimes even on Saturday. (The same meal may cost double in the evening.) Checking out these promising establishments may involve driving an hour each way or taking a week-long trip for a lunch prepared by a renowned chef. Was I out to lunch to want to live life at lunch? Demonstrating such unrelenting reverence for food would have seemed crazily obsessive in years past. But not so after deciding to spend our Third Age, as the French call retirement, in Provence, a region with transformative powers. Ironically, the lunchtime revelation began while I was trying to work off lunch—at a tennis club.

Hard court, clay, composite, you name it—wherever we are, my hubby and I will take a tennis court any way it comes. If the net is ripped and the surface cracked, it doesn't stop us, because tennis is our go-to, play-together sporty game. Even on vacation, we scope out the tennis courts if only to watch a few games. It offers a peek at authentic local life in motion. We're not tennis bums by any stretch, but we love the game and try to bat the ball around at our friendly tennis club in Saint-Rémy at least a couple of times a week, weather permitting. Of course, when the fierce mistral raises its ugly head, all bets are off for a day or two or three or more. But for the most part, it's just a question of getting ourselves up, out the door, and onto the court, just a short bike or car ride away.

Each day we play tennis is a memorable day for me, even though I lose nearly every single match, every single time. But during each set, Ralph lets me win a game here and there, and the fact that there is no real contest doesn't detract from the experience. I'm delighted when I do get him on the run or send over some serves that he can't easily blast back at me. Just being out there trying to improve, making the occasional good shot and having creative rallies is wonderfully gratifying. And we play by the rules, of which there are three: have fun, get some exercise, and nobody gets hurt. If one day a serve or backhand or volley fails, no whining. If a serve or backhand or volley is in fine form, no gloating. It should be a positive experience for each player.

On a visit to California, before beginning a match with my brother and his wife, we reviewed these rules and everybody agreed they were very fine rules. Sadly, however, my brother didn't take them to heart. Wanting to not just beat but crush his little sis, his competitive spirit took over, and he overstretched to reach a ball, ripping a quad in the process, which landed him on the cement in some serious pain. Fortunately, he avoided surgery, but it took him months to recover.

That incident reinforced our commitment to start each warm-up session with a renewal of our vows to observe the three cardinal rules. That way, an upbeat ambience was more likely to flourish even if someone was having an ornery day. Under those circumstances, we would play left-handed for a few minutes—this never fails to send one or both of us into fits of laughter. In a nutshell, any cranky, grumpy urges tend to melt away, allowing smiles to emerge, making the tennis court a happy place for us.

In France, most often a town's municipal tennis facility is run by an association and isn't free. One can pay an hourly fee, but the annual membership is more cost effective, even though it's a couple of hundred euros a person. That price tag was an especially harsh pill to swallow when we were living in Aix and finances were tight, but we knew the investment would motivate us to get out on the courts as much as possible. We scouted out different possibilities, visiting several major multisport clubs that included tennis. Eventually we gravitated to a small club with just a few courts in a little suburb called Puyricard, a ten-minute drive north of our apartment. We loved the low-key, pastoral countryside setting just on the outskirts of the village.

One pretty Sunday morning, we dressed in our tennis togs and headed over to the club with a stash of euros—we didn't have French cheques yet—fully prepared to join up. Jaunty Paul and his spunky wife, Agnès, greeted us warmly. We soon found out they were the parents of the owner, Hervé, who lived in the attractive yellow house next door. Mom and Dad manned the store when Hervé took a break. We explained to Paul and Agnès that we wanted to join the club. "Super," they said. "Take Court 3."

Ralph and I looked at each other, puzzled. *"Merci, mais …* we pay before we play, *n'est-ce pas?"* I asked.

"Non, non—plus tard," they said, shooing us off the terrace in the direction of the courts.

Wow, that was a welcome surprise. Fun first, business later. After our set, we strolled back to the clubhouse to do the paperwork. Paul and Agnès had been relieved by Hervé, their tall, tanned, lanky son, who flashed us a gleaming smile.

"Bienvenue au Tennis Club Puyricard. Vous êtes les américains, n'est-ce pas?" he said, holding out his hand.

"Oui, oui," we said, smiling. *"Enchantée,"* I added, shaking his hand, and Ralph did the same.

"You want to join the tennis club, *oui?"* We nodded enthusiastically, and Hervé dug around in his desk drawer and pulled out a form, which I filled out in two seconds. He glanced at it, placed it back on the counter, and looked up, smiling.

"Tout est bon? Is it okay?" I asked, figuring that since I hadn't put my glasses on, I'd probably made some mistakes. The stack of euros rested in front of me, ready to slide over.

"Oui, c'est bon. Parfait," he said.

And now will he discuss payment? I wondered. Instead, Hervé commented on the heat wave and that going to the beach was a good idea.

"La plage ... bonne idée," I agreed.

"Do you know La Redonne? I go there."

"Oui, I've heard of it," I said as I tried to hand over the euros.

Hervé ignored the gesture and leaned in, staring directly at me. "Do you know where to eat?"

"Ah, no, not really," I said.

He pulled out his cell phone and worked it frantically before showing me the screen. "Here, write this down—La Belle Vue. For fresh fish, this is the best resto. It is right on a *calanque*, a rocky inlet, just by the water. You must eat here."

"Okay, great. *Merci beaucoup*, Hervé," I said, beaming.

"And do not forget," he added, looking over his shoulder as he made for the door to greet some players who had materialized on the terrace, *"Toujours réserver."*

I still had my fistful of euros. "Hervé, wait, wait! Here's your payment," I shouted with my hand outstretched.

Hervé turned, *"Ah, oui,"* he said with a surprised expression, as though he'd forgotten all about it. He took the wad out of my hand, not pausing to count it or write out a receipt or give us any kind of membership card. He sorted through some boxes in a cupboard, dropped the cash in one of them, and hustled past us out into the sunshine.

Ralph, incredulous, said, "Did he just put our entire annual membership fee loose into a cardboard box in an unlocked cupboard?"

"Yep, looks like it." I nodded in equal disbelief. "He is one trusting soul. Just hope he has a very good memory."

"Me too," Ralph agreed.

A few days later, we awoke to a perfectly windless, warm, sunny day—the beach beckoned. It was an excellent opportunity to try out Hervé's recommended resto in La Redonne (technically Ensuès-la-Redonne), and then we'd report back on how delicious it was, as I was certain it would be. Perhaps he'd then reward us with another tip, and soon we'd have a comprehensive portfolio of primo dining destinations, which, we were quickly finding out, was absolutely critical to successful integration into French life.

That day, the plan was to earn our lunch. We'd park in the appealing seaside village of Carry-le-Rouet and walk the coastal path over to Ensuès-la-Redonne, where Hervé's recommended eatery was located. The lunch would undoubtedly be wonderful, and we envisioned meandering back to the car, savoring the dreamy experience. All went according to plan—at first. It was mid-week, and we easily scored a parking spot by the Carry-le-Rouet marina, where a peewee sailing school was under way. The École de Voile instructors were frantically trying to herd a cluster of pint-sized sailboats, which were tethered together, into a line formation, to lead them out into the harbor. The instructors pointed vigorously and shouted instructions through a loudspeaker, but to no avail. The midget captains could have been mini Monty Python actors, looping this way and that, slamming into one another like bumper cars at an amusement park. For all their effort, the newbie sailors could not force their vessels to cooperate, so untangling themselves was not going to happen anytime soon. Fortunately, we were on a walkway about fifty meters away, overlooking the harbor and observing the chaos through binoculars, so we were hopeful the little guys couldn't hear us choking back hysterics.

Wiping away tears of laughter, we left the slapstick scene and marched east on the Côte Bleue toward lunch, spurred by the imagined delicacies that awaited us. After just a few minutes, we realized that reaching our destination would take much longer than we'd thought, so we quickly ditched our lengthy workout idea. To save time, we retraced our steps back to the car and drove a couple of *calanques* toward our goal. From there we set off on foot again.

As we descended the narrow road into tiny Ensuès-la-Redonne, our objective quickly came into view. A collection of colorful fishing boats bobbed just steps away from our oh-so-charming bistro, complete with a cute striped awning shading a cute menu box, featuring a cute note produced with cute curlicued lettering: *Jour de repos—mercredi.* Day of rest—

Wednesday. As in today. Boo-hoo. Tennis club Hervé's comments reverberated in my head: *Toujours réserver.* Always reserve. Grumbling and with pouty faces, we trudged back to the car, which was parked in front of a strikingly ordinary eatery where we had an extraordinarily forgettable meal. Bah humbug. Well, our fault. We hadn't played by the rules and had suffered the disappointing consequences. No repeat performances, we vowed. We were even hungrier now, and not just for noontime sustenance. Though we may not have realized it at the time, missing the promising repast that sunny day on the Mediterranean fueled an appetite for seeing food in a very different light.

Hervé at the tennis courts in Puyricard may have added pace to the Destination Déjeuner explorations with his spirited restaurant recommendation, sidelining our business dealings, but he wasn't our first encounter with France's unwritten Food First policy. That was introduced to us at another unlikely place—our bank in Aix. As the French partner of our US bank, it allowed us to withdraw funds in the form of euros from our US account—at a happy rate and with attractive fees. Soon after we'd moved into our apartment in Aix, we hustled downtown and into the bank foyer, where we waited in a line we hoped led to the information desk. When it was our turn, I explained to the bank employee in my baby French that we wanted to open an account. For that, I was told, we needed to see a bank counselor. Okay, fine.

"Is there one who speaks English?" I asked in my halting French.

"Oui," the helpful woman said.

Yea! And where could we find this bilingual counselor, then?

The information woman read my mind. "It's not possible today. You must make an appointment. I will check the calendar." She clicked away on her computer and then said, "The soonest appointment I can offer you is next week. Tuesday at ten?"

The following week, we showed up on time and made ourselves comfortable in some chairs arranged in the foyer. Soon our counselor, a slim, smartly put-together young woman, came to fetch us and led us downstairs to her well-appointed office, where she offered us seats. We exchanged greetings and smiles as she positioned herself on the other side of her neatly arranged desk. Then I revealed the collection of euros we had harvested from our US account and explained that we'd like to open an account.

"Yes, of course," she said, still smiling but not reaching for any forms. "How are you finding Aix?"

"We love it. We walk all over town, up in the hills, and play tennis too," I said.

Ignoring our interest in fitness, she asked, "Do you know where to eat?"

"Yes, a few places."

"Do you know La Fontaine? It's just around the corner, and it has a lovely garden where you can sit in warm weather and have a relaxed lunch. And then there's Le Comptoir. It also has a very attractive *jardin*. Here, let me get you that information." She turned to her computer and punched some keys. The printer whirred to life. Our counselor handed us a detailed printout on the restos, the local term for restaurants.

"Do you know about *vin rosé*?" she asked.

"*Oui*, we like it very much."

"Then you must go to Domaine Pey Blanc. It's really good. My friends run it." Again, she turned to her computer, and soon more sheets emerged from the printer.

As great as it was to be getting so many terrific lifestyle tips, what we really needed at this juncture was a bank account. For one thing, we were walking around with a boatload of cash that we needed to stash somewhere safe. When our bank counselor was satisfied we would be able to adequately manage our wining and dining experiences and her attention turned to the bank account, the process took two seconds. We couldn't have one. Since we couldn't prove we had a French residence, no account was possible. The rental agreement was useless and we hadn't been in our apartment long enough to get a phone bill. We had nothing official with our current address on it, hence, insufficient proof we lived where we said we did. To solve the problem, the counselor would mail us a form, which we would fill out and return to her, a process taking only a few days. Only then could she proceed with establishing an account.

So, an hour later, we left the bank much as we had entered it—accountless—but not empty-handed. Without a heist, we had managed to walk off with a valuable commodity. In our hot little hands, we clutched coveted insider foodie information. It wasn't the type that would inflate our financial portfolio, but it promised to please our palates. The prospect put a spring in our step.

Wouldn't it be something if even *one* of those tips turned out to be as wonderful as the golden recommendation we'd received years previously while vacationing in Saint-Rémy? The British owners of our B&B bestowed upon us a restaurant referral for which we are forever grateful. We made it a point to go to the restaurant whenever we came down from Germany *en vacances*. We appreciated it then, but not nearly as much as we do while living in Saint-Rémy, only twenty minutes away.

Our wonderful restaurant is situated in a perfect *bijou* village in the shadow of Les Alpilles. We have been faithful to our promise to that terrific couple (who became friends) to discuss the restaurant only with folks we had thoroughly vetted and had deemed worthy—and who had made the same promise to us. That was a point of honor. And an honor and a pleasure it always was to introduce new friends to its wonders.

And so it was when Sally, the mother-in-law of my good buddy, Ellen, in Aix, was coming to visit from the United States. Ellen and her hubby, Rick, appreciated the establishment as much as we did and had told Sally about it. How she'd love to eat there! So Ellen had organized her mother-in-law's trip to fit in a visit. Happily, Ralph and I were invited.

"Can you guys make it the first Tuesday in the new year?" Ellen asked.

"You bet," I said without hesitation. It had been many months since our last lunch there, and I was anxious to return. Because it was such a special treat, it was important to space out our visits, but we were ready. Over the years, Ralph and I had eaten there dozens of times, and the food never failed to reveal unexpected combinations and flavors. That explained why, during the four weeks leading up to the event, I'd periodically catch myself thinking about the menu, wondering what would be on offer. Lunch menus weren't online, so like waiting to see what Santa would bring, I had to be patient and look forward to the surprise. I did decide, though, that I'd go for the meat dish and not fish. I typically ordered fish, but in winter, meat seemed more appropriate. My expectations were mounting.

The night before our rendezvous, I picked out my outfit and called our iron into action to avoid last-minute floundering around. That would have interfered with the relaxed frame of mind I was hoping to attain before the special lunch treat. Even Ralph had decided what he would wear, a small miracle. Okay, I confess to suggesting he do that, and with good reason. Typically, five minutes before we were to hit the road, he would call out from the bedroom asking me whether his sweater or shirt or pants needed ironing. "Yes," I'd reply, without even seeing whatever he was holding, and immediately unfold the ironing board. Not that our resto had a formal dress code—far from it. Monsieur Gilbert, our builder-landlord, told us that one day he'd taken a break from work to join a client for an impromptu lunch there, and he went in his dusty overalls, steel-toed boots, and all—and felt perfectly comfortable.

The morning of the big day, we ate only a little yogurt with fruit—just enough to stave off hunger. Horror of horrors, to be starving when you arrived at the restaurant and wolf down the delicacies without thinking or tasting! We power walked our standard loop up to Les Alpilles to rev up the senses and prime them for action. And burning off some calories ahead of the lovely meal reduced the guilt of consuming a three-course lunch, thereby increasing the pleasure factor. A simple, light meal was on tap for that evening to help balance out our midday indulgence.

When we returned home from our walk, Ellen phoned from the road—ETA ahead of schedule—that gave them time to run their new puppy around the park first so she would be tuckered out and nap in the car during our extended repast. I told Ellen we would also arrive early—that was de rigueur. It was vital not to be screeching up in a mad dash, rushed and flushed. To fully absorb the experience, it was necessary to be calm and relaxed when crossing the threshold.

Today both our cars found empty spaces in the parking lot in front of the restaurant, luckily for me and my daunting car-to-bar heels. (For special occasions, it's fun to wobble around ten centimeters taller.) We all hopped out of our respective autos and spent the next few minutes patting the pooch and blowing kisses all around. In Aix, a kiss on each cheek was the custom, but in Saint-Rémy and environs it was three, so the greeting between the five of us took awhile. I checked my watch. "Yikes," I said, "showtime!"

"Yes, let's go," said Ellen, all smiles.

Madeleine, the delightful owner, greeted us warmly, like old friends. "Is everyone okay? How were the holidays?" she asked. We chatted as we moved to our table, which was positioned in front of a four-meter-high arched window. Beyond the gravel courtyard with its muscular, leafless plane tree, the view featured the distant church tower that loomed over the rooftops of the sweet village. Floor-to-ceiling white linen curtains were open, puddling on the cool tile floor. The soaring cream stone walls were unadorned, except for some softly glowing sconces. Overhead, the one dash of splash, a contemporary glass-beaded globe, gently reflected slivers of light around the room. Young Albert, the waiter, took our coats and whisked them away, all without making a fuss. The sun was streaming in, enhancing an already warm and inviting ambience that appeared refined but felt casual. It was stylishly minimalist, tastefully restrained.

At that point, I wanted to push the slo-mo button to simply absorb the atmosphere and appreciate the culinary adventure ahead of us. All the white noise of the outside world was hushed. We were ready for a taste treat, delivered graciously, in lovely surroundings, confident the bill would be easy on the eyes. We settled into our seats and surveyed the table scene. Starched, folded napkins lay at a graceful diagonal at each place setting, tall stems stood next to low, plump water glasses, all sitting upon a pristine white tablecloth. Only a little round box of coarse sea salt with a cork top and blue label added a pinch of color. No flowers, no candles—richly spare.

Efficient yet engaging, Albert slid up and asked if we'd like an apéritif, but we all agreed the *deux verres* (two glasses of wine) with the meal would suffice. He handed each of us a hard-backed menu. I was sitting next to Sally, so I explained how the process worked. During the week at lunch, a special three-course *formule* was offered, which consisted of two choices for the appetizer and two for the main course, followed by either a cheese plate or dessert, of which there were usually at least two choices but often more. A glass of wine came with each of the first two courses. You chose your color and could switch between courses. Sparkling or still water and coffee were included. And with coffee, a little tray of cookies would appear. And the price per person for this thoroughly delightful, refined-but-not-haughty culinary adventure was not going to break the bank—just a tad more than you'd pay at an ordinary brasserie for a forgettable appetizer, unremarkable *plat du jour*, and a glass of bland wine from a ten-liter box.

Decision time. Madeleine arrived to take the orders for the *entrées* and *plats*. To start, Ellen chose the *tourte de caille* (quail torte), accompanied by endive with walnut oil, and then pork cheek with potato purée with leek. Rick, Sally, and I chose the same, but Ralph went for the cured salmon with crispy veggies, followed by cod and a variety of *légumes* in a bouillabaisse broth.

While Albert asked about wine preferences, his colleague arrived with the sparkling water. On a cloth-covered table in the middle of the room, bottles of *vin rouge* stood next to a transparent bucket filled with ice, holding the *bouteilles* of white and rosé. Albert plucked out a *vin blanc*, glided back to our table, and poured.

With big smiles, we clinked glasses. *Santé!* After a brief interval, the starters began to arrive. With care, Albert positioned the plates of artfully arranged delicacies in front of each of us. "*Attention, très chaud.* Very hot," he said as he pretended to tap the plate but pulled back his fingers at the last second. We all clinked glasses again and the feasting began.

"Oooh, this is delicious," cooed Sally, dabbing her lips with her napkin and relaxing into her chair. Everyone echoed her reaction. While managing some chit-chat along the way, we were mostly savoring the delicacies on our plates. I shared some of my wonderfully earthy *tourte de caille* with Ralph, and I sampled his cured salmon decorated with a tangy bloop of bright, lemony cream. We proceeded slowly, placing our forks down from time to time. It was so scrumptious, it was hard not to gulp it down; I had to remind myself to ease up the pace. The bread basket filled with a variety of plump rolls made its way around the table. With difficulty, I resisted as I was trying to cut down on those pesky carbs and wanted to save calories for the puréed potatoes with leeks. The plates were cleared, and Albert came to ask about the wine we'd like for the next course. I switched to red, so Albert brought me a fresh glass. Soon pork cheeks were placed before four of us, and then Ralph's fish appeared. We picked up our forks and tucked in. The tender pork cheeks were nestled in a rich, tangy sauce that was remarkably light. A crispy parsley sprig rested on top. The thick disk of humble potato-leek purée had a fresh zing to it.

"Honey, you have to try this," I said to Ralph as I passed a forkful over. He in turn let me have a bite of his *cabaillaud*, making sure the piece had soaked up a good amount of the bouillabaisse broth that quietly summoned the essence of the sea, home to its primary ingredients.

Unusually, the place wasn't packed. In all the years we'd been going there, I'd rarely seen an empty table. But in early January it seemed, people were still recovering from holiday overindulgence. Though I did miss the full-on buzz a little, the calmer ambience allowed for an even more relaxing experience.

We were already finishing the main course, but I didn't want it to end. As slowly as we ate, eventually every morsel was consumed, along with the wine. Albert's helper materialized for the dessert order. Four of us chose the cheese plate, but Ellen opted for the macaroon with *fruits rouges* accompanied by a healthy bloop of *fromage blanc*. After the cheese and dessert, coffee followed, along with a little tray of cookies. We lingered as long as we could, but eventually we realized we were stalling and asked for *l'addition*. We couldn't just camp out there—as much as we would have liked to. Madeleine swung by with a restaurant brochure, a corner of the bill discreetly peeking out at the top. After we settled up and heaped on the accolades, Albert appeared with all our coats. We reluctantly said our goodbyes to Madeleine and the rest of the crew and wandered outside to the courtyard.

We all agreed it was an experience that deserved the highest level of my very subjective Destination Déjeuner designations. Lunch was delectable, not fussy, and was served in a chichi-free zone where there was no room for poshness, pretense, or indifference. Above all, it was down-to-earth and genuine. And the owner and staff exuded personal and professional pride that was at the same time modest and exemplary in its natural ease.

Plenty of passion had been poured into our culinary experience, and it lifted us to another plane. There, for over two hours, we all floated blissfully content in a carefree bubble. All worries and problems faded. Serenity prevailed. Never mind that the staff was probably working their socks off behind the scenes. Out in the dining room they seemed to work as effortlessly as Roger Federer's magnificent backhand rocketing down the line.

Now, in the parking lot outside of our insulated bubble, clearly the party was very much over. Reality struck. I silently commisserated with baby birds that have been ushered from their delightfully comfy nest with its reliable catering service and now have to fend for themselves. In the real world, there were screeching noises, strange odors, bad tastes, dark clouds, and natural and man-made disasters. Lunch was finished, but life went on with all its messiness, stress, and distress. I had to buck up, because it was the thing adults should do, and also because withdrawing back into the bubble wasn't an option. The bubble was now closed—*fermé*. At least until dinner service. The letdown was real. Deflation set in, and not just because the wine glow had dissipated.

The same empty feeling surfaced when we left other Destination Déjeuner venues, even those with more modest price points within the foodie spectrum. There was a rustic village bistro in the middle of the Luberon where we often met with friends who lived east of the market town of Apt. It was a convenient halfway point, but that wasn't why we loved to congregate there. It was because the cuisine was good,

215

comforting French country fare, and the young owner and staff were very welcoming. The service always came with smiles and a twinkle in the eye, and the cost was astonishingly reasonable.

The bistro had no printed menus—several choices for each of three courses were all recited by the staff at the table. The first course was typically a vegetable *velouté* (creamy soup) or salad served family style and was accompanied by a huge platter of *chaucuterie*. Hearty grilled salmon, chicken breast with local mushrooms, or pasta pesto were typical *plats du jour*. After the second course was cleared, a huge cheese platter materialized—and remained on the table for as long as you liked—followed by dessert classics such as crème brûlée, *mousse au chocolat*, or *tarte aux pommes*. The wine *en carafe* was included too, and though perhaps unremarkable, it was perfectly quaffable. Not surprising, then, that the place was typically crowded.

One table at the front was always reserved for one special regular, an elderly gentleman who lunched at the restaurant daily. If he didn't appear as scheduled, one of the staff popped over to his house to check on him. Now that was certainly beyond the call of customer service. The staff genuinely cared a great deal about their clientele, and that heartfelt interest had special appeal. After a hearty meal in such a convivial, warm atmosphere, you wanted to call out to the staff, "Group hug, please!" Instead, we gave our compliments to the chef and left something extra on the table.

Just as when we separated from our favorite refined restaurant near Les Alpilles, when we found ourselves back on the sidewalk in front of our favorite country inn, outside its comfy bubble, the same letdown moment soon followed. During one of those out-of-the-bubble moments recently, a little voice spoke up in my head. Hang on just a minute. You've been coming to these places for several years now and enjoying the experience so much, and then you leave deflated. What is going on? There must be a way to avoid the melancholy. Think about it.

And then it dawned on me. Even if we couldn't live at the restaurant, maybe we could *live our lives at lunch*. Maybe we could always be out to lunch even when we weren't. What if it wasn't just *what* was brought to the table, but what *we* brought to the table? When we were connected to the moment—relaxed, senses alert, heightened expectations—then voilà, life was miraculously enhanced. Life seemed to shine brighter in those moments, and that was good. Not just tasty good or touchy-feely good but inherently good. It wasn't so much *going* out to lunch, but *being* in an "out to lunch" spirit that was the key. It wasn't such a crazy concept after all, was it? Perhaps Provence was not just a playground but a master mentor, helping me come of age in the Third Age.

Live life out to lunch.
When sensory systems are awake,
all possibilities beam brighter.

Chapter 20

Euphoria Formula

Saint-Rémy-de-Provence — Winter 2016

The clouds, thunder bursts, and general grimness that had
persisted the day before had given way to a calm, bracing blue
sky. It was perfect weather to clear the cobwebs, bolster our
can-do attitude, and face the sous-préfecture in Arles. Ralph
and I knew it was time to get the ball rolling on our ten-year
cartes de séjour. After five years of living in Provence, *the* day had
arrived.

It was Tuesday, 23 February 2016, and our current cards
were going to expire on 2 May. The French government
rulebook stated that it was necessary to apply for the new *cartes*
within two months of the expiration of the current visas and
not before. So were we or were we not in the sweet zone? The
fuzzy part was the date used for "apply." Did that refer to the
postmark on the dossier that we'd send to the sous-préfecture
or the date stamped on the official form the sous-préfecture
would give us that went into our dossier? We were hoping the

former. By the time we prepared the dossier, we'd be within the proper window of opportunity. The risk was that the sous-préfecture would be having a stickler kind of day and would insist we return later. Since we were anxious to have the bureaucratic burden behind us, we were willing to dedicate a few hours to test the system. If it didn't work, we'd continue on down the road to Saintes-Maries-de-la-Mer in the Camargue for some refreshing sea air, fresh fish, and a *verre* of crisp *vin blanc*. That type of afternoon was always uplifting. Then, we'd wait ten days and try again, one more time with feeling.

Our whole day was dedicated to that single yet vital activity because the length of the wait at the government office was impossible to gauge. And waiting was an art form we'd perfected over the years in France. Operation View-Finder had been born after the eco house rose up next door, blocking much of our blue sky *vue*, and that was now a year and a half ago. We'd searched for a new vista for months but finally mothballed the program. It occurred to us that from the point of view of the sous-préfecture, who granted the ten-year *cartes*, stability might be crucial. Our plan was to revisit our desire for an upgraded panorama once we had our ten-year cards, the process we were beginning today.

The least crowded days at the sous-préfecture were posted on the internet, but we discounted them because who knew if they factored in holidays and weather? Schoolkids had returned from their two-week "ski" vacation and were due back in school on Monday. So perhaps parents were now free to take care of business, which could mean Monday would be crowded and maybe Tuesday less so. Or maybe parents had not prepared for Monday since they'd had the kids the past two weeks, which would mean Tuesday would be a bad day. In any case, we decided to attack our task Tuesday. The sous-préfecture was open for visa business only in the mornings from nine to noon, so we would arrive about ten o'clock to miss the morning rush yet have enough time to get processed before lunch, unless everybody and their visa-running-out relatives had applied the same convoluted logic we had.

We dragged ourselves out of bed by eight (early for us retiree slugs) and had a quick breakfast. I left my usual second cappuccino on the kitchen counter—the sous-préfecture didn't have a public loo. The closest WC was a few blocks away, down ancient stone steps through a little park around the corner from a magnificent Roman theater built somewhere near the first century AD. Its grandeur was clearly visible through the iron fence, so while scurrying past it to the facilities, I'd be treated to a World Heritage Site.

We had packed our usual array of water bottles, snacks, reading material, passports, and current *cartes de séjour*. En route, we rehearsed the French lines we had memorized to impress the sous-préfecture folks, as well as those we'd memorized *not* to say. We agreed not to ask anything about a language test requirement if the sous-préfecture official didn't. Let sleeping *chiens* lie was our motto.

Parking was tougher than usual but after driving through a few packed parking lots, Ralph spotted a wide space and zoomed in. The walk to the government office took us another ten minutes, so it was 10:10 when we plucked our ticket out of the customer service machine. Our number was 358, and the electronic sign showed "Now serving 338." Twenty customers usually equated to two hours' wait, so there was plenty of time for a quick archeological loo run. I put down my stuffed backpack and hustled off to the WC in the park. Upon returning, I joined Ralph in a corner by the counter serving car registrations on the ground floor. We knew we had to go upstairs to the *cartes de séjour* department, but the seating *à l'étage* was usually cramped, so we planned to stay downstairs until number 352 was served. Ralph read a French magazine article on extraordinary homes in Corsica, and I went over my daily planner. At number 351, Ralph decided he needed to pay the WC a visit. That last-minute dash made me anxious, but he vowed to make it snappy. Before I could get too worked up over his absence, he reappeared after only one customer. "Wow," I said, "that really was fast. Did you find a bush?"

"Too funny," he said, smirking, and up the stairs we went, less than an hour after we'd arrived. The *fonctionnaires* were making good time. On the way, I noticed a spiffy new coffee machine tucked into the curve of the stone staircase. A thoughtful upgrade and yet, without a handy WC, didn't that counteract the customers' briefly expanded comfort level? It probably had something to do with Dualism that Descartes could easily explain, but I'd research the philosophical conundrum later. Right then we had other pressing issues.

Upstairs, only a dozen folks were waiting, so there were lots of open seats. An unusual but pleasant surprise was the absence of squirming kids and squealing tots in prams. Three women in dark, precisely wrapped headscarves were engrossed in their cell phones, but the rest were men, most of whom were mature except for a pair of twenty-somethings wearing earbuds and backward baseball caps. From the intercom, we heard both a female and a male voice. We figured the male voice came from a gruff fellow we'd dealt with the past two years. He was at *guichet* (counter) H, which meant the woman was at *guichet* G. A couple of women had helped us in the past, and both were congenial. How nice it would be to deal with one of the cheerful ladies, especially with the extra pressure of the ten-year card at hand. It wouldn't be long before we had our answer. Bingo, our lucky day. Number 358 pinged—*guichet* G.

With an upbeat, perky smile, Madame Congeniality welcomed us and gestured to the plastic chairs for us to sit. She asked what she could do for us, and I reeled off my lines about coming for the form and instructions for the ten-year *cartes de séjour*. We pushed over our passports and current *cartes de séjour*. After scrutinizing them, she said with a kind smile that we were too early. I began to object, but then she squinted at my card again and corrected herself.

"*Ah, oui*, I can do it," she said. Whew, first hurdle out of the way. To reinforce the rightness of her decision, I said we would mail the dossier after 2 March, within two months of the date our current *cartes* would expire. She searched for some forms, which we were to fill out and sign in two places. She asked Monsieur Misérable about a few items before swiveling back to us and explaining that she didn't process the ten-year card very often. I could understand that—spending five years on a type of probation before getting the ten-year card might dissuade a lot of instant-gratification types. She then pulled out a special sheet to add to the packet, explaining that it listed extra items for the ten-year card, things like a letter of motivation, information about health insurance, and other regulations. Everything we could understand made sense, so we nodded away. Without a copy of what she was reading, however, I wondered if she'd skipped over something important. While she was arranging the packet to tuck into the envelope, I took a risk and asked if there was anything extraordinary on the list. We needed to get as much clarified as we could right now to reduce delays later, and we were motivated to close this baby out. She considered my question, then used the word that struck fear in our hearts: *"Diplôme."*

My body shifted into clench mode. *Diplôme* usually corresponded to the *Diplôme Initial de Langue Française,* or DILF, earned via the dreaded language test. We had come to understand the DILF really wasn't a set-in-stone requirement, but we had studied for it and felt sure we'd pass. It was mostly out of curiosity that I'd registered to take the test—given only once a month—in a couple of weeks. But mentioning that might only complicate our situation. I'd found out later that it takes an entire month to receive the test results. I'd have no official language document to include in the dossier, anyway. Ralph's plan was to help me pass the test, and I would then help him pass the test at some point in the future. As if Ralph had been zapped by an electric prod, he jerked, experiencing a linguistic misfire, and from his mouth flew the phrase that we had agreed would not be verbalized: *"Comme le* DILF?" I cringed reflexively. Oh my God, he said *it.*

Madame Congeniality must now have assumed that when we'd received our first *cartes de séjour* we'd been offered French language training and had gone on to take the DILF test. Naturally, we would have passed it, because we were obviously so very capable. It was a good sign that she was so positive and trying to be helpful, yet language testing was a subject that was damaging to our case. We had not taken the course, and we had not taken the test. In Marseille, where we had processed our first *cartes de séjour,* I'd asked the official about the free, state-run language training, but he said we, as nonworking retirees, weren't eligible. Madame Congeniality now asked if I had the diploma.

"*Non,*" I said guiltily, feeling a flush of red creeping over my face.

"Oh, it's at home?"

"*Ah, non,*" I mumbled.

"You lost it?" she asked.

"*Non, madame,* I don't have that diploma." She looked puzzled. Then she shifted direction and asked about a French driver's license.

I lit up, grinning. "*Oui, j'ai un permis de conduire français!*"

"*Voilà!*" she said with a smile.

That confusing and humbling experience unsettled us for the rest of the day. All we could think about was compiling our dossier. And of course we had to rehash the conversation with the congenial sous-préfecture employee. Had we said too little or too much? It had felt like a job interview to keep a job we already had—not conducted by our local supervisor, who thought we were doing a fine job, but by a personnel manager from the head office who barely knew us. We were anxious that perhaps company (or government) policy had recently changed, necessitating some "downsizing." We'd hoped to convey what stellar employees we were—valuable assets with many remarkable attributes. We were punctual, followed the rules, paid our dues, brought cookies to the company picnics, bought our own office supplies, and spent a substantial portion of our income at the company store, particularly in the wine department. With such commendable characteristics, surely we'd be tagged as precious assets to retain, at least for a decade. But was that the impression we'd given?

After a good night's sleep, we awoke refreshed and with rejuvenated confidence. Upon reflection, we realized we'd combatted the rigors of the sous-préfecture and prevailed. In our hot little hands, we had the officially stamped forms we needed to proceed with our ten-year card and our future in France. We were gonna be all right. We had a plan, and it looked like this:

❖ Have professional photos taken for the dossier.

❖ Mail the packet on 3 March 2016.

❖ Receive notice it had reached its destination.

❖ *Not* have an incomplete dossier returned.

❖ Receive the temporary visa—the *récépissé*—within six weeks.

❖ Receive the letter requesting pickup of the real visa in another six weeks.

❖ Buy the *timbres fiscaux* to pay for *multiple* years.

❖ Pick up the real-deal visas from the sous-préfecture.

❖ Confirm the expiration date was not one year later but a whole ten years later.

❖ Tuck those precious babies safely away right there on the spot.

❖ Present the sous-préfecture officials with a batch of homemade chocolate-chip cookies.

❖ Be thanked for our thoughtfulness.

❖ Avoid an attempted bribery charge.

❖ Celebrate the real-deal visa (and not doing jail-time).

❖ Reactivate Operation View-Finder and find our new view.

For sure that was how it would go down. Bursting with new-found hope, we set to work.

The primary difference between the requirements for our five previous *cartes de séjour* and the ten-year version was a letter of motivation and proof we were "making steps to integrate into the community." Compiling the list of "Reasons We Like France" was a snap—terrific weather, fantastic wine, great food, fascinating culture and history, welcoming people, easygoing lifestyle, and those beguiling surprises that enhance the intrigue factor.

One of those extra-special surprises had occurred early one Sunday morning, the day after we had witnessed a triathlon in Saint-Jean-de-Luz, near Biarritz, in the Basque region. Bleary-eyed, I'd shuffled out to the balcony of our ocean-front apartment with my first cappuccino to take in the view of the waves and perhaps catch a glimpse of some shorebirds scurrying around on the sand. There may have been actual birds, but I couldn't say. My attention was drawn to the wildly impressive activity about fifty meters down the beach. Five young men—presumably triathlon participants, judging from their fine fitness level—were striking poses for a photo shoot ... in their birthday suits. They weren't without props, though. There was a bicycle, a swim cap, a helmet, running shoes, and a pair of sunglasses—all superfluous, in my humble opinion. Maybe the purpose of the session was to create a calendar, sell sports gear, or promote the triathlon—I had no idea. Whatever it was, from my perspective, it was a compelling example of the noble, nineteenth-century French aesthetic *l'art pour l'art*, art for art's sake. Also a reminder to keep binoculars handy for those spontaneous, educational moments. Long live lifelong learning. But out of respect for the valor of those magnanimous, manly models, the least I could do was demonstrate some semblance of discretion by omitting the tale in our motivation letter, even if it would be the poorer for it.

When our letter—*en français*—was finished, it still had a ways to go. It had to be made comprehensible to a French native. That task went to our generous bilingual friend, Julie. She corrected the glaring grammatical errors but not so much that it didn't sound like our genuine baby French, which we hoped the sous-préfecture folks would find endearing. We also hoped they'd be impressed with my Huguenot-ness, regardless of how faint. My paternal grandmother was born a Michaux, a family name that could be traced a long way back to a hardy bunch who called southwest France home.

As far as the community integration went, Julie insisted we provide proof called *attestations*. She enthused, "Oh, how the French *love* testimonials." We'd made many connections over the years, yet we were hesitant to ask for help. Eventually, we did and were gratified by the enthusiastic responses. Our supportive landlord wrote one, and so did a French friend with whom we'd shared many an *apéro*. Our sharp-witted Parisian neighbor Didier volunteered to write one too. "I am a very good liar," he said. If we'd asked him, we were sure he would have included some doozies. I almost wanted to let him do it just to see what outrageous remarks he'd come up with—like how our French was *magnifique* and how we formed the *coeur du quartier,* heart of the neighborhood. Chances were good that the sous-préfecture officials, not known for their expansive capacity for humor, would not appreciate the exaggeration, no matter how heartfelt it might be. They would, however, relate to the un-sugarcoated tone of the letter from my French conversation teacher in Aix. She wrote that when I had arrived in France my French was very *faible* (weak)—ouch—but over time I'd improved so much. We mentioned my tap-dance and health-club classes and included verification of our membership in the local tennis club, as well as Ralph's active support of the Ligue pour la Protection des Oiseaux. Julie proclaimed our dossier so impressive that the sous-préfecture folks were sure to hire us as *carte de séjour* consultants.

After crossing the *t*'s and dotting the *i*'s, and checking and double-checking the documents, we pronounced our dossier ready to go. The only thing I wasn't happy about was my set of professional photos. At the time of the shoot, I was having a good hair day, but my expression wouldn't cooperate. The photographer shot several photos, but she could not persuade my eyes to smile without my lips following suit. No grinning for the official photo—neutral expression only, she had admonished. My sourpuss grimace made me look as if I'd just swallowed some bad *foie gras*. At least my pathetic photo would give the government officials a good chuckle, which they sorely needed—no thanks necessary.

On the third of March, we sealed our packet and trotted off to the *poste* to send it on its way. En route, we chatted about the various postal worker bees we'd come to know and hoped we'd get the "bravo" lady. She wasn't on duty, but another, highly competent but more formal one was. This particular middle-aged postal person had iron-rod posture and an approach to match. Our dossier would be in good hands. After the requisite *bonjours*, I plopped our fat packet on the counter and explained it was the dossier for our *cartes de séjour* for ten years. *Très important.* She nodded solemnly as she tucked a loose gray lock behind her ear. I showed her the two *lettres vertes* (envelopes with embedded stamps) and the accompanying registered mail/return receipt requests—one for the dossier going out and two more for the envelopes that the sous-préfecture would send back to us. I explained that each envelope had to have a total of exactly 4.92 euros' worth of stamps to cover the cost of the paperwork being sent back to us, but I didn't know the worth of the stamp embossed on the envelope. It had to be perfect for the sous-préfecture people! She nodded again as she picked up the packet. Together we moved to a self-service stamp machine, where the woman did the key-punching. *"C'est lourd,"* she remarked. Yes, it was a hefty one, taking care of a twenty-euro note.

Back at her counter, she slid the whole stack of documents back into the envelope, pounded a few rubber stamps on the front, and flipped it over. From my backpack I pulled out a huge roll of transparent tape and scissors to seal the flap, but the efficient postal woman said, *"Non, non, non,"* and proceeded to affix the return receipt request on that exact space. *"Voilà, c'est tout!"* she pronounced. All done. We wished our dossier *bonne chance* and thanked the woman. She had fluidly carried out multiple tasks, and I wanted to further express my appreciation to her personally. I asked her name. When I saw her startled expression, I realized I might have committed a formality faux pas and wished I could have retracted my question.

But then a soft smile emerged as she replied, "Denise."

"Mille mercis, Denise, pour votre aide. Bonne journée."

The one thing I forgot to do was to write our address somewhere on the back of the packet. Last year another postal woman had given me a big bravo for remembering to include it. This *fonctionnaire* hadn't looked for it. After all, it was on the forms for the return receipt request. As long as that particular form didn't come detached, all would be fine. It could find its way back to us, if necessary, and not languish in postal limbo.

Like the drill for the previous year, now all we had to do was wait. There was some added suspense this time, though. We didn't know what the price tag would be. The precise amount of the payment wouldn't be revealed until we received the letter informing us our new cards were ready for pickup. Until now, we'd paid just over a hundred euros each for a one-year card. But this year, we had our hearts set on the government asking for a boatload more, the cost of a ten-year card. That would be a bill we'd be eager to pay.

After leaving the *poste* we crossed the Place de la République, dodging cars trying to nab a parking spot, and continued up past Saint-Paul-de-Mausole, or Van Gogh's hospital, as we called it. It was a crisp 10° C (50° F) with azure-blue skies and puffy clouds, a perfect day for a walk. Along the way, we couldn't stop talking about how we hoped the dossier would go through. Back home, we rushed through our weights and stretching, then showered and changed.

To celebrate submitting our dossier, we were meeting our spirited British friends, Caroline and Dirk, for lunch at a new bistro in a tiny village north of Saint-Rémy. We were delighted they were game to try an untested venue, and we couldn't wait to catch up. In the past year, they had been transforming the total ruin of a mill into a holiday rental apartment in a hamlet on the south side of the Alpilles, and they'd made all sorts of incredible discoveries—a capstone engraved with the year 1660 and a pristine black horsehair top hat. We were eager to hear their latest tales.

At the bistro entrance, kisses flew from cheek to cheek. After ordering, and clinking glasses, wishing luck to our dossier, we heard the renovation update. Everything was on track for an April opening of the *gîte*, despite a few setbacks involving the repainting of the entire project due to a single tiny error. As usual, our upbeat buddies took the not-so-inexpensive hiccup in stride. I was positive, however, if Ralph and I were ever tempted to buy and renovate a property, I wouldn't be able to keep calm and carry on as admirably as Dirk and Caroline.

Surprisingly, the lunchtime crowd in the sleepy village bistro was mostly nattily attired young professionals. Apparently, the word was out that this newly opened eatery was a cool see-and-be-seen kind of place. My hopes were rising that the food would be as pleasing as the ambience. We tucked into our meal with high hopes. Though the celeriac starter had too much mayo and the quinoa crowned with *cabaillaud* held too little heat, both dishes were flavorful and artfully presented. But sadly, for this resto, on this occasion, no Destination Déjeuner designation. It hadn't passed muster. I hoped our precious ten-year *cartes de séjour* dossier would not suffer the same fate.

Back at Chez Fou, with our dossier homework done, we turned our attention to enjoyable pursuits like finding a great destination for our twenty-fifth wedding anniversary in May. The place we were looking for had to have not only water views but sunset-over-water views, of the stunning variety, *s'il vous plaît*. Spain, Portugal, Corsica, Corfu, and the Italian lake district were contenders. So many tantalizing choices. We had agreed that the actual location wouldn't make or break the celebration. Wherever we ended up to mark our special occasion, it would be particularly memorable, tinted with euphoria, and not just because of the special bottle of bubbly Ralph was bringing. We would marvel at the fact that after two and a half decades of marriage, we were still a *we*, a couple, and happy about that.

But were we a *deliriously* happy we? For Ralph's opinion, I hollered downstairs where he'd been doing some trip reserarch. "Honey, you're deliriously happy, right?"

When no immediate response came, I peered out my atelier window to see Ralph wielding the *piscine* skimmer, fighting pool scum. I opened the window and repeated my question.

"Absolutely!" he yelled up at me.

To be honest, he may have heard, "Honey, you'd be deliriously happy if I brought you a cold beer, right?" No matter. Ralph would be the last to dispute the significant delirium levels registered in our home on a regular basis. After all, it was called Chez Fou for good reason. Crazy times aside, after five years, just maybe we were starting to get the hang of hanging out with France. Our relationship, too, may have been a work in progress with no surefire answer to any euphoria formula, but I took Ralph's "absolutely" as a yes.

20

Connect, connect, connect.
Building bridges delivers surprising rewards.

Chapter 21

Time—Pencils Down!

Saint-Rémy-de-Provence — Winter 2016

The piercing *thwop* that came from the back of the classroom interrupted the muffled murmuring and slammed into my eardrums like a stinging slap on the cheek. My body clenched, forcing my hand to jerk, messing up the tidy oval I was carefully penciling in on page two of my test booklet. Geez, what the heck was going on? It sounded like a ruler had been brought down viciously on the laminate desk. I hoped that was all. Did I need to duck for cover? I was alone in the first row. What was going on behind me was alarming, but I didn't turn around—not even when the shouting started. My head lowered, my eyes glued to the work at hand. The strongest voice sounded like the director of the education center. A chair screeched. Then came some shuffling of papers. More metal on concrete, as another chair was pulled out and scooted back in. More strident admonitions followed and then quiet. Apparently, some students had thought the language exam was a group effort. All the ruckus was merely their misconception being addressed—in no uncertain terms.

It was the first of March 2016, the first Tuesday of the month, the only day the exam for the *Diplôme Initial de Langue Française* (DILF) is administered at the official test center in Arles. I'd planned to take it in February, but when I'd called the center in early January to sign up, I found out I wasn't early enough. Sign-ups for the February test had to be made at least one month prior. I was a few days late. *Zut!* Also, I was informed, there had to be at least five others wanting to take the test at the same time. Double *zut!* It looked like preparing for the French language test was only part of the battle. My capacity for bureaucracy perseverance was also being tested. But in any case, I had to submit a cheque for thirty-five euros to hold my spot. On the good side, waiting until March to take the test would give me an extra month to study. On the bad side, since the test results wouldn't be ready for a month, and we were submitting our dossier a couple of days after taking the test, our dossier would include no proof of passing the DILF. And yes, I was counting on passing.

Ralph, on the other hand, was not going to put his language skills to the test—he'd discovered an escape hatch. Some tiny print on the Bouches-du-Rhône website indicated that those of a certain age were exempt from the language requirement. For my own part, over the previous months of studying, my fear of the DILF had morphed into a bring-it-on mentality. I'd been through the DILF practice test booklet up one side and down the other multiple times and was determined to get some sort of validation of my efforts. Also, as a former language teacher, I was curious about the whole French language testing process. Or maybe it was my masochistic self talking.

On the day of the exam, I got up at 6:45 a.m. after a restless night. After a reviving shower and some strong espresso, it was ready-or-not time for me and the DILF. The trip to Arles was thankfully uneventful. Ralph dropped me off near the entrance of the test center. He would read in the car in a nearby parking lot, and I'd meet with him there to take my triumphant bow.

I took a deep breath as I rounded the corner and walked into the test center. It was 8:20 a.m. The large room was packed with dozens of people, including some young students who were maybe in their late teens or early twenties. They filled the two classrooms and lined the hallway. I didn't know if they were there for the same test or were taking courses of some sort. What *was* clear is that they were *not* happy. None emitted the weakest of chuckles or revealed even a hint of a twinkle in their eyes. The area could have been mistaken for a waiting room at a colonoscopy clinic. They all looked whupped from the preparation and were ready for the procedure to be over.

As I wiggled my way through the crowd toward the reception area at the back of the building, I spotted a professor directing people to the second floor. It was the DILF line, so I joined the swarm. A few minutes after settling in, another professor informed us we were in the wrong room and needed to relocate to a classroom on another floor. Like well-mannered, obedient schoolkids, we followed orders.

As we shuffled upstairs, I couldn't help but notice the profound state of disrepair of the building. Huge swaths of paint were peeling off the wall and a piece of cardboard was taped over a broken window. In the classroom, piles of books and resource materials were stacked high on an industrial-type table, not a bookcase in sight. While I hoped infrastructure resources would be forthcoming, my hopes for a precisely organized test were fading. Ten of us eleven students congregated in the back rows, but I settled in up front. My rationale was that if I needed to ask a question or request confirmation on something, I could more easily do it with the professor right in front of me.

At nine o'clock, two professors entered and passed out the test booklets. One reviewed the various segments of the test, including a listening comprehension portion, and the length of time allotted to each section. All went fine at first. I listened intently to the recording, understood all the questions, and didn't hesitate when choosing the answers. I heard whispering behind me, followed by a sharp rebuke from one of the professors. More talking and more admonishments from the professors. Then came that sharp *thwop*. After that, there were no more interruptions, thank goodness.

Despite all the distractions, I concentrated on the last portion of the test, which was a writing exercise. The setup was that you're a professional who has to work late without time to go shopping for little Pierre's birthday party. You were to make a shopping list for a friend who would pick up the necessary items. Photos of wrapped gifts, fruit, soft drinks, candy, and a cake with birthday candles provided hints. I started my little essay with *"Chère Julie,"* and from then on, tried my best to make it short, sweet, and above all, natural, if only in baby *français*. I reviewed my missive a couple of times and put it down. A professor came over and stood in front of my table. She picked up my test, read it, and smiled. She showed it to the other professor who also smiled. Though they remained silent, I felt pretty sure I'd done pretty darned good. Finally, one of the professors called time. Whew! Only one more segment to go—the one-on-one oral interview, which would start at 10:30.

I ran outside and around the corner to find Ralph in the parking lot.

When he saw me hustling toward the car, he popped out to welcome an embrace.

"So?"

"I'm pretty sure I did okay. There was some hullabaloo, though—some students were talking and one of the teachers slapped something hard on the desk. I think it was a ruler."

"Are you kidding?"

"Wish I were. There was some yelling, and then I'm pretty sure one student got moved to another seat."

"Wow, that's crazy. Like third grade," he said.

"I know. It sure was disconcerting at first, but once things settled down it was fine. Those profs are tough—they made it clear—their classroom, their rules, period. I've got to get back now for the oral interview."

"Bon courage!" Ralph said.

"Thanks, sweetie. Back soon," I said, glad I had only one more hurdle to hop.

When I returned to the main desk, the director appeared and motioned to me to follow her up a short flight of stairs to a small glassed-in office. We sat on opposite sides of a table, and she asked me to tell her a bit about myself. That was a less-than-compelling monologue I'd recited a thousand times before, whenever we met someone new, but at least I had the verb forms and vocabulary down. "I'm American. I was born in the state of Washington, went to high school and university in California, worked in Washington, DC, and later lived and worked in Germany for many years. My husband and I lived in Aix for eighteen months and now nearly four years in Saint-

Rémy. We love the life here—*la cuisine, le soleil, le bon vin, tous les produits, la joie de vivre, les traditions, les marchés …"*

I imagined what she heard was something like "*Pi-ta-ti, pi-ta-ta,*" the French version of blah-blah-blah, but she didn't interrupt until I took a breath during the recitation of my favorite French treasures, and she was able to insert a single syllable—*bon*. She shuffled through some papers and pushed over a photo of a pair of jeans. She pointed to the price tag— 42 euros—and asked me the cost. Without skipping a beat, I rattled off the price. She let out another *bon*, and that was it. Finished—*fini*. She said I'd done very well. Hooray! Before leaving the center, I received an official *attestation* confirming that I'd taken the test.

That unexpected document had been a proud addition to our dossier. Even though it wasn't the actual *diplôme*, it did indicate that I'd negotiated one set of bureaucratic rapids. Admittedly, my linguistic canoe was badly dented and sported more than a few cracks, but it was afloat.

21

Be the teacher's pet.
Know the rules; follow the rules.

Chapter 22

Vantage Points

Saint-Rémy-de-Provence — Summer 2016

Presto! Magical mail service happens sometimes. Just two days after sending off our fat ten-year *carte de séjour* dossier, we received notice that it had been delivered to the sous-préfecture in Arles. Just one day each way—impressive. We were off to a super start but knew we had to keep our expectations in check. Our experience had taught us there was a possibility we'd have to send in a revised packet. Each morning for the following two weeks, we approached our *boîte aux lettres* with trepidation. Would we find our precious packet with a letter from the sous-préfecture indicating what documents were missing? Those weeks passed without a peep.

The temporary cards did not arrive within the expected six weeks but seven weeks and five days later, with only two days to spare before our current *cartes* expired. That was a close one. I had been gearing up for contacting the sous-préfecture, something I truly wanted to avoid. A phone conversation was risky business. There was the potential for being asked questions that I didn't understand, didn't have the answers to—or both. As much of a relief as it was to receive the precious interim documents, that relief was only temporary. The main prize was a pair of residence cards. When and if they would arrive remained uncertain.

Instead of dwelling on our *cartes de séjour*, we turned our attention to our enticing neighbor, Bella Italia. For our twenty-fifth wedding anniversary, we were heading to a sleek, contemporary apartment that boasted a massive terrace with a panoramic view of Lake Como and majestic alpine peaks beyond. It was located outside of Varenna, not far from Mr. Clooney's estate, as a matter of fact. No doubt we'd get together for drinks, time permitting—our schedule was fairly full.

We'd blown the budget on the villa, so our hopes were high the apartment would be as high-end as it appeared in the internet photos. We took our time driving the six hundred kilometers, stopping to see friends in Céreste in the Luberon, making our way carefully over a wiggly mountain pass to Avigliana, near Torino, and then one last stop in tiny Oggiono on Lago de Annone. Once at the Lago di Como apartment and out on its terrace, we were astounded—the view was far better than the photos had suggested. The stunning vista of the shimmering Como waters, distant towns of Menaggio, and dramatic, snow-capped peaks was mesmerizing. Even during a rainstorm, it was gloriously enchanting.

Getting to that point hadn't been all peaches and Prosecco, though. After retrieving the keys from the self-check-in lock box upon arrival, we realized the management team had suffered from amnesia, and not a slight case. They had forgotten to include the correct gate key, fix the hot water for the rain shower, repair the washing machine, install a microwave, activate Sky TV, provide more than a single pillow each, replace the threadbare towels, and fully equip the *cucina*. But it had a fridge that perfectly chilled that special bottle of Moët et Chandon Brut Impérial that Ralph had brought along. Even sipped from unmatched, chipped dollar-store flutes, it was divine, a good reminder of what was important—no corkscrew required for bubbly! But even more important to remember was that fizz was sublime in any vessel, particularly when shared with your *amour* with a feisty twinkle in his eye.

After ferry rides to Bellagio, Menaggio, and Lenno, hiking the steep hills, marveling at the stunning lake views, strolling some outdoor markets, sampling decadent pasta dishes and local wines (but sadly, no Mr. Clooney encounter), it was back to real life in Saint-Rémy. There, we were livin' *la vida* in limbo, every morning listening intently for the buzz of the postman's scooter. Would today be the day we would receive the letter requesting pickup of the real-deal cards?

Less than six weeks after he'd received his temporary card, Ralph's letter arrived. Normally, receiving a smaller, rather than a bigger bill, is optimal. Not in this case. We were hoping the letter would demand payment of nearly three times the amount paid for a one-year card, because that would indicate the validity of the card would extend beyond a year. Hooray! The letter asked for 260 euros, which most likely meant he was getting a ten-year card! We couldn't be sure, however, because the letter simply stated, "Your card is ready for pickup," without any qualification. We expected that my letter would come the next day. It didn't. And not the next day. Or the day after that, or the day after that, which was the day we were leaving for the Camargue to celebrate Ralph's birthday. We'd rented a little apartment with sea views in Saintes-Maries-de-la-Mer, a short walk to the beach, where we had hoped to completely relax with our shiny new ten-year resident cards in our pockets. But a single resident card wouldn't do the trick—we needed a pair. My good buddy, Julie, teased that France was keeping Ralph but sending me back. Not funny!

In an effort to pry myself out of full fret mode, I decided to take action. Before we left for the beach, we tracked down an email address for the immigration section of the sous-préfecture. Yippee! Writing the government agency was far better than calling. I could check my grammar and take all the time I needed to interpret the response. I composed a concise message, explaining that Ralph's letter had arrived five days prior and how normally the second letter followed within a day or two, but it hadn't this time. Was it lost? Did they want to send another letter? Did they want me to wait for the original or come to the office to pick up a copy?

Within a few hours, they sent a reply with an attachment—a new letter, generated that day—for me! What a relief! That is, until I read the amount required for the new card—only 106 euros, the one-year price tag. My heart sank. Back to the laptop for another note to the sous-préfecture. Boldly assuming that I was getting the multiyear card just as Ralph had, I asked for confirmation that the ten-year card they were issuing to me cost 260 euros. By close of business, there still was no response, making for a tossy-turny, sleepless night. But, the next morning the answer was waiting for me in my inbox: *Oui*. At last, we could both take a deep breath. We planned to pick up our precious cards the following Monday. In the meantime, we could enjoy our Mediterranean getaway.

❧

The weather cooperated in the Camargue—calm and sunny but not too hot and not buggy. Ralph always says that any day he can spot thirty different bird species, it is a good birding day. In each of two days he made that number plus a couple of bonus birds. On the last day, he called me on my cell phone to report that he was on his way back to the apartment, but he'd be later than expected because he'd stopped to watch several hoopoes on the lagoon by some thatched-roofed fishermen's cottages. Hoopoes are cool birds. They're black and white-striped with bright orange highlights and an outlandish feathered headdress. I really wanted to see the spectacular creatures. Was that possible—would they stick around? Ralph suggested we return to the location later on our bikes on the way to dinner.

By the time we revisited the spot where he'd seen the hoopoes, the sky was quiet. I scanned the scene for the flamboyant birds when I saw what I thought was a beaver swimming around in a canal. It was a nutria, I found out later, and it's considered a pest. I'm glad I didn't know that then because it would have spoiled the sweet nature moment, watching the furry fellow make slow, lazy laps in the canal, seemingly with no pressing agenda other than to chill. (He didn't *look* as if he was up to no good.)

While we waited for the hoopoes, Ralph pointed out an elegant black-winged stilt with red toothpick legs that seemed to go on forever. I liked it almost as much as the pied avocets with their long, shimmering teal legs that we'd seen in a marshland on a bike ride to a lighthouse the day before. Ralph had pointed the birds out to me on previous trips but at a distance. Just like the sixth stranger you're introduced to at an *apéro* party, their names hadn't stuck. That time, seeing the striking creatures up close made a real impact. I felt a surge of confidence that I'd retain their names, which suggested I might not be a completely lost cause at birding. While I pondered that unexpected possibility, Ralph yelled, "Hoopoe!" The bird swooshed across the sky, dove deep into a thickly leafed tree, and down to the ground behind a bush. I kept watching, and finally it strutted out in its full regalia. Stunning. If it was en route to a costume party, it was sure to win Most Chic Chapeau.

᳗

We arrived back home to Saint-Rémy on Saturday and spent the afternoon regrouping, leaving until Sunday the buying of the *timbres fiscaux*, the stamps used as payment for the residence cards. I hoped there wasn't a law prohibiting the sale of fiscal stamps on *dimanche*. After all, the stamps are sold at a bar, which did a bang-up business on Sundays, selling all manner of alcoholic beverages. I was confident there wasn't much risk unless there was a No-Business-Only-Fun-on-Sunday statute. If a problem arose, I planned to run into town early Monday morning before we left for the sous-préfecture. It would be a rush, but workable.

We showed up at the *bar-tabac* around 11:00 a.m., where a few locals were hunched over the zinc-topped bar polishing off probably not their first beers of the day. I told the bartender we needed 520 euros' worth of *timbres fiscaux*. He and his young female coworker flipped through a book of plastic sleeves filled with stamps, just like in the post office. Mademoiselle counted out the amounts on each page, then sighed as she said, "I don't think we have enough." We realized that 520 was a hefty amount and prepared ourselves to go elsewhere, hoping other bars in town sold them. In Saint-Rémy, that particular bar was the only one we'd ever used for fiscal stamp-buying.

"Let me see," the fellow said. He flipped through the pages. More sighing. "*Oui. There are enough.*"

Mademoiselle spread out the stamps on the counter, and we verified the total was the correct amount, then verified our verification. The bartender placed them carefully in an envelope and stapled it, ensuring none of those pricey, sticky squares slipped out. No room for error.

"*Merci beaucoup. Ils sont très, très chers,*" I said. Very, very expensive.

"*Oui, c'est ça,*" the woman said, nodding.

At 9:25 on Monday morning, we took off for Arles for our precious ten-year *cartes de séjour*. We'd doubled-checked all our required documents, a very good thing, as I'd forgotten one original in the copier. I'd made my chocolate-chip cookies and packaged them in a patriotic red bag with blue and white tissue paper peeking out from the top. On the front of the bag, I clipped a thank you card for the entire sous-préfecture team. Then I zipped the goody bag safely away in my backpack. My plan was to see the expiration date on the new *cartes* to make absolutely certain it was a decade away. Only then would I present my little treats, made with my dwindling supply of precious, semi-sweet chocolate chips, imported from the States.

As we drove through the dappled light of the plane tree tunnel between Saint-Rémy and Saint-Étienne-du-Grès en route to Arles, I tried to calm my agitated nerves. We'd worked so hard and long for the ten-year cards. I was looking forward to getting the bureaucratic machinations behind us, planning a celebration, and looking to the future. Ralph was carefully watching the speed limit—eighty kilometers an hour through the plane trees but fifty through the built-up stretches. Soon we were buzzing through open fields and could crank it up to a full ninety kilometers an hour. On our left, a large group of agricultural workers was preparing for their day. We wondered what they would be harvesting—strawberries, maybe? On the right, perky sunflowers stretched to the horizon, followed by vast expanses of wheat and then the landscape dearest to my heart, *vignes*, grapevines. We were moving at a good pace. Last year, we'd hit a very stubborn *bouchon*, setting us back nearly a half hour. In the distance to the east, the ruins of Montmajour Abbey were backlit against a streaky pale blue sky. I could see through the rows of windows, making it look like a huge, vintage computer punch card. Then came the massive yellow flags of a car dealership, madly slapping the two-story-high poles they were attached to, a reminder that the fierce *mistral* wailing on the day before was not over yet.

The *gratuit* parking lot in Arles where we normally parked had become a pay lot, which wasn't surprising. Just recently, a bunch of ticket machines had sprouted like bamboo all over downtown Saint-Rémy. We lost a few minutes circling around trying to find a free spot. Time being of the essence, we reluctantly opted for a pay spot before hustling off to the sous-préfecture. Crowds of tourists by the imposing Roman arena blocked our path, so we had to weave and squeeze our way through. Inside the entrance of the sous-préfecture, Ralph plucked the ticket from the dispenser at 10:05. It was number 375. The electronic "Now Serving" machine read 338. Ouch. It was going to be a long haul, and I hoped we'd get in before they closed for lunch. We really should have set the ol' alarm clock earlier that morning.

Since we had time to kill, I took the opportunity to skip down to the language school, about five blocks away, to pick up my language test diploma. Madame Professeur had emailed me that it was finally ready and I could pick it up at the reception desk, but she would not be present. That was a shame, because I really wanted to thank her in person. She'd kept in close touch since I'd taken the test in early March, eventually emailing me that I had earned the coveted *Diplôme Initial de Langue Française.* As I trotted down the street, I regretted I hadn't made her chocolate-chip cookies too. I should have at least written a thank-you card, but I suppose I was too focused on the sous-préfecture. I made a note to rectify that oversight when I got home. Inside the education center, I made my way past the gaggles of students to the main office at the far end of the hall. A youthful, chipper teacher attended to me immediately. While a secretary combed through a file holder for my diploma, Madame Professeur appeared. She was there after all. Removing my diploma from the large envelope, she presented it to me with exaggerated formality.

"Très beau, n'est-ce pas?" she said, smiling.

Grinning back, I agreed, *"Très, très beau!"* I asked if it was possible to know my score. She pulled out another sheet of paper that showed the breakdown of the four sections of the test. The total was 98.5 percent.

"Pas mal, not bad," I said proudly.

"Ah, oui, c'est très bon," Madame Professeur said, nodding.

I could definitely live with losing 1.5 percent, yet I was puzzled that I'd dropped the point and a half on the listening comprehension part, and not on the written part. I asked if she knew what I'd missed.

"Maybe an address?" she guessed.

"Maybe," I said, but suddenly I knew it had to have been that blasted ten-digit telephone number question. During the test, we'd listened to a number several times and had to choose the correct listing from the five written in the test booklet. I had understood all the numbers as they'd been spoken, but at one point I remember having lost track of the order. I vaguely recalled making a last-second correction to my original answer. So that was the pesky devil that had cost me a perfect score, my overachiever self whined silently. On the other hand, my commonsense self countered, if I'd aced the test to the tune of 100 percent, folks might jump to the erroneous conclusion that my French was flawless. Fully flawed was more like it. I interrupted my internal debate with a wave goodbye to Madame Professeur, accompanied by, *"Mille fois mercis à tous,"* and I headed back to the primary task of the day.

When I reached the sous-préfecture, I unveiled my *diplôme* to Ralph with dramatic fanfare. His eyes opened wide, "Wow, honey, 98.5 percent—that's impressive. You *nailed* it!" The congratulatory kiss would wait for a private venue, but I gratefully received a hug. It was a brief one, as our attention was drawn to the electronic board. It read, "Now Serving 355." Seventeen down, twenty to go. It was going to be tight if they closed at noon. It would be one depressing bummer if they made us come back after lunch or another day. I wandered outside to check the closing time, posted on a plaque by the front sliding door. Twelve fifteen—that extra fifteen minutes could make all the difference. At 369, we picked up our stuff and started up the stairs. In addition to the new coffee machine by the staircase, I noticed a new water dispenser machine along with little plastic cups. That meant not one, but two ways to need a WC. Maybe the sous-préfecture would install one next year; I hoped we wouldn't be back to find out.

When our turn came, we reported to Monsieur Misérable at desk G. Madame Congeniality wasn't even there; in her place was the chief, whom we'd worked with a few years earlier—a low-key, reserved guy. Oh well. Monsieur Misérable knew his stuff. We'd be fine. After exchanging greetings, I slid over all our identification documentation—passports, current *cartes de séjour,* and the letter requesting us to pick up our cards. He sorted through it all, then went to the back of the room where he crouched down over a large box of files. He withdrew one and flipped through some more, exhaling noisily. Oh, *merde,* I thought, he's having trouble finding one of our dossiers. More noisy exhalations. Finally, the chief asked who he was looking for. He said he'd found the dossier for *Monsieur* Padgett but not for *Madame* Padgett. Oh, man, don't do this to me, I thought. The chief didn't respond but disappeared into his office and returned with a dossier, which he handed to Monsieur Misérable with an apology. "So sorry, I forgot I had that," he said.

Monsieur Misérable, in turn, apologized to us and in unison we said, *"Ce n'est pas grave."* No big deal. He performed his tasks with smooth agility before pushing over my card, along with a paper requiring a signature. My heart was pounding as I squinted at the small plastic rectangle, searching for the all-important expiration date. What teensy print. Reading my mind, Monsieur Misérable said, "Yes, it's for ten years." Finally, I spotted the 2026 expiration date! I signed the paper with a flourish.

He went through the same procedure with Ralph. When he was about to stick on the precious fiscal stamps, he said, "Oh, there's a twenty-euro stamp missing."

What? No! We'd counted and recounted the stamps at home, and I'd secured each stack of 260 euros' worth with a paper clip and placed them carefully in an envelope, which I had sealed. Monsieur Misérable retrieved the wadded-up envelope from the trash and looked inside—nothing. Math major Ralph stood up, leaning over the desk as he recounted the stamps. *"Non, non, il y a deux cent soixante,"* he said to Monsieur Misérable, who proceeded to retouch all the sticky wisps of paper.

"Oui, oui, oui, vous avez raison. Two hundred sixty. That's right," Monsieur Misérable said, letting out a weary sigh.

For the second time in a few minutes, Ralph smoothly delivered another *"Ce n'est pas grave,"* just like a native.

"So sorry, it's been a tough day," Monsieur Misérable said, shaking his head. Tough day was right. While I had been at the language school retreiving my diploma, Ralph witnessed a verbal altercation between Monsieur Misérable, who looked as if he spent a fair amount of time at the gym, and a disgruntled, middle-aged man in the lobby. We'd never seen any of the immigration officials down in that area, so that in itself was surprising, but to witness one losing composure and using an angry voice was disconcerting. They had gone at it for a while, apparently over an invalid document, until Monsieur Misérable abruptly told the client, *"Bonne journée, monsieur. Au revoir,"* and marched back upstairs. So very glad I'd missed that—my nerves didn't need any additional frazzling.

After Ralph tucked his card away—but not before checking the expiration date was ten years hence—we stood and prepared to leave. Before turning, from my backpack I withdrew the spiffy scarlet gift bag. I placed it on the desk in front of Monsieur Misérable, who looked worried, which in turn worried me. Maybe officials weren't allowed to receive gifts from clients? Or was he formulating an attempted bribery charge? Our intention was not to cause any disruption but thank the staff in a unique, and above all, legal way. We appreciated the demands of the mind-numbing work they did day in and day out. In my 98.5 percent Initial Level French, I tried to say that we knew their work was difficult and that it involved many details, so it was necessary for them to have a lot of energy. Here were some cookies I made with *pépites de chocolat des États-Unis,* a specialty from the US. They were for the entire team to share. *Mille fois merci!*

Now Monsieur Misérable was looking more puzzled than worried. I had inadvertently used the word "cookie" instead of the French word, *biscuit,* so maybe that had confused him. I pulled one of the cellophane packages from the bag. When he saw the sweet treat, his eyes lit up and he grinned, saying, *"Très gentil, merci beaucoup."*

I glanced over at the typically poker-faced chief. He was beaming too. After one last round of *merci beaucoup* and *bonne journée,* we walked to the door. As we passed by the chief's desk, he waved and called out, "Thank you very much. Have a nice day"—in English.

The mélange of relief and exhilaration we felt far surpassed making our day a "nice" day. It qualified as a stellar day. A day to remember and to celebrate. Our new cards not only were good for ten years, but they also included the line, *"Toute Profession en France Metropolitane."* That meant we were allowed to work, a prospect not available to us previously. The possibility of working hadn't even occurred to me because the dossier required a statement that we would *not* seek work. Not that we were interested in full-time jobs, even thirty-five-hour-a-week

French ones, but now, should an enticing opportunity or idea present itself, we could engage.

A few years ago in Aix, we had been contenders to be extras in a film being made in Marseille. It would have been a hoot. But our legal status dashed our hopes of a silver-screen debut. Now, no restraints—red carpet here we come! And most importantly, with our ten-year cards came the security of being able to relocate without having to prove our worthiness—a stable address being a key element—to a sous-préfecture every year. Now we could rev up Operation View-Finder and head wherever that elusive panoramic view might be. Or perhaps buy a small property that we could renovate for our sole use or run as a B&B. Or I could be a meet-and-greeter for holiday homes, offering valuable, insightful travel tips to new arrivals. Or I could peddle chocolate-chip cookies—I'd already received a significant endorsement from Julie's young son, who had gushed over my last batch and suggested that I open a shop. We could be business partners—I'd man the kitchen and after his soccer practices and homework, the tyke could make home deliveries on his bike. A world of opportunity awaited an inspired spark to ignite imagination.

Whether we opted to apply ourselves or practice being bums, we still had a shindig to plan. Our silver anniversary excursion to the tiny village on Lake Como in Italy had been a private affair. It had allowed the two of us space to review life and reminisce about our meanderings so far—the exhilarating ride from Washington, DC, to Heidelberg to Provence. It was easy to track major events that had led us to France, but just the same, we marveled at finding ourselves living our retirement in lavender land. Yet (not to diminish the celebratory merit of our two and a half decades of nonstop marital bliss), we had even more to cheer than *past* time together. Now that we had our ten-year cards, allowing us to legally live it up in La Belle France for a decade, we'd assemble our friends, blow up balloons, and pop corks. It was time to toast the future and fête the fun to come.

How to celebrate our ten-year *cartes de séjour*? It was a simple question without an easy answer, because we had to factor in timing, weather, and space. It had to be an outdoor affair because the *jardin* was the only place that could hold more than a dozen *amis*, and our list was growing to double that. An afternoon garden *fête* wasn't a comfortable option in the middle of summer with temps topping 38°C (100°F), and waiting until after the heat subsided meant a two-month delay—*pas possible!* Our excitement was bubbling over and needed to be shared right away.

An *apéro* party, we decided, would fit the bill—casual and festive, short and sweet. That kind of *soirée* would suit folks with jobs, agendas, and wee ones. The big day would be Sunday, 24 July, at six o'clock, when it would be cooling off on the terrace. In keeping with our low-key approach, I sent out an electronic invitation, written *en anglais et français*, flawlessly, of course—all twenty-five words. There was just one stumbling block. English invitations usually come with a request to "RSVP," (*Répondez, s'il vous plaît*), by la-de-da date, but did the French use French in that way? Or was it one of those false cultural friends like *entrée* on a menu? In France, *entrée* is the first course, literally meaning "entry," but in North America, it had somehow become the main course. Anxious to move on to my own menu, I decided to ignore that formality and hope for the best. Within a couple of days, we had a confirmed guest list of thirty including six kids and one toddler, half of them *français* and the other half all forms of Anglo expats, including English, Irish, Scottish, South African, Australian, and Canadian.

Now for the hors d'oeuvres. I would prepare delicate little pastry cups (*merci*, Ikea) stuffed with herb-laced cream cheese, smoked salmon, and capers; more little pastry cups filled with ricotta, a drizzle of pesto, and twist of prosciutto; a seafood mixture of baby shrimps, crab with lemon mayo, and spicy Old Bay seasoning atop endive leaves; and round toasts spread with black olive tapenade with a dollop of crème fraîche and a fresh basil leaf from our very own *jardin*. No quiche this time, as I wanted to save myself from the inevitable—an inedible scorched version due to forgetting to check the oven, which I most assuredly would do in the last frantic moments before guests arrived. I love the idea of having downtime before a party starts—a pause in the action to leisurely check that everything is in place and take a deep breath. But seriously, when was the last time we'd been able to orchestrate *that*? Better to have everything cold. The menu would also include platters of a cheese and *charcuterie*, including sliced chorizo and salami, baskets of baguette slices, and a veggie platter. Making an exception to the no-dip rule—the French tend to steer clear of dips—I'd put out little tubs of tzatziki and hummus. Add to all that small bowls of mixed nuts, olives, crackers, and potato chips, and that would cover it. Oh, and maybe a large bowl of watermelon chunks with toothpicks at the side.

Beverages were easy—there would be *le bon vin* of all shades, and no shortage of it. Next, bottles of beer, still and fizzy water, and flavored *sirop* for the kiddos—they could mix their own drinks just as they liked them. I had another idea for the young set. Our neighbors, Robert and Maureen, had three delightful girls aged ten to sixteen, and together with Ellen and

Rick's pair of sweet daughters, Caitlin and Cameron, they formed a five-gal hospitality team. I'd ask them to arrive early to assist me with an art project—name tags. Most of the guests knew each other, but not all. The kids might enjoy putting their artistic talents to work on some stick-on labels, decorating each individually, and I hoped the guests would get a kick out of the novel idea. Could be a fun icebreaker and boost the festive mood of the event.

Along those merry lines, this was a perfect time to display my collection of new and vintage French and American flags. I'd place them in a tall ceramic vase on the table next to the red, white, and blue napkins and matching paper plates I'd found before Bastille Day. Though nonceramic plates seemed acceptable, only real glass would do for the adult beverages. Our stock didn't yield enough matching wineglasses for all, but I could supplement with an assortment of short, sturdy, *verres*, some adorned with the popular bee motif and others with the iconic fleur-de-lis pattern.

On the day of the event, by the late afternoon, the heat had fortunately simmered down and the winds had calmed. I covered two folding patio tables with white linen cloths that hung nearly to the terrace tiles—one for the beverages and the other for the edibles. We placed several other small bistro tables and folding chairs around the yard. There weren't enough seats for everyone, so some would have to stand, but we figured that would encourage mingling. When the children arrived, I gave them the guest list, labels, and colored pencils. They finished their masterpieces in short order and then dutifully manned the folding "reception" table by the garden gate, rolled back far enough to allow passage. As the guests drifted in, the brightly smiling bilingual kids asked for the first names, found the appropriate peel-off name tag, and carefully smoothed it on each guest. In the United States, partygoers might goof around by repositioning their labels upside down or placing them on the wrong people, but our crowd was very well-mannered and cooperative. Well, we had one bad boy. Jokester Didier, a big race car aficionado, refused his name tag decorated with a bunny and insisted on the tag featuring the spunky Citroën Deux Chevaux even though it read "Bob." Professional as our reception team was, they promptly created Didier his very own personalized label, upgraded to a version of a Lamborghini.

By shortly after 6:00 p.m., most of the guests were on the terrace, refreshments in hand. The first of multiple toasts to our ten-year cards was carried out. *Santé!*

"Wait a moment," Didier interrupted. "Where *is* this card exactly?"

Ralph pulled out his and handed it to Didier for a thorough examination. Didier squinted at the small piece of plastic until he found the expiration date and pursed his lips, as if to say, "No big deal." His hand holding the card flew skyward, attempting to jettison Ralph's legal right to remain in France into the stratosphere. Ralph and I, along with everyone else, gasped loudly. An impish smile broke out on Didier face as he handed the card back to Ralph. "Well done," he said in English, slapping Ralph on the back. As Didier headed to the bar, he deflected all the cheerful admonishments for scaring the heck out of all of us—with ease. Methinks he'd had a lot of practice.

After the excitement over Didier's mischievous antics had subsided, my attention turned to the edibles. My proactive volunteer hospitality team had already begun making the rounds with the platters of hors d'oeuvres, so Ralph and I were free to mill around and chat with the guests. Most of the folks were sitting or standing on the terrace—except one. Dirk, our typically energetic, perfectly bronzed housebuilder friend, was alone at a bistro table on the grassy area at the east end of the pool. I wound my way over to join Dirk, who was around seventy but looked and acted a decade younger. He explained he'd been working marathon days on the mill conversion and really needed a break in the action. He and his wife, Caroline, were eager to schedule a *déjeuner* date with Ralph and me. While we bantered about potential lunch venues, I noticed his glass was empty. I told him not to budge—just relax—and I'd return in a jiff with a refill of rosé. In short order, Maserati Man poured a glass—he'd taken over bar service, and Julie's partner, Benoît, was assisting. All under control.

As I made my way back to Dirk with his wine, I dipped in and out of conversations, a jumbled babble of *français*, *anglais*, and *franglais*. William, the Canadian representative who owned a vintage Porsche 911, was trading car stories with Didier. Julie and Lana, both holiday apartment owners, were sharing tales about the summer's tenants. Ellen, who had just returned from Dublin, was chatting with Irish Elaine about her hometown, while her hubby Daryl was entertaining Giles with golf stories, switching back and forth between English and French. Anna, originally from Scotland, made plans to meet with Valérie for a French-English exchange over coffee. Belgian Violette helped two-year-old Ariel retie the bow on her blonde locks, while her mom went to see what mischievous eight-year-old Lucas was up to (chasing the girls). And so it went. Seeing everyone mingling, laughing, sipping, and munching gave me a warm and fuzzy feeling. Édith Piaf, Jimmy Buffett, Andrea Bocelli, Zucchero, and others were crooning their hearts out, but you could scarcely hear them over the convivial din—exactly what we had hoped for.

By 8:30, we'd exchanged our last *bises* for the night, and Ralph rolled the garden gate closed. After "The Little Sparrow" finished "Non, Je Ne Regrette Rien," all was quiet. We plopped on a pair of slingback garden chairs on the grass and marveled at the depth of the contentment we felt. A home-sweet-home sensation washed over us. With a warm breeze came a rusty-tailed redstart that flitted across the pool and perched on the edge of the terrace awning. It looked down on us, giving us a beak nod and a chirp as if to say, "Bravo!"

"Thanks, buddy," I said, "I think it was a success too." Ralph leaned over to deliver a tender kiss.

"We did it, honey," he said.

"Yes, we pulled it off. Our long-term residency cards and our *apéro* party ... everyone seemed at ease and content."

The region's charms, along with our supportive friends and endearing neighbors, had affected us more deeply than we had realized until now. That sense of bonding with our adopted country was further enhanced by a special gift from our across-the-street neighbors. A bottle of local wine or olive oil is always a welcome treat and much appreciated, but this present was particularly touching—a tome of beautifully photographed legendary Provençal landscapes. The inscription read, *"Bienvenue aux nouveaux Franco-Américains de Provence. Bises de Jeanne et Didier."* The word *Franco* was underlined—three times.

Perhaps Jeanne and Didier's message implied we *were* becoming Frenchified, if just around the edges. And there was no denying our affectionate attachment to our Saint-Rémy neighborhood was extra special. Though we'd lost lots of our *sky* view framed by frilly, undulating bamboo stalks to the solid mass of brittle tiles that was the "green" house, it seemed we were gaining a new *point* of view. At that moment, as we basked in the warm afterglow of our convivial evening, the thought of separating from our *quartier* seemed extreme, even in trade for a stellar vista. No doubt Saint-Rémy's most notable native son, the renowned oracle Nostradamus, would have agreed. Had he read our minds just then, he would have been nodding his head and thinking, "Finally, they are getting it. Views are a *centime* a dozen, but *belonging*, now that's hard to come by."

Maybe the famous seer *could* have called it—that half a millennium after his birth, this city girl and her homebody hubby would settle in his tradition-rich hometown in the south of France. Despite the long odds, it had happened. Here we were, an ocean away from our American roots, embracing *l'art de vivre* in a Provençal village where intriguing surprises continued to captivate.

Channeling my thoughts, Ralph said, "Provence has worked its magic on us, hasn't it?"

"*Mais oui, mon chéri*, and the allure endures."

Take in the views—from all angles.
A sense of belonging can make a house a home and, just maybe, lead to *La Belle Vie*.

Epilogue

Ralph's search for the Grand Duc continues. Many of the "must-haves" from our storage unit in California have found their way to Saint-Rémy. Operation View-Finder was tabled. In place of our little backyard grassy area, we now have a meter-high deck. To the west, we can see over the wall to the olive grove. And glorious sunsets.

Acknowledgments

Mille mercis go to a long list of publishing professionals and dear ones in Europe, Canada, and the US, who played critical roles in transforming my dreamy book idea into a tangible reality:

Editors Arlene Prunkl, Kelly Lamb, and Caroline Kaiser, for their expertise and wise counsel.

My marvelous first readers, Mary Ellen Cravotta, Helen Staren, and Debbie Zedalis, for their comprehensive feedback; Barb Kelley and Susan Stone, for sharing their superb technical skills; Shelley Pick, for persuading me to share initial drafts; Beth Woodford, for the insightful French culture lessons; and Deb Ahern, for inspiring me to begin this journey.

All the treasured members of my informal booster club, for their endless, enthusiastic support of my project. It's my heartfelt wish that each one feels greatly appreciated.

Special thanks go to David and Mollie Regan, for their exceptional creative contributions and lively encouragement. Their boundless talents and positive outlook never cease to astonish.

Also, I owe a debt of gratitude to the owners of our first apartment in Aix-en-Provence, for taking a chance on us; our Saint-Rémy neighbors, for their inclusive spirit; and to our *propriétaire*, for his kindness and extraordinary generosity.

And last, to my love, Ralph, for our life together, our French life, and for bringing life to *Passion for Provence*. His infinite patience, technological savvy, and good humor kept me on track throughout the journey.

Now, on to more adventures!

About the Author

Gayle Smith Padgett, a UCLA graduate, has two master's degrees, neither in French. After studying in Mexico and South America, she worked as a language specialist in California and Virginia and later as a management analyst and US government liaison in Heidelberg, Germany. In 2011, she and her husband moved to Provence, where they continue to crack French cultural codes.

To find out more, go to:
www.gaylesmithpadgett.com

Made in the USA
Las Vegas, NV
17 June 2021